Tomorrow Will Come

TOMORROW WILL COME

by E. M. Almedingen

Little, Brown and Company · Boston
1941

My dear Audrey,

This book ends in September 1922. Less than a year later I met you in London. I brought you a handful of hazy ideas, and not much else. I was tired, ill, and more than uncertain of the future. I must have wasted hours and hours of your time in the following years. I brought you work which anyone but you would have dismissed with a despairing shrug. You were patient enough to read it all. Your friendship and patience were given to me from the very beginning: they deserve a poem. In my poky back room in Bloomsbury Square I sat and worked, and the sense of a possible defeat was warded off every time I remembered your faith in me. You urged and you argued and you even bullied sometimes, but always you left me with this sense of your faith.

There is a room in my life tenanted by those who have given me so much and to whom I could give so little in return. Esther is in that room and many others, and yours is a special corner in it. So I want to give this book to you as a most inadequate gesture of gratitude.

Yours ever,

E. M. A.

Shropshire,
May 1941

CONTENTS

Chapter One

DREAMS, GRANITE, AND WATER

1

‮~~~~~~~~~~‬

T HE STORY of a life may begin on a
nursery floor or in an April wood, with a slab of chocolate
or a broken, beloved toy. It may start with a fantasy woven
round a face, a song, or even a picture on the earliest remembered wall. This record must needs begin with a city,
whose child I was.

St. Petersburg . . . I can almost hear an impatient murmur: "Why the old name?" but I can make no apology for
the use of it. In 1914, the old name was changed to Petrograd, but the change, fathered by frenzied circumstance,
could not interfere with the spirit of the city. All my earliest
memories of her go back to the time when the name "Petrograd" was preferred by none except a meager handful of
Slavophile freaks. Indeed, "Petrograd" does ring a heavily
Russian note and suggests a kinship with the fat, indolent,
hospitable Moscow. "Petrograd" is a beard, a glass of tea
flavored with lemon, a piece of carving painted red, yellow,
and blue. St. Petersburg invited no such satisfying, easy
comparisons. She was created by a man whose devotion to

[3]

all things foreign equaled Hitler's worship of the Teutonic. She was born half-German, half-Dutch. For nearly a century she flirted with purely German tastes. Later she toyed with a rather tawdry stage setting borrowed from France. She ended by being her own, slightly grotesque, cosmopolitan self, aware that her scene could never give hospitality to any narrowly nationalistic expression. Most foreigners felt at home there. Purely bred Russians abused and also despised her. They never forgot that the ancient privilege of the Tsar's anointing was retained by Moscow, the true sovereign city of Tsardom. St. Petersburg would have staggered under the privilege; her own sanctuaries were newcomers in that world of well-nigh static orthodoxy.

Leningrad now stands on the banks of the Neva. Leningrad is more or less certain to rise from the charred desolation inherited since 1917, but Leningrad, known through brief newspaper reports, is a remote and alien sound. I wish it well, but I shall never know it.

Deep purple, soft gray, and a peculiar green, which had silver and blue mingled in it, purple in stone, gray in cloud, blue-green in water. . . . In St Petersburg none could escape either sound or sight of water. The Neva has countless tributaries, and almost round the corner lie the wide reaches of the Gulf of Finland, with its clusters of little islands.

I have no map except the one still etched in my memory. On that map, the Neva runs wildly and whimsically, a queenly river, girdled in purple-gray granite, powdered with snow during so many months in the year. Across the Neva were many bridges. Best among them I knew Nicholas's, which linked the Vassily Island, where we lived, to the Mayfair of St. Petersburg, where I was born and where

[4]

we should have lived. Nicholas's Bridge had exquisite gryphons for railings, and they were friends.

"Please come to life. . . . If I stroke your curly mane, will you be angry? You look so fierce, but I believe you are kind because you are strong and beautiful. . . ." Suddenly the magic worked, the gryphon was free of his bronze bondage. He plunged into the river, away from the bridge arches, towards the land of pearly mountains and unfading flowers, far beyond the sea. I was riding him, silent and triumphant — until a fat, bearded policeman decided that the thin little girl, her eyes far away and her hair gracelessly untidy, had stood long enough by the railings.

"Please, *baryshna*, have you lost your way home?"

"You are a wicked, interfering dragon," ran my indignant thought; "you have made my gryphon turn back . . ." and a very small voice, its dignity imagined rather than otherwise, stammered: "No, thank you, I have not lost my way. I am going home."

The Vassily Island, seen from a belfry, would have suggested an irregular piece of some check material. It had five horizontal lines, intersected by fourteen vertical ones, much shorter and more narrow. The wide strips were known as Quays and Prospects. The narrow ones went by the humbler name of Lines, and they were numbered. The Island had been planned by Menshikoff, Peter the Great's favorite. The Lines were to be canals, linking the Neva to her small tributary. The canals were never made, but the breadth of the Lines remained. Some of them had trees planted in the middle all along their length. To me, those wide, straight thoroughfares were what the Atlantic must have been to Columbus.

The Island had clear caste distinctions: certain of the Lines were almost aristocratic, others merely possible, and the rest quite slummy. The distinction was repeated in the Prospects: *Bolshoy* was very *comme il faut*, *Sredny* (Middle) more than doubtful, and *Maly* (Small), lying farthest from the Neva, housed the human dregs of the Island. The huge ocher-colored buildings of the Mines Institute at one end of the Nicholas Quay and the massive dark red bulk of the Stock Exchange at the other marked the Island's boundaries so far as the Neva was concerned.

The Bolshoy Prospect was flanked by tall elms, and the curve of the Nicholas Quay, fronting the river, was pleasantly broken by several deep green splashes, the Roumiantzeff Square and the University Gardens among them. To the Roumiantzeff we went on the days when excursions further afield were made impossible by the state of the family exchequer. Peter's Park, the Summer Gardens, the Zoo and the Alexander Gardens, near St. Isaac's Cathedral, were all delightful, but distant.

Across the Bridge, facing the Island, lay the Venetian sweep of the Quays, stretching to the right and the left. In the early mornings, the Quays were washed with light. Then the spires and battlements of the Peter and Paul Fortress over the water leapt into delicate gray-golden splendor, magical stories could be heard in the least audible phrase of the river running under the bridge, and there seemed music even in the clang of hoofs over cobbles, the shouts of tall, dirty-faced Tartars, meandering from street to street in their search for secondhand clothes.

Away from the Quays, behind an enormous gray palace, stretched the deeply leafed length of the Horse Guards

[6]

Boulevard. For one week in the year, in late Lent, it was given over to the lovely pandemonium of a fair. Toys; balloons; apples carved of wood and apples stewed in honey; chunks of sticky walnut cheese; hideous plaster statuettes of the imperial family; exquisitely carved boxes of *chinara* wood from the Caucasus and coarse gray lace from the Valdai Hills; wooden Easter eggs daubed with all the colors of the rainbow; suspiciously colored sweets, which smelt of paraffin and tasted of flour; jostling, hurrying, laughing, swearing, singing, and sweating crowds of men, women, and children moving up and down between shoddily timbered stalls! Smell of hot waffles, sweat, greening branches, carved wood, and humanity blindly enjoying an odd hour of noisy rapture! The annual *verba* was more than a fair. It was the gesture made once a year by St. Petersburg as a reminder that, after all, a corner within her gray gates belonged to a Russia of loud voices, unreasoned merriment, inelegant table manners, and rude public behavior, of time wasted most gloriously, and of the splendid contagion of geniality.

Yet the *verba* was a brief annual intrusion. It never answered the city's deeper urges. St. Petersburg endured that fierce, chaotic splendor for one week, and then forgot it. Then the tall elms of the Horse Guards Boulevard learned of peace and dignity once again, and you could walk down quietly until you came to St. Isaac's Cathedral. Massive and violet-brown, it broke on you like some phrase of an archangelic choir. The wise architect had given it wide belts of space all round. Services in the cathedral were not for me, but a few moments spent in a corner, with a fresco of Christ on the opposite wall, grew into so many tentative approaches to a world greater and much more satisfying than the one known to the senses. No noise of traffic broke into St. Isaac's heart, tourists were few, and their small, scattered groups could never invade the whole place.

In chiseled and graven stone, in sloping roof and flattened dome, in the voice of several nations, in wide streets and narrow alleys, and always, predominantly so, in the insistent phrases of her waters, do I remember St. Petersburg. There may have been, indeed there must have been, ugly patches on that richly colored carpet. . . . True, there were slums behind her grandeur which would have turned White-chapel into an imagined replica of Grosvenor Square, and the social upheaval which I was to witness so many years later brought worse things to the foreground. Nonetheless, St. Petersburg was very lovable.

"A city — built on skeletons, a breeding place of trage-dies!" remarked a casual observer in the long ago. Well, she was no fun fair, nor a circus, yet even at a fun fair there may be tears over a burst balloon, and hearts and limbs occasionally get broken on a circus stage. I have known her frivolous, mad, and merry. I have known her sober and be-mused under her cloak of darkness since 1917. But even in her charred and naked desolation, St. Petersburg could still offer some sanctuary from fear which invaded her walls.

If ever a place befriended a rather unwanted and lonely child, she so befriended me. If ever a place was articulate, St. Petersburg certainly had a voice, and she compelled me to listen. "No national anchorage? Have I any? Yet it may be possible to achieve things beyond the immediate environ-ment, even to learn the pure lines of form through sheer formlessness. A man's wild fancy urged me to life, and I had to borrow beyond my own swollen waters and bleak marshes. You, too, can build yourself a house which may yet be happily tenanted by others than yourself." Her gifts, at least, were true and good, no counterfeit coin ever came from her mint, and in 1914 I said in my diary: "Were St. Petersburg in England, she would be perfect."

2

LIFE came to me in shape, color, and smell. The first snow falling, "Silver smells like it," and a bearded cousin laughed in a most unmannerly fashion. "Little fool, silver never smells." Of course it did, a cleansing white smell, a star and a snowdrop together. Therefore it was easy to remember the smell of the first snow; the music of sledge runners; the tiring dryness of summer pavements (when luckier people deserted St. Petersburg for Finland or the country); big straw hats; an enormous garden, full of old lime trees, and a brother saying, "This is a public park, but trees belong to the world, and so they are yours and mine"; the hard granite pavement on the quay; my tiny feet running, my hair all down my back, and a huge, black-whiskered policeman at the corner of the Moshkoff Alley standing to attention and saluting.

There was an enormous room with rows of slender, gilt-legged chairs ranged along the walls, and I stood by the door, observing that sea of polished parquet. I moved and tumbled down long before I had reached the middle of the room. I had meant to slide down the whole length of it, and the disappointment brought tears, and then I knew myself cradled softly and safely. I smelt violets, my cheek nestled against a sleeve of lilac sprigged with tiny white flowers, and the room was a kingdom because it held my mother. In the middle of that empty ballroom, on the cold, uncarpeted floor, I learned myself belonging to her in a secret and special way. We stayed on the floor, she held me tight, my small, dusty hands round her lovely neck, and the great room rang with her laughter. Something unseen in that room must have bidden a child's memory seize on that laughter and grave it deeply. I heard it then. Never again was I to hear it.

"You have an unbridled imagination," said a tiresome aunt about a century later. "You can't remember that house. You were born there. You left early in 1901. You were just two and a bit." She looked suddenly curious. "Anyway, what happened there to make you remember that room?"

"Gilt chairs," I said, "and mirrors between the windows — "

"Chairs and mirrors did not happen. They were there."

I said no more. I could never talk about my mother to my father's people.

My mother was the clean, sweet smell of lilac to me, skies in the morning, an answer to the nightly falling darkness, the reason for everything, including God. She was my Saint George to the dragon of a frequently puzzling life.

She remained the unsullied, proud symbol of race in a humble and circumscribed environment. So far as I was concerned, she stood there at the very beginning of things, not only a face or a voice, but someone whose nearness and love were as natural as the air.

But my father's people for years remained footsteps, voices, faces, even mere names. They walked along their own street, and the seventh child of a younger son meant little, if anything, to them.

The senior branch of his family moved north to St. Petersburg in the seventies. The estate near Tver, given by Catherine the Great to a forebear in 1793, still belonged to an uncle of mine, but nobody lived there. A century of living in Russia had not given them any roots. Country life implied an anchorage and led to tiresome obligations. They chose St. Petersburg in a rare flash of wisdom. As to the rest, their story, when I came to learn it, suggested a variant of the Wandering Jew theme: from Spain they leapt to Saxony, from Saxony to Austria, from Austria to Russia. My uncles loved telling a meager handful of stories about these peregrinations, but I saw little in them. "We are like gypsies with Europe for a tent," I complained to the head of the family in my own day. "Seven hundred years old, you say? What's the good of it? None of them ever did anything — not even lead a decent army into battle" — which was not a fortunate thing to say to a soldier.

"You have no family sense."

I had none. But I could not be blamed for its lack. A family sense might have been fostered by a rooftree or by something a little more tangible than a cluster of legends.

My grandmother had thirteen children, and all her nine

sons were soldiers except my father. All were married.
This suggests a clan rather than a family, and, on very rare
occasions when they met, they were apt to behave in a
clannish manner, but fortunately this did not happen often:
they were scattered all over Russia, Finland, and the Baltic
provinces. St Petersburg had a few uncles, aunts, and a
handful of cousins. The rest were strangers.

Alone in the family, my father turned his back on the
army and became a scientist. My grandmother used to say
that "someone in the family had once dabbled in it." Nobody knew more. In 1924, in the Reading Room of the
British Museum, I found a clue: there is a small Latin book
on pyrotechnics, published in Vienna in the middle of the
eighteenth century by Count Ludwig von Almedingen
zu Harrsch, grandfather of the man whom Catherine the
Great was to welcome as "her beloved subject."

The ballroom with its gilt chairs belonged to a past which
was already remote by the time I was six. We were poor,
though we still kept four domestics, because wages were
sinfully low in Russia. We lived in one of the humbler
Lines of the Vassily Island, the Ninth, rather far from the
Quay. The flat was in the yard, a further sign of social
deterioration, because all worth-while tenants had their
front door in the street. But the house in the Ninth had a
garden, and the rooms were large enough for seas and con-
tinents to be imagined in. We moved there from the house
where I was born, near the Mariinsky Theater, and the flat
in the Ninth had neither study nor library.

My earliest remembered world was unpeopled by the
least consciousness that I had a father still living. He left
us in 1900. I dimly realized that I possessed an elder brother,

George, and two grown-up sisters. I knew their names, but they all lived their own separate lives. Rarely enough my sisters would fill a room with rustling silk, enormous hats, and unfamiliar voices. They closed the door, hands gloved in impeccable white kid. They seemed to demand intimate reaction, but they remained strangers.

My immediate world was small enough. It housed my mother, two brothers, both older than myself, a never-ending army of Finnish domestics, a gold-bearded man at the oil shop down the street, — remembered for his gifts of fireworks, — my mother's sister, Aunt Hermione, splendid and incredible, two great Newfoundlands, a kindly hearted *dvornik* with slabs of mint gingerbread in the pockets of an enormous blue coat, our landlord's wife, fat and genial, remembered in a startling gown of green silk, my tiny Danish grandmother, and a woman who brought fish to the back door, dirty, nice, and immensely lovable because she smelt of the sea. In the flat on the Ninth, Gay and I lived alone. Cyril, my other brother, was at the Naval College, and came home for brief week ends only. My mother must now earn her living, and she gave English lessons from morning till night. Our life was outwardly uneventful, our clothes looked shabby, our toys were few, but each day ended gorgeously with my mother's return. The front door clanged, our slippered feet pattered down the narrow passage, our eager hands clutched at her before the maid could take off the snow-powdered coat.

"Your Mamma is tired. Keep quiet, please."

We were quiet. She was home. The shabby dining room looked nicely dim in the light of an oil lamp. The white cloth shone like snow, and the samovar came in with its song. We watched her hands move among the white and blue cups. Her hands were safety and music to us. She must have been tired in those days: horse buses cost money, and she saved her fares, though, of course, we did not know it. There were no comfortably upholstered chairs to ease her tired body. But her face never showed fatigue, her mind opened widely to receive our day's small chronicle, until the copper samovar grew into a fantastic tree, and we were sent off to bed.

3

∿∿∿∿∿∿∿∿∿∿∿∿∿

ST. PETERSBURG was so much flesh of Finland's flesh and bone of Finland's bone that when I first went to see my grandmother at Loksarjarvi I had no sense of being in a foreign country.

The Finnish Station on the Wiborg Side did not look beautiful the day I first saw it. We came from the Ninth Line down the river on board a tiny steamer, and when I looked at the ugly face of the station, I wondered if we could have left St. Petersburg far, far behind. The day was hot and the huge square smelt of asphalt, squeezed oranges, and dirty straw. The green-yellow face of the station was unfriendly; it seemed to be saying, "Well, you are going to Finland, I am the ugly gateway and you can't escape me." My tiny hands clutched the string satchel with biscuits and a slab of chocolate. Nobody must rob me of my treasures. Hold seemed the most important thing in the world. Gay, my little brother, was by my side, but the crowd heaved up and down, and the pink-faced Estonian maid looked so indifferent that I felt certain she would not care if an ogre came out of the station gates and swallowed us up. But all dangers were over, and I found myself sitting in what I thought was a moving house, watching the drab outskirts of St. Petersburg flash past the window.

I was in the train for the first time in my life. We were traveling third class, all through the endless hot day and part of the night. The early morning came, with new colors and smells; the window gave the pleasure of a world where everything seemed painted in soft colors, and the air was sharp and pleasing — sea and pine needles together. I drank some milk and slept again until we halted and got out. There was a village, all tiny squat wooden huts, a slim blue spire of a church. A woman with a seamed brown face, her gray shawl embroidered with red, came to meet us, and we drove off in a cart which smelt of hay and fish, to the lip of a lake where the bearded ferryman lifted us off the cart.

So we came to the island where, in a low, white-painted house, my small grandmother welcomed us with saffron buns, gingerbread, and milk again. Neither of us could eat or drink. We forgot our manners, our kisses were perfunctory. We turned our backs on the house and stared at the lake. "It's the Neva in a lovely dream," I must have thought. The opposite shore was enameled with multicolored mosses. Beyond a sloping field the tapering mass of a pinewood lost itself in the clouds. It was a paradise, unspoilt by cobbled streets. We explored it slowly, almost afraid lest it were to vanish, leaving us alone and desolate in the ugly station waiting room. Space and distance meant nothing to me in those days, and my reaction must have been of astonishment that anything so lovely could have come out of a journey begun so dismally. Early the next morning I woke and lay still, afraid to tiptoe to the window and see the world. Had it changed in the night? But the window gave me the lake back again, and I shouted, "Gay, it is still there, it was not a dream." My voice brought my grandmother up the narrow wooden stairs. "A dream? Little one, what curious words you use! Why should the lake be a dream?"

Against the white walls of her island house my grandmother still stands, a tiny woman, almost a doll by the side of my tall mother. They were so alike that outsiders often imagined a link of blood between them: it was the expression of peace on their faces, their quiet hands, their softly chiseled mouths. I could never put my grandmother into the gallery inhabited by the rest of my Almedingen relations. She was so different — Northern, granite, pine, and soft moss together.

"Grandmother," I should like to say now, "my mother and St. Petersburg gave me life and something lovely for my own. You gave me the wealth of detail. You taught me to love grass and moss, ants and butterflies. St. Petersburg had talked of water: you taught me to be at home in it. You gave me my first trees and my first sunset, mushroom hunts and the bliss of long walks. There was something in you like the island which housed you, eternal and clear-cut. What did you say once — 'Beauty need not be a dream. . . . Sorrow need be neither burdensome nor ugly. . . .'?"

Such reflections, of course, never crossed my tiny mind at the time of my first visit. All I knew was the joy of having the morning lessons in a huge barn with sunlight stippling the straw and the wooden bench where we sat, my brother struggling with an irregular French verb. I sat by lazily, a picture book on my knees, my mind on the lake. The barn was gorgeous, the kitchen even more so. Its queen, Maria, enormous, fresh-faced and blue-eyed, loved company and chatter. From her we learned many important things. Always, when going after wild strawberries, were we to leave one clump untouched — "for buttons," said Maria; "little folk like scarlet buttons to their shoes and they run about so fast that they will lose their shoe buttons, and they must find new ones every evening."

"Suppose," said my brother, "we took all the strawberries. What then?"

Maria answered promptly that all sorts of things might happen. "Little folk are tidy people, they hate walking with their shoes unbuttoned, and they would get cross."

Once a week the ferryman waited for my grandmother at the tiny landing stage. We all joined her in that expedition to the nearest market place. She wore black serge, and a bonnet with jet trimmings. Shoemaker and butcher, grocer and stationer, the wool woman and the fishmonger — she went everywhere, to talk as well as to shop, and the jet-trimmed bonnet was worn to turn every call into a social gesture. Under her guidance, our own social horizons widened considerably. We ate Wiborg buns, hot and spiced, and drank cool milk with a few strawberries crushed into it. The pastor's wife tried to teach us singing; she knew no other languages than Swedish and Finnish, and we spoke little of either. She fetched a German psalter. On the flyleaf "*Vater Unser*" was written in big purple letters, and we repeated it word by word. All the way back to the island I wondered whether God understood German.

On the morning of our last day at Loksarjarvi, we were called into the barn for "parting prayers." Small, hard-backed chairs stood in a semicircle, from the open door came the pungent smell of hot grass and pine needles, and I sat still, longing for the magic carpet to carry me through the air to my mother in St. Petersburg. I had no wish to sit in "the moving house" again, nor to see the dismal, dusty platform of the Finnish station. My grandmother must have read the misery in my eyes, but I thought that a fairy must have inspired her brief extempore prayer for a safe and pleasant journey. She used simple enough words, I listened, and my misery vanished.

4

IT WAS winter, and we were in St. Petersburg. The frost sang and cracked all down the street, and we huddled in front of the brown porcelain stove in our nursery. Suddenly Gay pushed the big globe towards me, laid a grubby finger on a brown spot, and told me that it was England, where our mother had come from. I stopped painting a cow bright vermilion and craned my neck. The brown speck looked very remote. It seemed incredible that she should have come from there, and I said so.

"She did not walk," Gay said patiently, "she came by boat."

I could understand that. Foreign countries meant nothing to me, but boats were nice intimate things. Cyril, my second brother, could build them out of just anything. All our rare treats and excursions were always by boat, either up or down the river. Our most precious toys were boats again — mostly humble cardboard models of imperial yachts.

"Look," Gay was saying, "they go through the North Sea."

I followed his forefinger on the face of the globe. The route he was tracing spelt nothing to me, but I would not have admitted it for the world. I knew that he was working hard for an entrance exam at the Cadet Corps, and I thought it the greatest honor to have him talking to me during his lessons.

"Then turn to the east, into the Gulf of Finland," he finished, and a secret troubled thought, which had been embedded in my mind for more than a day, burst out in an awkward question: —

"Gay, do all the people in England never smile at all? Mummy does not. . . ."

His blue eyes darkened and he ruffled his untidy hair. "Well, she's got such a lot to think about . . . there are so many of us for one thing. . . ."

"But they are not here," I protested. "George is away,

and so are the others. Cyril comes home so seldom. . . ."

"What's worrying you, Poppy?"

I said there was nothing. I waited until Sunday when Cyril came home, and I chose a moment rather carefully.

"Two silly girls at Uncle Alexis's laughed at me and said we were all funny. What does 'Papa' mean? I mean, who is he? Where is he?"

Cyril explained, rather bluntly. He said that some time before, when I was quite tiny, my father and mother had decided that it would be better if they were not together any more. I could not understand it at all.

"Then we've got him? He's ours. He belongs to us. Why must he keep away?"

"I have told you."

"He is ours," I insisted. "I want him here, unless he's a wicked man."

"Never even imagine it, Poppy. He's clever, brilliant; one day you'll be proud of the name he's given you."

"I don't want a name," I sobbed, "I want him. He should be here if he belongs to us. It's all unfair."

"Poppy, you'll understand some day."

But I would not listen. I felt that I was being cheated in a way I could not grasp. I mumbled that nobody could help me except my mother, and Cyril picked me up in his huge arms.

"You must never speak to her about it. It would hurt her too much."

"Why?"

"Because she loves him," Cyril answered, and the mystery deepened still further. Nobody seemed able to explain it, but I must promise Cyril that I would not go to my mother about it. The promise made me all the more unhappy: I had never hidden any of my troubles from her. The brightly lit nursery became as bleak as an ogre's den because it housed my misery. It was the darkest day in my small life. My mother came back so late that we were in bed, and I pretended to be asleep, my face hidden in the pillow wet with my tears. A little later I heard the patter of bare feet across the floor. It was Gay, coming to tell me the little he remembered about Father — a ride in the Summer Gardens, the smells of chemicals in the laboratory, and a big conference somewhere where Gay had been taken as a tiny boy. "Father stood on a platform. He spoke, and they all clapped. I was so proud, Poppy."

Both of us decided to start praying for his return, and all through my childhood I went on hoping that my father might come back and grow into a real friendly person. There were no portraits of him anywhere, but my fancy wove its own picture of him — someone in a flowing black cloak, with silver locks falling down on his shoulders, a beard, and piercing black eyes. All the remote Spanish legends I had ever heard were poured into that imaginary mold. Gay could not remember him clearly enough. Cyril I would question no more. My fancy had to suffice.

Meanwhile, one morning there was neither milk nor bread for breakfast. The windows looked out into the yard, else we would have seen the clumsy, ugly barricades erected here and there down the Ninth Line. We ate porridge and nibbled at some rusks. Down the passage, from the kitchen came the bourdon of excited voices, and, forgetting all bans, we crept towards the kitchen. The young *dvornik*, in a dirty white blouse, sat drinking tea at the table.

"*Revoluzia* is not a wench, you fools," he was saying. "It is something that happens — bang out of the blue. . . . You just come out and watch. I shall be sitting in the Winter Palace tomorrow, velvet chairs and all!"

The cook saw us, and we were turned away. But the day was strange. The weedy young man from the University, who tutored Gay, never came. Anna and Maria kept aloof and taciturn. Only in the kitchen did they burst into ceaseless chatter. "*Revoluzia*" rang again and again. My mother was back in time for our midday meal, and she told Anna that we would not go out that day. We were still eating when a tempest of noise broke out in the yard. I leapt to my feet, but my mother ordered me away from the window before I could realize what was happening. There was a sound of running feet, followed by screams, a thud, and a sharp dry noise.

We were told nothing about it, but I remembered the scream and the thud, and years later I understood their meaning when, from a window, I saw a small crowd of men and women attack a policeman.

But in January 1905 we could not be told about people being fired at and trampled to death. We knew something was happening; we were kept indoors for a few days, and even the huge gates leading into the street were kept bolted. The world beyond sounded noisy enough. One night we were awakened by the roar of what sounded like the sea. Outside in the passage, a candle in her fat hand, stood Anna, in a shapeless nightgown, a shawl over her shoulders. "It's the workmen."

"Are they Tartars?" I asked sleepily, because some time, from somewhere, Tartars had poured into Russia. She sniffed angrily. "Workmen," she said, "from the Baltisky Works . . . Queen of Heaven, will they shoot at them also?"

"Who will?" demanded Gay, and Anna, hearing my mother's steps down the passage, sniffed again and vanished.

Soon we were taken for a walk. Anna kept away from the Nicholas Quay and made towards the Exchange Bridge. That old wooden bridge joined the Vassily Island to the Petersburg Side, a rather slummy borough of the city.

It was a gray, woolen kind of day. It had snowed earlier, I slipped now and again, and Anna urged me to go faster. The streets seemed disappointingly usual; they were empty, and no red banners waved against the woolen gray background of the skies. But when we got within sight of the Exchange Bridge we were stopped by a police picket. The policeman spoke roughly: Anna had no business to bring children there.

We heard vague shouting from across the river and Anna needed no further persuasion; she snatched my hand and ran back. But she ran too fast; I slipped and loosened my hold. She kept urging me to hurry. I heard Gay's small anxious whisper beside me. I plodded on as fast as I could, and then I knew that a thickly woven curtain of snow was falling all round us. It did not frighten me — I was too familiar with the blind, gray wetness — but I stumbled, picked myself up, and shouted for Anna and Gay. Nobody answered. I imagined myself lost in a world of screams, thuds, and snow, and I fell again. This time I shouted louder. No reply came. I turned back quite blindly, what slender sense of direction I had now gone to the winds.

Snow fell and fell, and my courage fell with it. But I had to move, because I knew that no one must stand still in a snowstorm, and I plodded on. I must have been shouting all the time without being aware of it, because suddenly an arm seized me and a strange voice asked whether I had got lost. I remembered police, workmen, Tartars, and fear turned me dumb. I think I fainted because I remember myself in a terribly hot, poorly furnished *dvornik's* lodge, a bearded man and a shawled woman standing and looking anxiously. They asked me the usual questions, but I could not tell them my address. They murmured "Police," and, very much later, my mother and our own *dvornik* arrived in a hired sledge. Her face seemed to have lost all color. Anna had run home all the way, sobbing and saying that the workmen by the bridge had got hold of me. Fortunately, I had not wandered very far, and the *dvornik* who had rescued me must have got in touch with the local police station, which happened to be our own.

The first revolution was over.

5

∿∿∿∿∿∿∿∿

IT FELL on the last day in March. I had a cough, and my mother decided I had better stay indoors. Sadly I stood in the nursery, sucking my thumb. Gay, his cap in hand, called out to me from the door that I might

finish building the huge cardboard fortress we had begun
days before.

"Get those gates together. Don't upset the glue. We'll
get the ramparts up when I am back."

Off he went. Our cousin Andrew joined him, and I
lingered by the window trying to see them cross the courtyard, but the icy traceries on the glass pane refused to melt
under my breath. I turned to the table and began working
at the gates.

Nobody came into the nursery that afternoon. Suddenly, unaware of the time, I knew that Gay and Andrew
should have been back long ago. It was getting dark. I
could not go on with the fortress gates. I slipped out into
the passage.

I saw a thin scarf of light coming from the slightly
opened door of the hall. I heard a vague rumble of voices.
I tiptoed towards the door and peered hard, but I could
not see anything, and the strange deep voice rather scared
me. The deep bass was asking if my mother lived in the
flat, and Anna's tremulous voice affirmed it. Then I thrust
my head through the door and saw a burly black-coated
policeman in the doorway. The sight of him shocked me.
A policeman in Russia was always a terror.

I kept still. He spoke again in a very low key. I could
not catch a single word, but the gap was successfully
bridged by Anna's sudden shriek: —

"Go to, I don't believe you . . . Queen of Heaven,
save us."

My earlier dread vanished. I darted into the hall. "Anna,
Anna. . . ."

But she and the policeman between them hustled me

away into the dining room. They talked so rapidly that I could not follow them. All I understood was Anna's plea that I should be good and keep quiet. She lit the big bronze lamp hanging over the dining table. Left alone, I sat on the edge of a chair. A world had broken, but I knew no more. Maria, the cook, presently came in with a glass of very hot tea and lots of cherry jam in a china dish. She put the little tray by me and ran away as fast as she could. But I was past asking questions. Tea was a forbidden beverage, and cherry jam a rare luxury on a weekday, and I drank the tea and ate several spoonfuls of the jam, even though the unexpected treat helped to deepen all my suspicions about the collapse of a world.

Cyril, who was never at home during the week, stood in the doorway. I stammered something about Gay, fortress gates, and the cherry jam, but he said that my mother wanted me, picked me up, and carried me to her room. I found her sitting in a chair, facing the door. Her white face brought back an earlier experience, and I thought, "Gay and Andrew must have got lost, like I did — but why don't they come back?" And I ran towards her blindly. She began speaking very quietly.

Gay and Andrew had gone to Gavan for their walk. Gavan was a part of St. Petersburg adjoining the slummy corner of the island, and there the gulf ran past one of the quays. Andrew had insisted on walking across the ice. Gay had argued with him; it was the last day in March and the ice showed signs of getting thin. Andrew would not listen, and the ice cracked under him. Gay jumped in and pulled him out. She stopped, and I clapped my hands. This was a splendid, lovely story. Now Andrew would never dare to scoff at us again! The candle spluttered and my mother said very softly: —

"It is a splendid story, darling, but Gay must have been very tired when he had done it — he could not get back." She paused again, and I stammered that he would tell us all about it. Gay had such a way of telling things that they became part of everything round us. . . . She said again: —

"Darling, don't you understand? He is with God now. You remember, he used to read so much about great men like Achilles and Agamemnon. They were brave men. Gay was a bit like them."

"But he must come," I said. "You see, I had him only." I could not understand.

The rest of that week was blurred. People came and went. Masses of white flowers were piled around the small white brocade coffin. I learned the hitherto unfamiliar smell of wax candles and incense. I listened stupidly to the low-keyed chanting of monks as they went through the requiem psalms. Ice began drifting down the Neva, Easter was near; dirty gray snow melted in the gutters; sparrows came chirping and twittering to look for crumbs on window sills, and winter clothes were being put aside.

I understood nothing. The lid of the coffin stood against the wall in a corner of the dining room. A long footstool stood by the big table. I crept in, raised myself, and looked at that face, cradled in white satin and hyacinths. It was like Gay asleep, only it was not Gay because I called and could not waken him, and I knew that he would never fail me. My mother's door was closed. In those days nothing would have astonished me. I almost expected the chanting and the flowers to continue forever. Andrew, too, had gone. I never saw him again, but I did not think much about him. People who came had a kiss and a word for me. I avoided all of them.

At last the small coffin, hidden under the white flowers, was carried out shoulder-high by my uncles and my two brothers. Someone helped my mother downstairs. A cousin picked me up and put me into a stuffy carriage. We went off very slowly. Once I craned my neck out of the window: an interminable file of carriages trailed behind us. I sat stiff and silent between two red-eyed aunts, and said nothing until the endless drive came to an end.

For the first time I found myself in a church. It made no impression on me. I stared around and suddenly I saw a tall man in a black coat, with flowing white curls, a big nose, and striking black eyes, come forward and take his place just behind the coffin. I forgot all else in the world. Of course, I recognized him, but the whole world had become so bitter and strange that the most usual thing in the world, like saying a word to your own father, would have been impossible. I kept still, staring at him, and the day's emptiness grew strangely, sweetly filled. A dream was coming true — when I saw my mother's hand on his shoulder, for a mere moment, when he stooped over the coffin, and the thin, olive-colored face looked real and familiar in its sadness, as though he indeed belonged to my own life. I took my eyes away, and when I looked again he stood remote and upright. The choir had stopped chanting, and people began moving.

An aunt tried to claim me, but I let go her hand and lost myself in the crowd streaming out of the church. An old, shabbily liveried man noticed me, shook his head and picked me up in his arms. We went along a muddy, narrow path. Then we halted, and the man held me shoulder-high. I watched them lower the white coffin into a deep, black-brown hole. I heard the sharp, thudding noise, as lumps of half-frozen soil fell on the white lid. I looked away and stared at my mother's face, sad and closed. I knew she could not lie, but someone must have lied to her and succeeded in deceiving her: God had never taken Gay; the cold, un-friendly soil now imprisoned him. I scrambled out of the old man's arms and ran over to my mother. Somehow it seemed necessary for me to make her understand that I knew. But I failed. Standing there, tugging at her sleeve, I could think of nothing except our unfinished fortress and his face against the white hyacinths. Tears came instead of words.

6

SEVEN times seven makes forty-six," I repeated loudly, "and if it does not, what does it matter?"

The untidy, ill-shaven young man from the University used a word I could not understand. His hairy, spatulate fingers were savage over a textbook. It was a hot morning and the collar of his faded pink shirt was unbuttoned. He looked shapeless, hot and annoyed. I disliked him. His name was Peter Ivanowitch; he came for two hours every morning to teach me arithmetic, geography, and Russian. I knew he was very poor — he had once told me that he lived on luncheon sausage, bread, and weak tea because a proper meal at the University canteen cost twenty kopeks (about fivepence), and he could not afford it. His manners were appalling, and he used to ruffle his flaxen hair and whistle through his nose whenever my obstinacy got the better of my manners.

"Forty-six?" he bellowed. "And how much is seven times five?"

I could not remember, and he got up.

"You are nearly eight and you are stupid," he thundered; "you can't speak Russian properly; you can't tell the difference between the genitive and the accusative; your mind is all bits and pieces."

I retorted that I had got to Michael Romanoff in Russian history, and to Richard II in English. "I can also speak French. I heard you speak of a letter to my mother, and you said 'le lettre'! This is worse than the genitive case." I thought hard for a moment. "I also know 'Our Father' in eight languages — Slavonic, French, German, Latin, English, Swedish, Greek, and Bulgarian."

He ruffled his hair again and said heavily: —

"What did I say? All bits and pieces! In eight languages! It would not do you any harm to forget it altogether."

That was the end of Peter Ivanowitch. An envelope with three ten-ruble notes was sent to him that same day, and my mother decided that no more tutors from the University were to come to the flat. Peter Ivanowitch, she said, was a very clever young man, but in four months' tuition I had made very little progress. I was not told that Peter

Ivanowitch's theology had earned him such a speedy dismissal.

My mother had taught me my letters, and now she took me for three hours every morning. Somehow things were learnable with her. I asked puzzling questions, and she, too, would look puzzled: a book in her lap, her forehead knit in a frown, she would say, "But I have forgotten myself. Poppy darling, it is ages since I read anything about it, you must give me time." I waited, and her honesty inspired me. I struggled with the Multiplication Table and the abominable fractions, and the no less abominable French irregular verbs, and the thorny mysteries of *der, die, das*. My greatest reward was history, and even now the desk seems littered with the books long ago perished in Russia: Mrs. Markham's *History of England*, drab-brown and well used; Dr. Werner's *Hellas*, which I almost knew by heart; an exquisite edition of an old French *Life of Joan of Arc*; and the thick volume, bound in faded crimson leather, of Froissart's *Chronicles*.

It was not only theology which had sent Peter Ivanowitch away. Anna and Maria had gone. We had moved and lived in a still slummier Line of the Vassily Island. In the narrow, bleak kitchen Fekla reigned alone, Fekla who came from Novgorod and whose accent was well-nigh unintelligible to my mother. Fekla was small and squat, her face the color of well-seasoned mahogany, her hands like beetroot, and her hair hempen in color and texture. She cooked badly and sang worse; but she always sang an interminable song about the boats of one Stenka Razin, a pirate of the Volga in the long ago. The flat was small and Fekla's lusty voice carried far. She would be asked to moderate her vocal fervor. Then she covered her face with an invariably soiled apron and sobbed that the birds of the air had more freedom than herself. She was kind and loyal, and Stenka's boats ended by being endured.

It was a queer period. There was no Finland that summer of 1907. I had already outgrown my gingham frocks, they looked faded and shabby, but I went on wearing them. We lived in the Eighteenth Line, in the gloomy annex of a house which belonged to a Baltic baron. You got to the front door by a narrow court, part of which was glorified into a garden for the tenants' children. It was an oblong piece of gravelly ground with neither grass nor trees, and the horizon was an abrupt red brick wall, but the Baroness had put in swings and a bench, and the garden was included in the rent. The Eighteenth Line was no pleasant thoroughfare: a ghastly warren, known as "the Red House," stood but a few yards away from No. 25. The Red House came to be known in terms of curses, queer smells, slovenly women standing at the doors, and indescribably miserable children. The police ignored The Red House, but it was unpleasant to pass it after dark.

The Baroness's "garden" afforded a few social opportunities. It was there that I first came to know other children of my own age. For a brief while, too, they were pleasant enough, but they had a sharp sense of caste. Our Fekla was a "general." Their parents could afford two and even three maids. We dealt with the local dairy and grocer. Their people, despising such places, shopped further afield. There were parties given for the children, and after two or three months' acquaintanceship, the Baroness's daughter-in-law invited me to a birthday tea she was giving for her small daughter. The party was given in the Baroness's own house.

I went, wearing a neat white and blue checked gingham. My mother had asked Fekla to starch it, and the rustle of my little skirt gave me a strange and novel satisfaction. My shoes were of humble enough white canvas, but in the summer, I thought, such footwear would surely pass muster. I went on to the great balcony, crowded with guests. Through the opened windows I saw long tables laden with cakes and sweets. I went up the steps and the Baroness's daughter-in-law smiled at me. The other children crowded round a man in a funny top hat. "He is a conjurer," someone whispered excitedly. They all wore lovely muslins and silks. I could see their feet in patent-leather slippers and neat white socks, and I hurriedly glanced down at my own, all of a sudden conscious of the white canvas. Then the Baroness appeared on the balcony. She saw me and beckoned to her daughter-in-law. The children were still crowding round the conjurer. I slipped behind the pillar, my cheeks crimson. The Baroness never whispered.

"Why is she here?"

"I — thought," the daughter-in-law stammered, "I asked her. . . . Mimi always plays with her in the garden. . . ."

"This is my house." (How I wished nobody had ever taught me any German.) "You must ask her to go . . . her mother has not paid the rent for four months. . . . What impudence!"

I should have been less miserable if she had railed about my gingham dress and canvas shoes. I knew nothing about any rent, and my confusion plumbed bitter depths. I stood behind the pillar, ears burning and hands shaking. Presently, Mimi's mother came up to me. She murmured something about a mistake and led me past the balcony into the dining room. The Baroness had gone on to join the children in the garden. Mimi's mother stopped by the table. "You will have some chestnut cake, my dear," but for the first time in my life I refused a sugared bounty. I ran home as fast as my feet would carry me. There in the dining room, which was the only parlor we had, my mother sat over some sewing. I halted at the door, too angry for tears.

"The old Baroness sent me away . . . she said something about you not having paid."

My mother stood up. Her face almost frightened me.

"Said it to you?"

"No, but I heard."

I never spent another morning in the gravelly garden. Wet or fine, my mother took me for a walk in the nearest public park.

Chapter Two

FOOTSTEPS AND VOICES

1

❧≈❧≈❧≈❧≈❧≈❧≈❧≈❧≈❧≈❧≈❧

MY MOTHER'S family, the Polto-
ratzkys, had "sat" in the Ukraine since immemorial days.
At the beginning they walked in humble enough lanes, an
orchard and a house expressing their manorial status. Early
in the sixteenth century they turned their back on cherry
trees and apple trees, and remembered that swords and
sabers were fashioned to a purpose. In Aunt Hermione's
notebooks I found an intriguing sketch about one Philip
Poltoratzky, who was born in 1598, fought Pole, Turk, and
Muscovite in turn, and died in 1710, having felled a tree
on the day of his death. Philip was illiterate. At his death,
the modest manorial possessions were increased a hundred-
fold.

Serge, my grandfather, married in 1845 one Helen Sarah,
daughter of John Southee of Beeksbourne Manor, near
Maidstone. They lived now in Moscow, again at Avchourino in the Ukraine, seldom enough in St. Petersburg. A
pure Saxon from Kent, she somehow fitted against the
Russian background; her eyes were dark brown and, unlike

the prevalent Russian idea about all Englishwomen, she was small and graceful.

But she was insular to her finger tips, and she had been bred in the strict evangelical tradition of the early twenties. The English chaplain became an intimate in the Poltoratzky house. Five children were born between 1847 and 1857, all duly baptized into the Church of England. Grandmamma was breaking the strictest law of the Orthodox Empire: in a mixed marriage, once one of the partners belonged to the official orthodoxy, all the descendants had to be brought up in its tenets. Grandmamma must have been unaware of the law, and certainly nobody explained it to her. Grandpapa neither knew nor cared: he was a convinced, if a secret, free-thinker. He lived absorbed in literature and because of his social position he could afford to do very much as he pleased — always within the margin of the law. Grandmamma took it for granted that the children of her flesh and bone should be welcomed into the same fold as herself.

Things went on smoothly enough until Christmas 1857, when my mother was born.

I never learned the complete story. An obscure version insisted that a French valet, dismissed by her for incompetence, turned informer, but the story is rather weak because a foreigner would hardly have been versed in the laws of the country. Another variant hinted at a profoundly pious Orthodox cousin arriving at the very moment when the English chaplain was baptizing the baby, and the suggested dramatic scene was certainly a temptation to the credulous. Still another account told of a governess, summoned to instruct my aunts and horrified at their ignorance of the least thing about the Orthodox observance. Any version may have had a germ of truth, but the root of the matter lay in the ultimate discovery. Grandmamma was astonished, but not perturbed.

"It is a mother's duty to bring up her children. I could not have brought them up in a different fashion. If the worst comes to the worst, we could go back to England."

Nonetheless, the story ran like wildfire. Unkind people hinted that the very last person to hear of it was Grandpapa. This may have been true. When the story reached the Holy Synod, he left for St. Petersburg reluctantly enough. Grandmamma stayed in Moscow, and when a cousin said viciously: "You talk about leaving Russia! Perhaps you will — I don't suppose you could call Siberia Russia," she realized that things were grave, left the children under the wing of a carefully chosen English governess, and flew to St. Petersburg, vaguely planning an immediate escape either to France or to England.

Grandpapa refused to share her feverish eagerness. The young Emperor, Alexander II, was no stranger to him; they had met before, and Alexander had once stayed at Avchourino. My grandfather's generosity in giving freedom to his serfs had called forth an appreciative personal letter from the Emperor. Yet the situation was too serious for any favoritism to come into play. Such an offense could not be condoned without lowering the prestige of church authority, and the latter was unthinkable. Grandpapa must leave Russia. "Then we shall go to England," cried Grandmamma, "and live in Kent." Avchourino must go out of the family possession. "My library! My library!" murmured Grandpapa, the only reproachful note he ever allowed himself. Prince Orloff offered to buy it. "It was an inheritance, not a purchase — I shall not sell it," said Grandpapa, and gave it to Moscow. So they went into exile.

First they came to England, where my two youngest uncles were born. They lived in Kent, Gloucestershire, and London. Shorn of all her glory, Grandmama was happy enough. Not so Grandpapa. He could never learn English. The food bewildered him, the open fireplaces filled him with despair. In a bad spell of foggy weather he went to bed, had his curtains drawn, consoled himself with tea, made *à la Russe*, and Lamartine. "An English Sunday," he wrote to a friend in Paris, "is a penitential Psalm or else a foretaste of the Day of Doom." In Canterbury his wife's sister-in-law found him absorbed in solitaire on a Sabbath afternoon! "Helen, is your husband a Christian?" Grandmamma, after seventeen years in Russia, was indulgent. Grandpapa was furious. Kuzma, the faithful valet who had followed him into exile, suggested going to France. "A Russian peasant may be illiterate, but he is seldom a fool," remarked Grandpapa, and began packing. None dared touch his portfolios, his canvas-sewn boxes of notes, clippings, odd eighteenth-century pamphlets in French and Russian, innumerable fragments of manuscripts, all the material he had been gathering for his monumental French Dictionary of Russian literature. Kuzma packed the valises. Grandpapa mounted guard over his literary baggage. They came to Dover from London. Grandpapa, leaving passports and tickets to Kuzma, began counting his treasures one by one. Two were missing. "Kuzma, we go back to London!" "But, *baryn*, the boat, the boat! We shall miss it." "Let us miss a dozen boats — I must find those portfolios. My most

precious notes are in them. I could not face M. Tourguenieff without them." The burly, red-bearded valet and his
small, slim master, taking no notice of the bustle and hurry
around them, started counting for a third time. Grandpapa
smiled. "They are all there! Kuzma, I quite forgot that
fifteen, and not seventeen, comes after fourteen."

My mother grew up in England — except for one rather
inexplicable year in Brussels, which she spent in the Sacré
Coeur Pensionnat in the Rue de Sèvres. Her brothers were
at school in England, and later they went into the army.
The name of Poltoratzky seemed to answer in Paris where
le petit grand seigneur was adored by all who knew him.
But in England it sounded far too strange and cumbersome.
Grandmamma's youngest sons bore her maiden name. At
least, it went well with their Christian labels: Lionel Ed-
ward Poltoratzky would have struck a far too exotic note.

The cosmopolitan leaven of the family branched out in
its daughters: the eldest, Helen, went to Italy, and there
married Conte Filippani-Ronconi, son of the man who had
helped Pio Nono escape to Gaeta in 1848. The second girl,
Hermione, traveled all over the world, then made France
her spiritual home, and took to literature. Settled in Paris,
she preferred the name of Poltoratzky to any other. My
mother grew up in Kent under the care of two maiden
Southee aunts. In 1880 she went to Paris. She saw her
father's study littered with books and portfolios, and an
engraving of Avchourino on a wall. She pondered over a
volume, bound in dark brown leather and stamped with
the words "Poltoratzky Library, Avchourino." To her
Russia was an alien country, but she wanted to go there. I
believe one of the Orloffs was then ambassador in France,

[41]

and Grandpapa went to him. There were difficulties. A
Russian passport was out of the question. Grandmamma
bridled up. "Go to Wiesbaden — we have friends there.
Or to Vienna. I could write to the Waldsteins." But some-
how, things were arranged. My mother traveled from
France to Italy, and then through the Black Sea to the
Crimea with a British passport, described as Olga Sarah
Southee. Poltoratzky was relegated to insignificant
brackets.

A year later she found herself in St. Petersburg. Cousins
ignored her arrival. Was she a Poltoratzky or was she not?
She settled the question by marrying my father in 1882.

Two years later Grandpapa died, and Russia remembered
all he had done, all the help he had given to men like Bielin-
sky, Dobrolyuboff, and many others, all his own efforts
to bring to light "many forgotten gems of Russian letters."
There were pompous memorial services and lavish eulogies
in the papers, led by Souvorin in the *Novoye Vremia*.
Years later Aunt Hermione regained some of the old family
glory with her work. She lived in France but she came to
Russia every year, staying with Madame Naryshkin, one
of the distant cousins. She went to the Golitzins, the
Gorchakoffs, the Sheremeteffs. Yet my mother remained
an alien, an Anglican, an Englishwoman, whose sympathies
were always and openly on the side of her mother's country. The shattered Poltoratzky splendor seemed to matter
nothing to her. Years later, she said to me that her loveliest,
happiest years had been spent in England.

To us, her children, Aunt Hermione's world seemed
exciting enough from a distance. Her comings and goings
furnished ample material for fairy tales. But the tapestry

was far too rich and costly for everyday enjoyment. In a sense, Grandpapa Poltoratzky was far more real than his incredible forebears and his magnificent daughter. We had never seen Avchourino, but some of his books were in the Imperial Library, and his portrait and papers were with us. Those were tokens of a tangible inheritance. Something far subtler and more significant lay in the fact that literature under our roof was accepted in permanent terms. We grew up with Pushkin, Lamartine, Molière, Homer, Virgil, Froissart, Karamzin, Tourguenieff, Milton, Tennyson, Macaulay, and others. This reads like a motley collection. It probably was. Yet there was nothing really pedantic in it: we were bred to respect literature of every nation, and I can now understand why an otherwise harmless but light novel of our young day was unpopular with my mother. "Beauty, depth, sense," she remarked one day when I brought the latest Locke from the English library, "are any of those in him?" I argued that he was a master storyteller, but she obviously demanded from a book far more than the skeleton of a story.

2

MY UNCLE ALEXIS was ill, my Danish grandmother was away in Siberia, and Aunt Hermione in Italy when the crash came early in the spring of 1909. We had long since left the Eighteenth Line, and were living in a cramped four-roomed flat in the Twelfth Line, miles away from the Quay. All the windows of the flat looked out into a narrow courtyard. The Maly Prospect, with its noises and smells, was almost round the corner.

It happened on the day when Cyril left for his summer naval cruise, and the world became very much smaller, darker and somehow prickly. It still held my mother, however, and remained endurable.

Late in the morning my mother sent the maid away. I can still see her face, rough, ill-shapen and bewildered, as she stood in the tiny, dim kitchen, listening to mother's carefully enunciated Russian. I can even see a neighbor's yellow cat jump through the open window. He rubbed against my bare ankles and miaowed for milk. The maid whimpered. My mother spoke patiently.

"Yes, your work is good. It is not that. I simply can't keep you any longer. I can't afford your wages."

The girl scratched her head. She understood and went.

We, too, left the flat. We walked across the river to the Nevsky Prospect. It was now long past our usual luncheon hour, and we came to the Philippoff pastry shop, where my mother bought six small meat patties. They cost five kopeks each and were lovely golden-brown things, fried in deep fat and served piping hot, wrapped in a tiny bit of thin brown paper. We ate them, standing by the counter, and next to me was a small fat woman in a silk dress, who had ordered ten such patties, and ate them quickly and greedily, and I watched the precious crumbs dropping on the floor. . . .

We left the Nevsky Prospect and found our way to the

Quay. My mother kept silent, and I did not feel I wanted to talk. We reached the Summer Gardens and sat down on a bench in the famous lime avenue. The afternoon had gone, pale silver light lay all over the trees, and I wondered if my mother could afford the boat fare back to the Vassily Island. My feet ached a little, and I felt hungry. We had some tea and biscuits at a cheap little pavilion at the back of the gardens, and then turned back to the Quay. My mother did not suggest a steamer, and I plodded on by her side. We got back to the flat. I saw her turn the key very carefully and slowly. I could see her hesitation. A small oil lamp hung on the staircase landing; her face was very near, dim and sad. Suddenly I realized how drawn and tired she looked. I, too, was spent, but her fatigue seemed different — just as though it had nothing to do with flesh and bone. I shed my usual reticence, reached up and kissed her cheek. She was always undemonstrative, but now, to my surprise, she returned the kiss and said "Thank you."

We groped our way into the tiny hall. I was the first to find the matches.

"Mother, someone has been here."

The hall floor was muddy and dusty. The room was bare of all furniture. I ran past her into the dining room, I saw empty walls stare at me. In the second bedroom I saw an iron bedstead, a heap of bedding, and two enormous trunks in a corner. Everything else had vanished.

"Mother . . ."

I turned. She was standing just behind me, a lit candle in her hand. Her eyes did not avoid mine.

"I could not bear to tell you beforehand. You see, there were some payments I had to make, and I had not enough money, so I offered them the furniture, and they came and took it away this afternoon."

"Took it away — "

I stared at the walls as though hoping to see some tangible memory of long-beloved things imprinted on the pale ochre paper. "Took it away. . . ." That moment a resolve was born in me never again to get attached to any inanimate things: parting with the least of them hurt far too much.

Wildly I remembered them, the few things I had grown up with. None of them were exceptionally valuable: my mother's slender-legged mahogany desk and bookcase, my own small walnut cabinet, the only sofa we ever possessed, the massive dining table, the bronze hanging lamps! That little mahogany table with a cunning nest of drawers underneath, where I had written my first poem, and our only real treasure, my mother's dressing table with a mirror which swung forward, revealing a whole world of tiny drawers, inlaid with tortoise shell and mother-of-pearl. . . . The corner cupboard, its handles carved like bears' heads, where she used to keep our modest silver. The books! Oh, Mother, not the books, not the beloved Shakespeare and Milton, *Joan of Arc* and my very own *Hellas*. . . . No, the books were in a trunk. Books did not fetch much, she said.

We went into the bedroom. I felt so desperately that it was my duty to behave in a heroic way, and there seemed nothing I could say except that now we had no need of three rooms and a kitchen. Bending over the narrow iron bedstead, my mother answered quietly, "You are right, darling. We are leaving here. I have paid everything now."

"Where are we going?"

[46]

"Into an unfurnished room. I am sorry I could not find anything cheap enough on the Island. It is the Petersburg Side."

I fought back my tears, but they got the better of me. The Petersburg Side had neither quays nor ships. It lay worlds apart from all familiar, beloved haunts.

"I — I just hate the Petersburg Side. It is nothing but traffic and narrow streets and markets — and people."

"There is a good garden not far from the house we are going to — "

But a garden was not enough to comfort me.

You can talk about straitened circumstances. You might write an essay about genteel poverty. But it is only after years and years that you can speak of penury in the midst of opulence, of hunger in the midst of almost sinful plenty. You must never speak of the immediate experience unless and until you have learned its consequent value. Otherwise you grow old in bitterness which is barren, and futile. . . .

We moved to the Petersburg Side, to a tall, bleak, grimy house in an alley. We moved into a one-windowed back room, and the sour-lipped Baltic landlady watched our "furniture" being carried in, a smirk on her thin, dirty face. The narrow room seemed fairly crowded with the iron bedstead, two trunks, two kitchen chairs, salvaged from the crash, and a deal kitchen table bought for forty kopeks from a stall on the way to the Petersburg Side. A bed was made for me on the top of one of the trunks. The other served for cupboard, sideboard, and anything else that we could think of. Our clothes would be kept on hangers and in the trunk which became my bed at night. A small oil stove was put into a corner, for now we must do our modest cooking in one room: outside meals could not be considered. Our belongings moved in, the landlady insisted on a brief interview in the passage. My mother returned to the room and fumbled in her bag. I watched her, my eleven-year-old mind able to grasp the situation. The rent paid, we went out for a walk.

The Petersburg Side was nothing but traffic, narrow streets, markets, and people who looked as though they had never seen a sunrise in their lives. It seemed noisy and airless after the wider spaces of the Island. We went into unfamiliar, unfriendly, queer-smelling shops. We bought a small enough portion of ham, a barley loaf, some coffee, sugar, and milk in a bottle. I remembered Peter Ivanowitch and his bleak diet of luncheon sausage and weak tea. The fly-blown, marble counter in the shop exhibited a great slab of most peculiarly pink sausage. It was cheaper than the ham, and I pointed it out to my mother, who shook her head. "There is more nourishment in ham," she said briefly, and my heart felt lighter: Peter Ivanowitch chewed his sausage because he could not afford the ham. We could, therefore we had not quite plumbed the worst depths. I hugged the small paper bags almost cheerfully on the way back to the alley.

But dusk had fallen, and the narrow staircase was dim, slippery, and very malodorous. In the hall, the cabbage-minded landlady pursed her lips at the sight of our purchases. I had a feeling that, had my mother not paid the rent, the woman would have pounced on the paper bags. As it was, she attempted a smile, and I thought of salad vinegar. "*Guten Abend.*" She spoke through her thin lips, and my mother replied politely. But I was glad to see the door close upon her: she reminded me of those Nuremberg witches I had once seen on an old engraving — all wiry, unkind, and cunning.

Somehow, I asked no questions all through that summer. I trusted my mother so entirely that I had not the shadow of a doubt that, if the catastrophe might have been averted, she would have succeeded in doing so. I grew that summer, and I learned much. I learned never to admit that I was hungry. I learned to be reticent with the few people who now entered our strangely narrowed world. I learned not to show pained surprise when our daily allowance of ham and bread was reduced by a half. I learned to put on my clothes very carefully because I knew that an unfortunate rend meant the purchase of a reel of cotton. I, whose greed had nearly always got the better of pride, now learned to refuse a sugared bun or a piece of toffee seldom and grudgingly offered by the landlady's pale and furtive husband. But I did not succeed in learning about thrift.

It was a fine summer, and we spent most of the time in the little public garden not far from the alley. I had a hoop and a big India-rubber ball, and I played alone. My mother went with a few books under her arm, and my morning lessons took place under a huge chestnut. Within the bright green-papered walls of our "home," I often read the poets aloud to her the while she was laundering or cooking or mending. Very few letters came to the door, and most of them were from Cyril, who was now at Kiel. Once a florid Italian stamp reminded me of Aunt Hermione, and I almost laughed — "Supposing she were to see us here. . . ." Mother smiled. "She would weep," I said slowly — "if we did, we could not live."

One morning, at the end of the summer, my mother said she was going out for the day. At the door she turned and added: "I should not like you to go out on your own. There's enough food. By the way, I believe things are going to be better. . . . Thank you, you've been rather a brick!"

For a long time after she had gone, I could not settle down to my books. My mind lived in her last words. They were rare praise from her who never indulged in extravagant eulogy, but I wondered if I had merited them. Surely, I must have whimpered and complained often enough, longing for a ride in a horse bus and for a glimpse of the Summer Gardens, now forbidden because of the fare. . . . I remembered all those sullen spells when I would curl myself on the lid of the trunk, turn my face to the wall and refuse to recognize her presence in the room. And yet she said I had been "a brick"! I knew that it was so worth-while to do the least thing for her. She took it, as it were, kept and cherished it until the right moment, and brought it back with a smile or a word, always an intimate friend as well as a mother.

That day, indeed, the Petersburg Side became a closed chapter. I was not told details at the time, but later I heard that my mother had won a case in the Law Courts, and a certain sum of money came to her. All I knew was that we went out and had a proper meal at a restaurant. Both suspense and excitement played an unkind trick on me. I came back and was disgracefully sick.

We moved back to the Island. Our fortunes had not improved enough for us to live in a flat. We were in rooms now, in a great block at the end of the Eleventh Line. The block had six floors, and each floor had a long corridor. Strangely assorted people lived there, but all the rooms had double doors, and a certain amount of privacy was still possible. Also the one window of our room gave a view of the remote Neva. Of furniture there was none except what we had brought over from the Petersburg Side, but we had a home, some clothes, and food. The block faced the annex of the University on the Tenth Line, and girl undergraduates soon discovered my mother. A few English and French lessons added to our meager budget.

But poverty troubled me no longer. By that time I would have gone to a palace, wearing a shabby gingham and canvas shoes.

Later in the year Aunt Hermione returned from Italy. The block on the Eleventh Line, with its queer tenants and a communal kitchen, appalled her far more than the proximity of the Red House had done. She paid a brief call, and she never came again. From that time onwards we went to see her whenever she stayed in St. Petersburg, the Serguievskaya, the Palace Quay, the Morskaya, the beautifully sheltered and paved Mayfair of the city. That world still glittered. The iced cakes she bought for us at Berrin's were still enjoyable, but I had outgrown the days of blind covetousness.

3

❧∿❧∿❧∿❧∿❧∿❧∿❧∿❧∿❧∿❧∿❧∿

BUT there were still days when I imagined myself unwanted, a tiny bit of flesh and bone, hedged about by laws I could not understand. Everything went wrong on those days.

The slightly improved circumstances once again enabled my mother to let me have a few hours' tuition every week. Unlike Peter Ivanowitch, the new tutor was all dry facts. One morning he said that unless I remembered the square root of forty-nine he would have to give me up. We were alone in the room, and I retorted, my voice shaking with fury: —

"Oh, go to the devil with your square roots," and the door opened and my mother looked at me as though she could not recognize me.

I fell ill soon afterwards, and for convalescence I went to Finland for a long spell, but even the beloved, familiar world came to be seen through a dim glass. Walls and fingers were hateful; walls were prison, and my fingers ached whenever I touched anything. I returned to Russia, and the first day I broke my mother's favorite coffee cup, one of the very few personal treasures salvaged after the spring of 1909.

"I am sorry," I stammered, "my hands worry me."

My mother said nothing, but she took me to a doctor.

With me there, he said I was growing too fast. Then I was sent back into the waiting room. Picture books were there, and the windows were open. The doctor, convinced that any foreigner understood Russian more easily if words were hurled at him, bellowed to my mother, and I heard every word. He shouted that I was too much alone, read too much, that, though my constitution was like iron, yet my nervous reflexes were shocking.

"Is she given to fancies? Does she tell lies?" I heard him thunder.

"I hope not. I have never known her tell a deliberate lie. She invents a good deal — she is always writing stories and poems — "

"Imagination overworked!" he bellowed happily. "Would you like me to speak to the Professor about a school for her — somewhere away — in Finland — ?"

There followed a brief pause.

"I am afraid not." I had never heard my mother speak so coldly.

"Well," he roared, "after all, he's her father. I am sorry. Thank you."

I crept away from the window. My face burned crimson. Going home, I confessed myself an eavesdropper.

"The window was open. . . . His voice was so tremendous. I hated him. His hands were like enormous slices of ham."

My mother looked at me searchingly.

"You heard? Well, I am sorry about the window," and she fumbled for coppers in her worn black purse.

I sat silent. I never discussed my father with her. But this sort of thing happened often enough. Once, at a picture

[53]

exhibition, a grave, white-haired man glanced at me, came near and began: "I heard you were Professor Almedingen's daughter. What a remarkable likeness!" and I jerked my head and answered brusquely, "Yes, I am, but I don't know him," and turned away. But a cousin overheard, and she was shocked.

"You have no family pride! How can you say such appalling things in public?"

"Well, everybody knows all about it. Family pride? What's the good of pretending?"

"You talk as though you did not care."

I said I did not. This was an untruth. I cared so terribly that I did not want anyone to know much about it.

St. Petersburg was not a big city, and its several worlds were apt to overlap on occasions. In the world of science my father went about his ways, an acknowledged leader and master. I did not know him, but what I knew of him had early enough filled me with a strange, inarticulate hunger. In that alienation, shaped by circumstances beyond my control and never remedied, lay rich material for an avidly imagined friendship. Somewhere, in a house far removed from the Eleventh Line, Vassily Island, my father and I read, talked, and argued together. Somewhere I went through my days, learning from him and drinking of his own great cup.

Early in the spring of 1912 he fell ill, and I heard about it by mere accident from my Aunt Catherine, who was the wife of Uncle Alexis and the mother of three brilliant and inaccessible people: Nathalie, who managed the publishing office after her father's death; Tatiana, who wrote for children; and Boris, who worked at the Mariinsky Theater, painting subtle and delicate stage settings for ballets, and who counted Golovin, Glazounoff, and Chaliapin among his friends. First cousins though they were, they seemed remote, and they always awed us. But Aunt Catherine was kind after her fashion, and that day she tried very hard to impress on me the importance of having such a father. She talked about his work at the University, about his own private school of chemistry where he took talented pupils and asked for no fees. "Indeed, I know him to have bought boots for some of them — otherwise they could not have come to the lectures. And he is so encyclopedic. . . . Science and classics together. Surely, you have read his *Ulysses!*" I had, and I loved it, but I could not discuss him. Her conversation was salt and vinegar together rubbed into an open wound.

Early in May he died.

I went to his funeral. The old cemetery had shed some of its bleakness. Young grass was struggling bravely in between the gray coping stones of ancient vaults, branches were greening here and there, and somewhere, almost vanquishing the dark mood of the place, rose the pure courageous song of the thrush.

There were enormous wreaths and interminable speeches. There was a crowd, and the corner of my mind certainly received an impression about his place in the world. But something more than the huge oak coffin was lowered into the soil: all the jealously unshared dreams of my childhood were put under the earth with each fresh spadeful. I could imagine them all, so beloved, so foolishly delicate, far more fragile than the masses of expensive lilies-of-the-valley heaped all round the opened grave. So stupidly cherished, so unreal were they, those endless skeins of secretive make-believe about a happily balanced, wisely chosen lifework, enriched by his companionship, made almost worth-while by his guidance. The unfledged, questioning mind longed to find some assurance from the thought which had left the flesh and the spirit which had ventured so far. . . . But the last spadeful of moist black-brown soil had been flung, and a black-coated stranger mounted on the planks by the side of the grave bowed and opened his lips.

This was not for me. To hear a stranger orate on what he had probably learned from personal experience seemed more mockery than pain. I worked my way to the fringe of the crowd and came to the gates where the carriages were waiting. There were no coachmen anywhere, but an old droshky man crawled by. I remembered I had some loose silver in my pocket, and I hailed him. He drove me back to the Vassily Island, through miles of cobbled pavements, past shops and cluttered market places, over one bridge and over another, until, having once stopped to water his horse at a gray-stone trough, he brought me to the Eleventh Line. Having paid him off, I mounted the five flights and came to our room. The mirror over my mother's bed gave me the picture of a tall, lanky girl, her untidy brown hair tumbling from under a faded black felt hat, her body awkwardly encased in a black coat and skirt and a white muslin blouse open at the throat. Under the black brim the face looked drawn and smudgy: I had had to wear black gloves for the funeral.

I was thinking about a wash when the block porter stood in the doorway and said sullenly that I was wanted on the telephone. The telephone had been installed for the use of the tenants, the rent had been proportionately increased, but the porter disliked summoning us because seldom enough he got a tip for his trouble. Now the silver in my pocket had gone, and I felt a sharp misery because of his sullen manner.

It was my Aunt Catherine — to lecture me for having disappeared before the speeches were over and to remind me that we were dining there that night.

"I could not wait," I said almost brusquely.

"You might have thought of your mother. And — wait a minute — Sonia says she heard you say that the Grand Duchess's wreath looked like a lot of scrambled eggs cooked in tomato sauce — "

"Yes — I said it — and it looked like it — "

"You are stupid," she said impatiently. "Is that the sort of thing anyone would say at their father's funeral?"

"Thank you, Aunt Catherine. I'll come," and I turned away from the telephone to see Cyril mounting the narrow stairs.

He had been away for nearly two years, and now, seeing him there, I felt shy and unnecessary. My face was dirty and my clothes did not fit me, and that day had been like a scorpion. I knew I was glad to see him, but I could not bring myself to say so. "If only he'd chaff me about my hair," I thought desperately. "Does he know? I'd forgotten all about his coming. How am I going to tell him?"

He merely thrust his arm through mine and we went up the endless flights. At last, the door shut behind us, he put both hands on my shoulders.

"Little kitten, I heard just when we docked. Boris sent a wire. Where is Mother? How is she?"

"We are going to Taurida Park, she is with them," I

replied woodenly. "We are to dine there. She is — just herself — "

"It will be much easier for her now. . . . People live and die, but dreams can go on. . . . Little kitten, don't put them into a coffin. . . ."

We tramped the long way to Taurida Park. We tramped in silence: with him, as with my mother, no words were necessary to build a bridge between mind and mind.

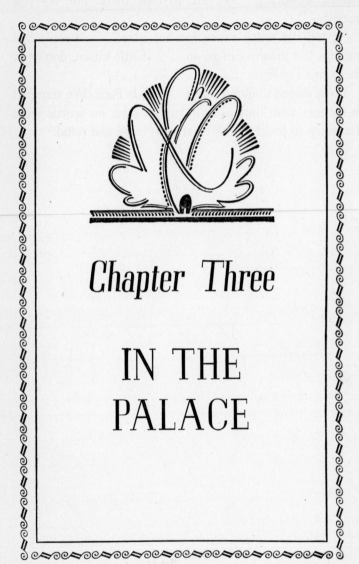

Chapter Three

IN THE
PALACE

1

PETER THE GREAT decided to educate Russia, but he was no feminist. The girls of Russia had to wait until Catherine the Great came into power. She sponsored any venture so long as it was original. It certainly seemed a novelty to introduce the French conventual pattern into Russia. She started her schools, and they increased in number under her successor, the Emperor Paul, whose wife, Marie, had liked the scheme from its very initiation. The schools were called Institutes; there was one in most of the important towns, and several in St. Petersburg. Education under such a roof gave any girl a distinct social *cachet*.

The Smolny in St. Petersburg was the female Eton of old Russia. Its buildings looked majestic enough in my young day. They were painted a watery blue and yellow, a profusion of colonnaded porches giving them a somewhat Italianate appearance. I am not quite certain but I believe Rastrelli was the architect. The Smolny boasted of a park within its spacious boundaries. My own Institute had a patch of ground, called "garden" by exaggerated courtesy. That patch may have been slightly bigger than Berkeley Square, though I doubt it.

We still lived in the Eleventh Line. We were still poor, though my father's death had brought the definite income of a pension to my mother, and the stark edges of want were not as evident as they had been. But the pension was small. There was no margin left for anything like an expensive private education. The word "institute" began to be heard within the four walls of our tiny home. I heard it and shuddered. On a few occasions I had been taken to a Sunday reception at the Smolny, and the starched decorum of the place had nearly deadened me. But Aunt Hermione, splendid and elegant as ever, was in Russia. From Volosovo, Madame Naryshkin's estate in the Tver Government, she wrote saying that she might be able to exert friends' support in having me received into the Smolny. I did not shudder. I wept.

But I knew that tears and other signs of rebellion would not be successful. My Aunt Catherine and her children began telling Mother that it would be better if I went to some school. Private establishments, run by Germans, were certainly good, but their fees were prohibitive. An Institute seemed the only possibility since, by virtue of my father's position, I might be considered a possible applicant for one of the so-called Grand-Ducal vacancies. At last, Mother told me she had sent in her application. It was early in 1913. I received the news in silence. The summer was going on uneventfully enough when one morning the postman handed me a big square envelope. I carried it to Mother, and she unfolded an enormous sheet of thick white paper, with the eagle embossed in black. Standing by her, I read the few formal lines which said that I had been found eligible for the Grand-Ducal vacancy at the Xénia Institute. An early date in August was fixed for my admission. My mother said warmly: "You will try and be pleased about it."

Dumb, hot with sudden anger, I stared at the paper. It was no letter, but a huge padlock made of cast iron. The key would be turned one day in August. A door would then be slammed behind me, isolating me from the only life I had ever lived. To go and live at a school among strangers, and at Xénia of all places! I remembered my father's funeral and all those wreaths, swathed in broad orange and yellow ribbons! Those had come from Xénia because he had been associated with Xénia for years, directing the senior science courses. I felt that they would want to talk about him and intrude into a corner where nobody had ever been given admission. I stared at the typewritten lines. I said nothing.

"You will try," urged my mother.

She had much to say. She reminded me that, at my age, I would be going there for less than three years, that, though she would have loved me to go to England, she could not afford it. She said Xénia had an exceptionally nice head-mistress, a distant cousin of her own on the Poltoratzky side.

"You'll meet girls of your own age. It is high time you did. Perhaps you'll also learn to keep your hair tidy." Her rare smile should have compelled me to corresponding warmth, but I spoke woodenly: —

"Perhaps."

The news was so hateful that a long and tiring walk

seemed the only remedy. I plunged down the Eleventh Line and made for the Quay and the bridge. But even the sight of the river could not take my bitterness away. "After a certain day in August," I thought, "I shan't be able to wander anywhere. . . ." St. Isaac's belfry pealed the vesper hour as I was crossing the great square, and I almost resented the sound I had always loved. In the Morskaya I ran into my cousin Boris. He seemed in a hurry and, ordinarily, he would not have taken much notice of me, but the misery graven in my face made him stop and fling a brief question at me, and I mumbled that I was being sent off to Xénia.

"I hate the very idea of it," I added.

"Hate it over an ice at Berrin's," he invited. "Perhaps you will feel better."

Berrin's was a place where people like us went about once a year, if as often. In a dim cool room we were given our apricot and cherry ices. I poured out my woe. Boris's swarthy, lean face looked so ironical that I almost regretted my candor. But he snatched at a menu, opened a box, brought out some colored crayons, and said hurriedly: —

"I have just got an idea. Have another ice, little monkey, and I am going to give you a drawing as a memento of a great day."

Comforted by the ice, I sat and watched him. He worked, his face very close to the paper, the colored crayons flashing in his long brown fingers. But he was slow: my second ice was finished, and he had not done. I must have begun to fidget because, his head still bent over the paper, he muttered, "Have a third — if you can survive it," and I buried the remaining shreds of my misery in the luscious chestnut ice, the most expensive kind you could buy at Berrin's.

At last Boris finished and pushed the drawing towards me. I peered at it. I could see something like a thin columnar piece of finely veined marble; at some distance from it a pillar of flame spiraled away into a faintly lilac background. Between the marble column and the fiery pillar was poised something like a shape, all hands, loose hair, and a face somewhere, with its eyes looking at the flame and hands stretched towards the marble. It was all clever and broad, incisive, as though he had used a chisel instead of soft crayons, but I could not make out the meaning.

"The thing in the middle is your own self," he said. "I saw you like that! Little monkey, at the moment you are hating much too fiercely. Do hate if you must, but can't you spend your hatred on something worth-while — not a stupid girls' school — "

"You won't be there," I said bitterly, but he promised he would come and see me, paid for the ices, and vanished. I took the drawing home, but I would not show it to my mother.

Years later, I challenged Boris to explain the pillar and the column, and he laughed.

"It was your own family — as I saw it. Uncle Alexander was a flame, and your mother always suggested marble to me. I didn't quite know what you would be like — so I put you in the middle."

"Very kind of you."

He stopped laughing.

"Little monkey, you aren't hurt, are you?"

I was not, but I looked puzzled.

"Between the flame and the marble. . . . Boris, this sounds a bit of a riddle."

"I dare say it is." He stopped suddenly as if remember-

[65]

ing something. "Do you know what Leo Tolstoy said once about you? You were ten, I think, and you talked to him about Homer. He told my mother he thought you might grow into a poet. . . . But a poet, little monkey, must have a language. . . . You couldn't write a poem in Russian, could you?"

I shook my head.

"You must 'live' a language before you can use it. . . . I've never 'lived' Russian — "

"No," he said, "you never have. . . . You might be like your Aunt Hermione and write in an alien tongue. . . . Spanish or Greek, perhaps — "

2

FROM the distance of several years it is easy to throw a cloak of glamour over those few years spent at Xénia. It was, certainly, a good school of its kind in Russia. A magnificent palace was its home. The uniform we wore, relic of the eighteenth century, should have pleased my fancy, always hungry for the least hold on historical fragments. The routine might have grown even amusing towards the end, because, at Xénia, any rule was made only to be broken with zest and eagerness worthy of some nobler purpose. Rebellion against authority, contempt of food and uniform and furniture, were all so many essentials for a true Xéniite, who was expected to be imbued with the peculiar *esprit de corps* of the place. Yet, though I found it easy enough to be a rebel in general, it was hard for me to fashion my rebellion on what principles were laid down by my fellow pupils.

Nonetheless, there were certain things at Xénia which ought to have won and held my sense of wonder. Such schools were greatly favored by the Imperial house. A sister of Nicholas II was Xénia's virtual head. The Dowager Empress Marie paid state visits at appointed times. At certain functions in the great paneled white hall it was easy to imagine yourself plunged into the court life of the late eighteenth century. The very details of etiquette may have been rigid, but to say the very least they lent a certain grace to the daily life.

The chapel should have stirred me into appreciative gladness. It was a detail of rare beauty, pure and restrained, a faithful copy of the church built over the traditional Nativity site at Bethlehem. There was some awe-inspiring depth, akin to the first chapter of the Fourth Gospel, in the peace found within those dark brown and gilt walls. A pious and gentle Romanoff prince took pleasure in it, and he preferred the girls' singing to that of any other choir in St. Petersburg.

The palace, for all its enormous size, was beautiful. The sweep of that regal, gray marble staircase, curving off to the right and the left, must have been an architectural marvel. We played in halls, their high ceilings supported by Corinthian pillars, their walls covered with most exquisite paneling. We read and studied in rooms with doors made beautiful in white and in gold, with lovely mirrors, framed in the scrolled and carven fantasies of great artists. We slept in dormitories, their walls covered by delicate frescoes. There was enough and to spare to feast one's eyes upon at Xénia. But I can remember all that loveliness only in a dry sequence of purely visual memories, utterly detached from any warm and personal reaction to the beauty I had lived with. I must have been far worse than a sullen rebel at Xénia: I was a stubbornly blindfolded fool.

To an uncertainly tempered, ridiculously shy, and shockingly gauche girl of fifteen all that glamour and beautiful dignity were less than nothing. The exquisite staircase was nothing more than a bitter reminder: its marble reaches swept down to a hall where a gigantic Cerberus of a porter, magnificent in scarlet and gold, stood on duty. The great front doors, splendid with carved wood and panes of cut glass, were nearly always closed. Outside, the lovely, free world of walks, books, self-chosen leisure, still remained —barred not for three brief years, but for all eternity. Within, another world insisted on taking most tiresome, immediate shape, insisted on being given recognition, and the process branched out in a tangled growth of quite unnecessary travail.

The routine, as such, was hardly responsible for that travail. Regular meals and fixed hours for sleep and work meant nothing new to me. It was not the discipline, either, since at the beginning, at least, I felt so bewildered by the environment that it would not have occurred to me to break the least important rule. It had nothing to do with uniform. Clothes had played a trivial enough part in my earlier life, and the cut of the old-fashioned "robe," its voluminous skirts all but trailing in the dust and its boned corsage cut surprisingly low, did not mean anything more than a few minutes' irritation in the mornings, when the white lawn accessories, apron, cape, and sleeves, refused to stay in their appointed places and made me late for prayers.

No, it was rather the fact that there had always been a secret corner hedged around in my field; the hedge was high enough, and nobody ever walked there. Now the hedge seemed thinned out, straggling and inadequate, and the corner seemed mine no longer.

The girls I now met had been brought together at an early age. They had so many advantages over me not only where the immediate Xénia world was concerned. They shared interests which meant riddles to me.

Admittedly, my own world had been small and soberly colored. I had never been to a dance or to a real children's party. I had never traveled beyond Finland. What human contacts could be considered mine were made among a group of men and women met at my Uncle Alexis's. Early enough I had learned to listen to arguments. I was still too shy to talk much myself. Most of my education had come from my mother. Some of it had been dull, like the French grammar. But she possessed a sharply defined catholic taste, particularly in literature.

Again, racially, I found myself an alien at Xénia. My loyalty was wholeheartedly given to my mother, her language, her religion, her way of thinking and acting. England meant the whole world to me. I had once found an underlined sentence in Mother's Macaulay, and I accepted it with all fervor — "England is so great that an Englishman cares little or nothing of what others think of her or how they speak of her." Such an allegiance was not a very fortunate asset to bring to a Russian school in 1913 when Germany was popular and England was not.

But I believe the thing they could not forgive me was my shameless admission of our poverty. They came from a more or less uniform level; some were wealthy, the majority just comfortably off. Most of their people lived a placid manorial life somewhere in the country. A few vaunted choice addresses in St. Petersburg. I came from one poorly furnished room in a humble line of the Vassily Island. They were horrified when they heard me mention my "bed-trunk." They were almost grieved when I admitted a predilection for the food we had at Xénia; we could not always afford meat at home, and bought jam was a luxury we had long since dispensed with. They were puzzled because I was one of themselves, and yet my mother had earned her living by giving English lessons. Our very modest silver still bore a crest, but the services of the near-by laundry were often beyond our means. What did it all matter, I asked in genuine astonishment, rather disappointed that it would be obviously impossible for me to give them a sketch of the Petersburg Side landlady. What did it matter? I was worse than a misfit: I had no sense of race.

It was the case of one against twenty-nine, and they won on all counts. They sent me to Coventry. I did not mind in the least. But they, at least, had their own world to live in. Mine had been wrenched from me. Pupils' private belongings excluded books. Much later, I learned the ropes of smuggling in unauthorized possessions, and so could turn to my books for comfort. The first term was barren of all such solace.

3

⁣ᱤᱜᱟᱹᱜᱟᱹᱜᱟᱹᱜᱟᱹᱜᱟᱹᱜᱟᱹᱜᱟᱹᱜᱟᱹᱜᱟᱹᱜᱟᱹ

Oₙₑ Sunday afternoon, when an incipent
cold kept me indoors, I ventured greatly and found my
way to the wing where the senior students had their quarters and learned higher mathematics, science, and art. I
came to a long paneled corridor and stopped at the very
end.

From the wall, in a row with three or four other portraits, the face, familiar only from pictures, looked at me.
I stared at the leonine head, the silver hair falling almost to
the shoulders in untidy locks, the magnificent dark eyes,
the aquiline nose, the sensitive mouth, half hidden by the
carefully trimmed beard, the beautiful hands.

"You are here — on this wall!" I wondered. "You are not
really walking about the place — or are you?"

It was a brief winter afternoon. I stood and stared until
the swiftly gathering shadows drove me away. I wandered
back to the *manège* where we congregated in bad weather.
It was a big, bleak hall, unfurnished except for two grand
pianos and rows of rush-bottomed chairs ranged alongside
the walls. I sat on a piano stool and tried to conquer my
foolish idea that the whole place was haunted by my father's
ghost.

I was not absolutely clear about the initial connection
between Xénia and him. I think Xénia was the very first

among its fellow schools to start supplementary courses for girls on their completing the usual seven years' curriculum. Those senior classes lasted three years, and science held its very important own in the program.

I went to Xénia a year after his death. Many of the seniors still remembered him. The building itself seemed to hold several associations with his work. That nickname "*le Marquis*" was given to him, as a condescending senior explained to me, "because he had such exquisite manners. He came to our balls in his court dress; he looked exactly like a Spanish grandee," and a little later my bitterest enemy chose to add to the story — "We were so glad when we heard that you were joining us. We were certain that any daughter of *le Marquis* would be marvelous. But nobody would even guess that you belonged to him!" And they took to discussing me as though I were not in the room: —

"Still, she has his eyes."

"Nonsense! His were magnificent! Hers are just twin currants."

"And wasn't he clever?"

"Clever? My uncle said he was a genius. He might have died a millionaire if he had ever marketed his inventions."

"Do you remember the ball the year we were in the Lower Sixth? We were allowed to watch from the gallery. . . . He danced like a Greek god."

At my desk I sat pretending that I was reading, and I longed for the next history lesson to come round, since history seemed the only ground where I could walk as a human being and not be considered as a worm of no consequence. I felt no anger against the twenty-nine. Rather, I knew myself beaten to something like dust. Outsiders and strangers, they knew so much about him. They remembered the way he used to smoke a cigar and the reason he preferred a blue-shaded lamp over his desk. They remembered the speech made in 1910 and his triumph two years earlier when two of his pupils were awarded special science honors at a German university. A senior, who had attended his lectures for one brief year, was supposed to have kept one of his handkerchiefs.

Outwardly indifferent, I listened hungrily. Even those inconsequential gossipy crumbs, given in no spirit of love though they were, seemed better than nothing. In a way I could not then understand, those meager details helped lay the ghost later on. Certainly it was good discipline — this strange experience of watching virtual outsiders meander in and out along the paths which should have been trodden by his children's feet. It was, probably, an experience worth having. In fact, it proved the only shred of good I scooped out of those three years. There was an Achilles' heel in me, and Xénia soon discovered it. This was good in that it helped me to rub my eyes and try to realize the very obvious fact that no single human intelligence could possibly count all the pebbles on the world's beach.

Nonetheless, the experience had something dangerously explosive in it, and one such explosion nearly ended in my being expelled from Xénia. As the first year drew to its end, the twenty-nine began to recognize my mother's quality. She came to see me twice a week, and she quite liked the twenty-nine. I never told her about the feud. Some of its ramifications might have led to the introduction of the one topic she and I never discussed: my father. On their side, they were quick to appreciate her sweetness, her generosity, her praise of their singing, a point of which they were very jealous. I knew they approved of her wholeheartedly, though this did not seem to narrow the gulf between us. One evening, in the dormitory, my bitterest enemy stopped brushing her hair and said loudly:

"You know, Mesdames, in spite of all we know about *le Marquis*, there must have been something caddish in him. Madame Almedingen is the sweetest woman I have ever met. He must have behaved abominably to her."

Across the great room I rushed, my right hand clenched hard. That hand came down on her cheek, and the row started to the accompaniment of most savage yells. The girls never told tales, and the battle would have been finished then and there had it not been for someone's locker overturning with a stump of a candle on it. A girl rushed to the door screaming "Fire," and all the powers that were on duty came running in. Next morning I was summoned to the Head.

I went, prepared for a thunderstorm, but her delicately veined face reflected nothing except bewilderment.

"I hit her," I admitted awkwardly. "I am sorry for the row, but I could not apologize to her because if she ever said anything like that again, I would hit her a second time. It is no use apologizing, is it?"

"You are a strange child," she mused. "I know what she said, and it was abominable. But you never knew him. I don't suppose you could ever have cared for him, and yet because a foolish girl says something impertinent about him, you run the risk of expulsion."

My face must have gone pale because she added hur-

riedly: "I hope it does not come to that. But her people
will be annoyed. Certainly I can't have that sort of thing
happen here. This is supposed to be a ladies' school, not a
bear garden, my child! And why did you do it?"

"He was my father. That ought to be enough. The rest
is no business for strangers to meddle with."

"I see," she said slowly and dismissed me. Christmas came
and I left for home four days later than the rest of them.
Nothing happened further. My bitterest enemy never told
her people about it.

4

My second year at Xénia broke in a dif-
ferent key. Delayed by illness, I arrived late in September,
1914. At the door of the classroom I halted, unable to believe my eyes. They all rushed towards me, hands out-
stretched, lips smiling. I made my way to the desk to find
it decorated with several clumsy Union Jacks and an enormous sheet of white paper blazoned with block letters in
purple ink. "Welcome. We are allies. The feud is over."

It was a swiftly passing mood. Quarrels crept in again
— though on a much smaller and far less violent scale. All
of us had people at the front. Nearly all my first cousins,
known and unknown, were fighting in the Baltic, in the
Black Sea, on the Eastern Front, and in the West, where

later the snow-capped fastnesses of the Carpathian Mountains were to shelter so many of them in safety, beyond the hurt of bullet and hatred. Now all my waking moments were filled with the hope that Cyril might be spared. I did not know that a day would come in the none too distant future when someone would say to me, "Thank God that your brothers were not alive at the beginning of the Revolution."

There were evenings when Michael, the Princess's old, grave-eyed footman, slipped into the classroom. Lessons forgotten, we watched him lean over the form mistress's desk, his tall, thin figure rather ghostly in his gray and silver livery. He whispered his message and walked away as quietly as he came. The mistress got up, and thirty pairs of doubt-clouded eyes were riveted on her face, thirty pairs of clammy hands clutched the edges of desks, and thirty hearts took refuge in wild, incoherent prayers: "O Lord, that it may not be for me — nor for any of my special friends," and then the mistress stopped by a desk, her blue-clad arm round a girl's shoulders, and the twenty-nine shivered at the words — *"La Princesse voudrait te voir à l'instant, ma chère. . . ."* A second later, twenty-nine mouths tried to smile encouragement, and here and there a voice found itself again: —

"There's an ink stain on your chin, darling."

"Let me put your cape straight . . ."

"Don't fuss her." The mistress checked all dangerous enthusiasm.

The girl went, and the big room stayed silent. That silence was kept like a requiem. Vocal sympathy seemed out of the question, and I can't remember streams of tears shed by anyone at Xénia. The Dowager Empress came and singled out all the black-aproned girls, whose number grew from week to week. On Saturday evenings, Prince John, Grand Duke Constantine's eldest son, came, as was his custom, to listen to the choir. The service over, the Prince moved from one classroom to another, encouraging and advising us all to work as hard as we could. They made a martyr of him in the turmoiled years which were to follow, and, for all the cruelty, this seemed a fitting end for one who had always felt far more at home in a church than in a palace. People said that his intelligence was below the average, that his very piety had something thin and childish about it. But, remembering him at Xénia, I know such judgments were harsh and unfair.

Prince John had something deep and fine in him. His very piety won you over by its simplicity. He went his ways, convinced that God was very near to him — in spite of his own unworthiness. He came to see us one morning before leaving for the front. "I want to say 'God bless you all,' " he said and made a sign of the Cross in the air. "You and I are friends. I want to have your prayers — not for my safety — because it is in God's hands — but for me to do the right thing — whichever it be. I want you to work and not to spend yourselves in pity."

I remember him standing in the chancel, close to the dark brown and gilt wall. Sometimes I could see that thin, ugly face etched very clearly, and always it gave me the impression that I was looking at someone who had found a home elsewhere. Not as an Imperial prince but as a very humble pilgrim he came to see us at Xénia, to comfort the black-aproned girls and to reassure those whose soldiers had been spared so far. His father wrote good poetry: he lived it.

As a pilgrim, unafraid and calm, he must have faced the gaping mouth of that disused mine shaft in Siberia three years later.

5

IT WAS during the next term that I came to change my white apron for a black one. Michael never brought me the summons from the Head. My mother came, and at her request I was allowed to go home for a few days. This was an unprecedented privilege, but I accepted it indifferently. The world was a cold, dark place once again, and the only shred of negative comfort lay in the realization that this once there would be no half hour at any cemetery. A little later I could afford to think and to picture him going out with the tide, the amber evening skies and the waters washing round the jagged lip of a rock off the Finnish coast. There must have been something of a delicately pantheistic streak running through our lives, because our very love for sky and water, for stone and tree and flower, had something like a hush about it: an eternal setting seemed so much to be everywhere that I can easily understand Cyril's rebellious remark about a verse in Revelation: "No more sea? What a poor idea of heaven!"

But, at sixteen, it is hard to find comfort in pictures and ideas. I spent three brief days at home, and I was almost glad to return to Xénia. Even geometry became something of an enchanted garden. In those three days, alone with my mother in a strangely empty room, I lived through several years; usually so reticent, she was most communicative about him. I heard about his efforts to help her financially. "In the spring of 1909 he coached some junior cadets in astronomy although his own examinations swallowed up most of his time. You know, he hardly ever had an idea of self. Before he went to the Naval College, when we lived in the Eighteenth Line, he used to spend hours at a cobbler's, who lived in the basement of the Red House, and he learned cobbling to save the expense of having our shoes mended outside. . . ."

The day I returned to Xénia, Mother showed me the letter received from the girl Cyril had hoped to marry. It should have surprised me. I had never heard of her existence, but I was past astonishment. I heard Mother say that she was the daughter of a retired naval captain and lived near Riga. I scanned the brief letter. Somebody else's world had fallen to pieces. I said nothing.

"She must have loved him."

"You knew about her?"

"Yes, and Cyril meant to tell you soon. She was coming here at Easter."

I thought, "You never told me, you must have thought I knew. . . . We had always known each other's business. Words were almost unnecessary between us."

At Xénia it was a relief to follow Prince John's advice about hard work. It was better to be tired in mind and

[79]

body than to allow hours to slip by, wasted in brooding and longing for a face never to be seen again. Prince John, on leave from the front, came one Saturday afternoon. Some-one must have told him, for he wandered to the end of the classroom where my desk stood.

"Is it your cousin — Alexander? I heard that he was wounded."

"No, Your Highness. . . . My brother."

"God have pity on you and give glory to him."

A girl in my class came back from a Sunday afternoon re-ception, her face flushed and her black eyes full of fore-boding. She had an aunt who dabbled in the occult and who had tried to read the future. Liza murmured: "She said it all looked like chaos in the country. She said we would live and die in that chaos," and my bitterest enemy retorted: "Nonsense! The war must end very soon. And we shall win because we must. Think of the world under the German heel. . . . It would be worse than Siberia — "

We all shivered and stayed silent until a Cossack girl whimpered that her father had not been very cheerful on his last leave. "Things are getting desperate, he said. It looks as though we were running short of boots and muni-tions — "

"Mania, stop scare-mongering. Liza, what else did your aunt say?"

"Nothing much — except that she had seen Petrograd absolutely topsy-turvy. Even the unimportant shops seemed to be standing upside down."

We tried to laugh it off. This sounded a foolish night-mare. The aunt must have imagined it all. How could a house stand upside down? But the girl took umbrage.

[80]

"Well, stop pestering me with questions! Aunt Marie is no fool. She saw things before the Japanese war, and they came true. Of course, you need not believe me."

We tried to soothe her. We wanted to hear more. When would the chaos break out? Liza shrugged. "She said any time next year, perhaps a little later," and we were reassured.

"We'll have left Xénia by then. Oh dear, surely, the war must be over in a year — "

"She never mentioned the war," Liza retorted. "She spoke about things happening here — not at the front."

A little later rumors grew and spread, unaided by the imagination of anyone's foolish aunt. There was vague talk of treason within the country. There floated disturbing stories about vast sums of money being sent to Germany from Russia. Newspapers were vetoed at Xénia, but they came in nonetheless, smuggled in mothers' and aunts' handbags and muffs. We devoured their contents in the dormitory, but censorship was rigid in those days, and the amount of real news was meager.

A few months before our ceremonial exit from Xénia I sat in the classroom one Sunday afternoon, my small diary open on my desk. I put the date down and sat still, chewing the pen. In a few months the ordered life of Xénia would be behind me, and I would be "out," though the uncertain temper of the day as well as our own poor circumstances allowed of no definite plans. There had been some vague talk about my going to Oxford. In secret I had decided to enroll as a student at the Petrograd University. I supposed I would take history. But that afternoon I was not thinking of history. I glanced through the pages of the diary. An entry staggered me by its terseness: "Mother came to take me home three days ago because of Cyril being killed." There was no other mention of him. Now I took my pen and wrote slowly: "I think I still believe in God even though Cyril is dead." The line looked naked and callous. I wondered if I should have put "gone" or "after what had happened to Cyril," but the grim, brief word stared at me, and I decided I had no use for silken euphemisms. The naked word rather helped to open a small window in my jealously shuttered house: for some months I had lived unfeeling, dumb. He had meant more to me than I could have expressed. I had gone to him with all perplexities. With him I had shared the passion for water and for cloud, for wind-blown sails and tarred ropes, and now I knew that I had never admitted sharing him with others, that I had never thought of what his going must have meant to others — to my mother, above all to that girl in her home near Riga. I had merely sat and brooded because a corner of me had been wrenched from its moorings. But to one person, at least, it must have meant the wrecking of the boat. I shut my eyes and tried to imagine it. Presently someone came to fetch me: my mother had come. I knew I was not fit to go out into the hall. My face was blotched with tears, but they had cleansed away the cobwebs of self-pity.

Chapter Four

ST. LUKE'S SUMMER

1

~~~~~~~~~~~~~~~~~~~~~~~

THAT summer of 1916! Had I but known it, it was St. Petersburg's song of sunrise and sunset at once, but I had no such premonition, and I spent some of its weeks away from her gates. I remember that summer as a field, carpeted with white flowers, big, bell-like petals with a touch of red in their stamens, long-stemmed and virile, sprung from the cool, pale green grass, flowers opened to the wind and the sun, allowed to live their lives out, rooted to the soil which had mothered their seed, never cut and condemned to bowls of water and to yellow weariness within any four walls.

I spent some of its weeks in Finland. I went to Loksarjarvi to see my grandmother. That summer all the earlier visits seemed gone from my memory: I looked at the white-timbered house; the jagged lip of a rock on the mainland shore; the little kirk, which was Finland, Sweden, Norway, and Scotland together; the sloping field where the wild strawberries and mushrooms grew — and it seemed to me as though I were being introduced to them all for the first time. The years of unconscious love and worship were

[85]

expressed in that astonishingly clear mood. I went to Tammerfors to see my grandmother's lawyer, and the journey continued the same note of some familiar and yet novel song. All the past months, spent in Finland, kept me company, and yet the scene they painted was one I had never seen before. I went south, through Åbo, to Hirvansala on the edge of the Åbo-Åland Islands, the tiny little islet where locks and bolts were a thing unknown. I had been there before, and had never seen it. Now the country got hold of me, gripping me so fast that I was almost hurt by its clean, stern beauty, its worth-whileness, its honesty, so much akin to the sea. At Hirvansala, in the little house overlooking a closed-in bay, I stayed with a cousin, married to a sailor. We avoided the war, but we discussed Finland. She did not know the country, and the taciturn, reticent people had nothing to say to her. She began telling me that she was afraid they were being disloyal. "They could not be," I answered. "Their loyalties are eternal — but they are not harnessed to anything temporal — you imagine they should be. . . . Finland may be a Grand Duchy on paper and by law. But Finland is pre-eminently Finland, and the Norse tradition will assert itself one day."

Those were idle words, I knew so little of the situation; but I would not withdraw them, and my cousin was not pleased. "What do you know?" she challenged me, and my mood found a ready outlet in words: "Know? I was bred here. . . . The little I know about the beauty in the world I have learned here. . . . St. Petersburg has more in common with Finland than with Moscow. . . . The little I know about the best in human nature came to me from these people. They are slow but sure. They are as genuine as their own firs. . . . They are as clean as their snow. . . ."

"They are slow and stupid," she asserted, and I was angry.

"Give me a Russian peasant for stupidity. . . . Leave Finland alone. You came here, and you took the ferry back to Åbo because you found no locks to any door in this house. How well you knew your Finland! So you got a Russian locksmith, and you had locks and keys made to fit every door here. . . . But of course, you are an alien. . . ."

She could see nothing except the obvious.

"How can I be — when Finland is in the Empire? I had no need of a foreign passport when I came here. . . . Locks? How could I sleep in a house with its door unbolted?"

The argument could not continue.

Back to St. Petersburg I went. Xénia was behind me, and I knew that sooner or later I should have to earn my living. An academic career was more or less of a foregone conclusion. Its financial advantages were hardly glittering, but fortunately people in that world never think of achievement in terms of a bank balance. Late in June, 1916, I had myself enrolled as a student of the Petrograd University. I knew well that a Russian university did not stand very high in Mother's eyes, so I kept it secret. But on my return to St. Petersburg I found her suggesting that I should do some war work. "It might help you to meet more people and to get on with them."

She was right. In 1916 my social contacts were few. Aunt Catherine's house provided certain channels, and the great Imperial Library was mine to explore at will. Apart from the English Church, the Library, and one or two houses, I went nowhere and made no friends. I was intolerant, critical, moody, taciturn, and ridiculously sensitive. I also imagined that because I had read Ammianus and Eusebius and was more or less at home in the centuries between the fall of the Roman Empire and the capture of Constantinople by the Turks; because I knew my Spinoza and dabbled in scholastic theology; because of an untidy, unsorted, casually acquired mass of information, shelved in between muddled reflections and incoherent judgments — because of it all, I was singled out from the rank and file. Those were hardly fortunate assets. My sense of humor lay hopelessly dormant: I could not even see what a fool I made of myself on many an occasion.

"Don't you ever read Taffy?" asked a cousin. "You simply must. She is a genius. . . . Fancy anyone being able to write funny stuff during the war! That story about a fat woman strap-hanging in a tram . . ." and I broke in with the pompous manner of a Chinese mandarin: "I have not heard of her. I never read light fiction."

She laughed and reminded me about my father and his passion for Mark Twain and Jerome K. Jerome. I frowned and said that I was reading Feuillet's *Histoire de la Philosophie*.

"Drop it," she counseled. "Go to the Gostiny Dvor, buy yourself a few archines of cheap pink silk, have a nice frock made by Agrafena Filipovna, and come with me to a merry little war party at the Zabalkansky Club. We are not grand — we are just alive. We dance and sing and talk about everything under the sun — sausages and the Western Front, stockings and the future of Europe."

I said a brief good-bye.

[88]

2

~~~~~~~~~~~~~~~~~~~~~~~~~~~~

BUT what about your war work?" asked
Mother.

I was not sure of it. Everybody seemed to be making
swabs and knitting scarves. My own efforts resulted in a
scarf which was all knots and tangles. Of course, there was
nursing. The magnificent Anglo-Russian Hospital on the
Nevsky, housed in the palace of Grand Duke Dmitri,
seized my fancy for a few days. Mother refused to share
my enthusiasm. "Nursing is a vocation. You have none. I
don't think you would turn sick at the sight of blood, but
you are so impatient and intolerant. You have not got
enough love for people as people." And I knew she was
right.

Nonetheless, St. Petersburg was burning with war-
work fever, and I met several Xénia girls wearing the short
white veil and the scarlet pectoral cross on their white
aprons. They looked tired but cheerful. Their Mecca was
the front. Their hands were discolored with disinfectants.
They discussed amputations, internal operations, gangrene
and gas poisoning, using important, obscure terms. Their
Olympus was peopled by doctors, their Hades teemed with
matrons, senior sisters, and patients' relatives. There was a
suggestion of carbolic, gray army blankets, and tepid
cocoa in their manner, and I wondered whether they

imagined that all the disasters befalling a human body had been called into being to give them a chance of realizing themselves in some fashion or other.

Yet such reflections in no wise solved the problem of war work. War work came to me in the end, but I never did anything spectacular in that field. Mine was a tiny basket to carry in a crowd of those who were mostly burdened with enormous crates. Yet the contents of that small basket proved more valuable than a whole library of books on abstract philosophy.

The English Ambassador's wife, Lady Georgina Buchanan, was wholly absorbed in war work. Every Monday there were sewing parties at the Embassy. The British Convalescent Home in the Vassily Island was run under Lady Georgina's close supervision, and so was the Anglo-Russian Hospital on the Nevsky. She had an enormous amount of energy, and she wasted none of it. Eventually, the Emperor made her Dame of the Order of St. Catherine, and this was no amiable gesture: she had fully merited the honor.

In 1916 she launched a fresh venture — the aftercare of convalescent soldiers and their families. Men sent to the important military hospitals in St. Petersburg had their names and home addresses sent to the Embassy. But the hospitals had sent in inaccurate reports once or twice, and Lady Georgina decided to get herself all the details she needed. She went the rounds of all the hospitals; each soldier, on leaving, had a bulky parcel given him for himself and his family. The gift was mainly clothes, and children's ages had to be verified before such parcels could be distributed. The scheme branched out in several directions.

Those who received the first batch of parcels went home convinced that the capital housed an angel from abroad, whose name they could not pronounce. They called her "Excellency" to her face, and "the English Ambassadress" behind her back. Once they reached their villages, they broadcast the story. They wrote poignant letters. Most were illiterate, and parish clerks were employed as secretaries to pen grateful epistles to the English Ambassadress. All of them fervently hoped for an answer. Lady Georgina knew no Russian. At some hospitals where she called, somebody would be found with a more or less adequate knowledge of French, but the services of such interpreters did not satisfy her. She wished she might have someone who, as it were, belonged to her, who knew Russian and was also at home in English. The volume of "convalescent" correspondence daily reaching the Embassy grew and grew, and she could not deal with such letters. When she asked if I would help her I agreed gladly, and together we drove in a common droshky to the Obuchovsky Hospital.

The Obuchovsky, its bleak, thickly serried buildings standing on one of the lesser Quays, was usually spoken of with bated breath. Built in the reign of Catherine the Great, it looked as though no spring cleaning had ever come near it since its opening day. Outside it suggested a prison. Within, the air was thick with carbolic, dust, soapsuds, and stale human sweat.

They had been warned about Lady Georgina's call, but the unkempt man at the door yawned, saw an elderly woman and a young girl alight from a common droshky, and turned his back on us. The door stood open; "Let's go in," said she, and entered; and the man's mottled face went unpleasantly red when I explained who she was. He bowed low from the hips, he sniffed and whimpered, he ushered us into a stuffy little room, lined with several dusty ledgers, dead flies patterning the grimy window sill. "Could the Fortress be any worse?" I wondered to myself. There were a few chairs, but we preferred to stand. We waited, and nobody came. After a few minutes, Lady Georgina decided to go upstairs.

Halfway up, a fussy, gray-mustached doctor swooped down on us, seized Lady Georgina's hand, kissed it noisily, and filled the building with the sound of terribly accented French apologies. It was dreadful, incredible. . . . Would she like some wine, any refreshments? He was so sorry — it was a Wednesday, they were always busy on Wednesdays, but she could rest assured that he had not known about her coming. . . .

Lady Georgina cut him short by saying her time was limited, she wanted neither wine nor biscuits, and on we went.

In and out of the numberless wards did we go that morning. Lady Georgina had a polite smile for sisters and nurses, but she managed to ward off their fussy servility by her determination to get to the men. The only language she could use to them was here a smile, there a brief but reassuring gesture. It answered, judging by the men's spontaneous and glad reaction. I followed in her steps, my own tongue cleaving to the roof of my mouth. The air in those dreadful colorless rooms was thick with pains as well as with iodine and carbolic. We began to work soon enough, and I tried to think of nothing except the naked facts of each case. It sounded something like this: —

"Michael Volkoff? Government? Borough? Village?
Married? How many children? Three? All boys? Ages?
Sorry, I have not got them right. Seven, four, and two, is
it? Thank you so much. Gavril Romanoff? Government?
Borough? Village? Married? Any children?"

Recorded in cold black and white, this may suggest soulless repetition. Yet, with the first ward done, the completed
notes clenched in my hot hand, I knew that to the tired,
white-faced men in the impossibly uncomfortable beds,
each of those questions must have come like a shower of
pure cool water. They put so much life into the answers.
Those who could move raised themselves on their elbows,
faces all lit up with the peculiar light of expectation. Their
eyes raced between the pencil and my face. Their replies
were colored with gratitude for a gift as yet not received: —

"Nice, your coming here. . . . Married? Yes, praise be
to God. . . . Eight years come next St. Andrew's day. She
is such a mate, *baryshna*, never a grumble in her letters.
Even when the cow died, she found something cheering
to say."

"Married? Yes, and my old woman is coming to fetch me
home. I will tell her all about you, *baryshna*."

"Children? Why, two of them given by God. A boy of
eight, such a sprightly lad, took to minding pigs before he
was five. And a girl, a baby one," wistfully, "I have not
seen her yet — "

My impression of the Obuchovsky, as such, was anything but pleasant. The hard hand of rough, tyrannical
officialdom had lain on it so long that the ocher-painted
stones of the façade and the manners of its personnel seemed

dangerously at one. The airlessness was incredible. The meals carried in anyhow by rough, slovenly nurses, loud of voice and heavy of step, were all steam, grease, chipped dirty enamel and tin. The walls were bleak. Gray army blankets, muddily gray walls, the yellowish cotton of none too clean pillowcases and towels, the drab yellow paint of the floor, the gray ceilings, and those grimy windowpanes which all but vanquished the fierce sunlight of a warm September day. . . . They disliked fresh air at the Obuchovsky, and the windows remained closed. As we went on, we noticed the feverish hustle with which flurried, red-cheeked nurses removed dirty white trays, stacked with used dressings, and their smell suggested something suspiciously stale. Not all the men were "tidied up." One with a face wound lay on one side when I came up. The dressing did not look fresh even to my lay eye; his pillowcase was horribly soiled with matter and blood, and the stains looked dry. I said I had better call a nurse. He shook his head. "They will do it some day," he murmured.

I found my hands full indeed during the following weeks. The Obuchovsky lists had all to be checked over, and I must go there time and again, until the thick musty air grew almost familiar. At the Embassy, I had "convalescence" letters to deal with. They arrived in thin, smudgy envelopes of all sizes and colors. Their postmarks varied from Archangel to Odessa, from Pskov to Tobolsk, from Nijni Novgorod to Blagoveshchensk. Some came from obscure Siberian villages where the post, apparently, functioned once a month. Others were sent from Caucasian hamlets, and the writers mentioned that the nearest post office was a good day's ride from their *saklia*. Some came unstamped and addressed very simply to "the English Ambassadress, Petrograd, *k Angliyskoy Poslannitze, v Petrograde.*" Few, if any, were written on proper letter paper. Some were scribbled on blank pages of account books. A few exceptionally lengthy missives were "calligraphed" in the local parish clerk's copperplate hand on lined sheets of thick foolscap. One, from a Pole, was written on the back of a loudly colored religious card.

All of them "saluted her Excellency" at the beginning and remained "with undying gratitude her humble servants" at the end. Most of them were undated, and a good many carried no address of the sender; in such cases a reply meant some search in the files. Sometimes the very signature defeated all efforts at deciphering.

Some were soldier-like, brief. They wrote they had arrived safely, were in good health, and hoped that hers was just as good. They thanked her for her gifts and "saluted" again. But such were comparatively rare.

Next came longer letters, embellished with a profusion of rather tangled detail about their journey and arrival. They mentioned a neighbor's *isba* being burned down and a wife's tears on unpacking the parcel from the Embassy. Plans for the future would also come in, and "the Ambassadress's" advice was sought on such matters as the purchase of a cow or a turkey. There were brief paragraphs about the children and the brave show they made in the village with their new shirts and socks. These richly narrative letters suggested painstaking efforts of a priest or a parish clerk. They were passably spelt, and the illiteracy of the sender was made obvious by the three crosses scrawled beneath the neat and lifeless signature put in by the scribe's hand.

But there was another category. It gave me furiously to think, and it marched parallel with the earliest impressions gathered at the Obuchovsky. Those were not real letters. They read like dirges, but something raised them high above the level of cheap and calculated whining.

Some such epistle came from a cavalryman somewhere east of Kazan. After the customary opening, he went on, "And I gave your parcel to my sister, and she thanks you and salutes you." This startled me because I well remembered the man's unusual name. He had spoken eloquently about "his old woman." Married? "Yes, God be praised. She is a treasure. She is carrying on singlehanded. And letters have been coming every month — by the deacon." His thin brown hand fumbled for a thick bundle under the pillow. "She never runs into debt. . . . Such a rare woman. . . . I am not half good enough for her, *baryshna*. . . ." Yet he had given his parcel to a sister. I read on. "And a soap merchant came from Kazan last St. Nicholas's day, and he had a lot of money, and my wife went with him, and my sister is looking after the baby, and I salute your Excellency, and God grant you health for many years."

3

~~~~~~~~~~~~~~~~~~~~~~~~~~~~~~~~~~

THE last months of 1916 were weaving a
feverish enough texture of their own. The city was brooding over a darkly uncertain future. The richly colored gossip, bred in market places and in food queues, had, of
course, to be discredited, but deeply disturbing rumors
continued seeping through channels which could not always be dismissed as untrustworthy. In our own circle we
met few enough people. We lived in two modestly furnished rooms in the Bolshoy Prospect, and we had to
gauge the situation through what openings our life afforded us. My mother seldom went out. Aunt Catherine and her circle were not very communicative. Aunt
Hermione was in Italy, and letters from Rome took ages
to arrive, and often enough whole pages were *"caviared"*
by the censor. But there were ample signs of growing un-
rest. Local food riots grew both in frequency and in scale.
Police and plainclothes detectives were more busy than
usual. Public meetings were strictly forbidden. Mounted
cossacks paraded up and down the main streets almost
every day.

I heard prophecies of defeat and of famine. *Revoluzia*
never came within my hearing. Had it done so, I might
have given my approval. A year of war work at the Obuchovskaya had convinced me that things were far from

well within an autocratic country. A policeman's brutality, witnessed in early childhood, was a faithful echo of the general attitude of all authority to "the black people." I had such thoughts, but I kept them secret.

It was the loveliest autumn ever remembered in St. Petersburg. It had been a very hot summer, and every bit of gray stone and purple granite must have absorbed something enduring from the sun, and now began giving it back without stint. Few of those autumn days brought the usual high winds and gales from the Gulf of Finland. It was sometimes so very still that the tall old limes in the Summer Gardens stood as though they had been sculptured out of living flames. An occasional blue-white mist from the Neva lent the trees an other-worldly appearance, coating the deep orange of oaks and the russet of beeches and elms with a faint pearly film. Against the dark trunks, the white marble of statues, once pillaged from the Saxon Park in Warsaw, became fierily rose. All was so still that the fall of a leaf on the ground sounded almost loud. The great lime avenue, leading to the white house built by Peter the Great for a palace, stood vested with an incredible silver dignity, and, as the shadows lengthened and insisted on cloaking the blue breast of the Neva, the usual bleakness of the ancient fortress softened, grew ethereal and almost tender, as if it knew itself incapable of resisting the urgent plea for pity and gentleness born of the twilight.

Farther down, at the mouth of the arrogant, crowded Nevsky Prospect, clumps of late asters in the Alexander Gardens burnt like gorgeously colored candles, and the gardens suggested a chapel of ease to St. Isaac's Cathedral. The primrose buildings of the Admiralty, low-roofed and graceful, looked like a picture cut from the pages of some German fairy tale. The Bronze Rider in front of the Senate sat his magnificent horse on the massive granite rock. On the Vassily Island, along the busy cobbled Quay, where Norwegian, Swedish, and French were heard side by side with English, Dutch, and Spanish, the great merchantmen stood at anchor, the pale Northern sun indulgent over their begrimed hulks. These grew fewer in number day by day. People talked of a severe winter. Most boats raised anchor and rode towards the gates of the Gulf.

Still, squalor and anxiety, increasing from day to day, marched by the side of all that beauty. By the end of 1916 shortage of food ceased being a distant threat and turned into a grim reality. The rich could buy anything and forget the meager rations allotted by the Government. But for people like us — and, after all, we were the majority — shops gradually became forbidden ground. Grocers' shops, in particular, were zealous in displaying empty windows and counters swept clean of all the stock they had once had, but the storerooms were full. Butter, bacon, jam, flour, sausage, and ham could be had — at a price; and such hoarding, for the benefit of the few, led to the gradual shortening of "legal" rations. A girl I had known at Xénia met me in the Nevsky one day and invited me to tea. The round table was laden with things I had almost forgotten to dream about. She made me a pile of liver-sausage sandwiches. Munching, I asked her: "I say, did you have a parcel from the country or what?"

She made no secret of the provenance. The local police inspector was indebted to her father. A chit had been given to her mother, addressed to the nearest important grocer, whose counters were now blamelessly empty. On the strength of the chit, the grocer supplied them with everything. "Not at the pre-war prices, of course," she shrugged, "but then the man must live, I suppose." Those men indeed lived well. Speculators in flour, beef, and sugar were busily amassing their gains. The ruble had not altogether lost its meaning, as it was going to do soon, and we did not discuss prices in dizzy millions, but fifteen rubles for a pound of butter was not considered extravagant.

From the point of our budget, fifteen rubles meant food and rent for a fortnight, and butter was a forgotten luxury. We preferred to talk about beef while eating chilled horse-flesh, and of sugar when dropping unpleasantly flavored saccharine tablets into our tea. But those were minor discomforts.

Always, through those months, something got hold of you in the streets. The Press became so reticent that such cramped and censored news as appeared in their columns led to fresh outbursts of scaremongering rumors. In early December, the *Novoye Vremia*, reporting a sitting of the Duma, mentioned that at a certain hour of the afternoon some news came to the House which electrified all the members. This was the only way they were allowed to mention the report of Rasputin's death, and the circumstances which surrounded it were, to the best of my knowledge, never made public in print. But the crop of stories! Some were too fantastic to be believed — nevertheless they were believed by apparently intelligent people; we lived in a world so unreal that the last vestige of all difference between the grotesque and the probable was fast disappearing from the common life. There were stories about the Empress praying for a German victory, about a Grand Duchess smuggling gold into Germany "in the coffins supposed to hold dead German prisoners of war," and the person telling the story added that the Grand Duchess had packed the gold herself, in dead secrecy. There were stories about premonitory visions at the front, and weird prophets began appearing here and there in the country. There was rumored to be a terrible increase of rats in Archangel, and the rats were supposed to devour all the flour allotted to the civilian population. Famine was no longer a distant menace. There was a great deal of hysterical talk about its horrors, but people who bewailed the ever-growing scarcity were usually those who could afford to slip into a shop and enrich their larder by a few pounds of butter and sugar denied to those with slender purses. The economic rottenness of Russia had been in evidence for some time before the Revolution. They said conditions in Moscow were far worse than with us, but I could not gauge whether this was true. Moscow was too much of an unknown world to me.

4

NOW the Quays were deserted. The streets were just queues, full of ceaseless, whimpering chatter. I still had an occasional hour of leisure, and I discovered that the Smolensky Lutheran Cemetery was not too distant.

I found peace there. There was a tidily kept avenue with a bench at the end. I brought my books to the Smolensky. Nobody ever came down the avenue.

That summer had been something of an earthquake. I had then left Xénia, and my human contacts had been thin and few. They had since increased greatly, but the general tenor of life had grown so disturbing that thought, as such, was getting difficult. The Obuchovsky experience had brought endless revelations. That work was over. I had a few private lessons. Like most people with humble incomes, our life was checkered by the incisions of almost constant want. I had once known it well, and it did not frighten me. But the tide of life around me was getting fiercer and fiercer, one's own self smaller and feebler. It seemed safer to be cradled in a crowd, carried along by its mood. Suddenly I said aloud: "And yet I can do so much more when I am alone. I get dried up and wooden when I am with other people. . . . It is a vicious circle whichever way I look at it," and a voice from somewhere behind a tree replied instantly: "Well, some of us are lonely animals by nature."

I thought of ghosts, my hands went cold, but the ghost came out and I was reassured: no ghost had ever been seen munching a fat, rosy apple.

She was small and slight. She wore a well-cut coat and skirt and a wide-brimmed felt hat. A pink blouse was the only touch of color about her. Under the wide brim her face considered me gravely. Its pallor was extraordinary, its eyes were as black as the clothes she wore. A long white scar ran from the left temple to the chin. The scar made her at once ugly and attractive.

She sat down on the bench and went on: —

"Some of us must be lonely animals. Herds are not for everybody. But I watched you come here, and I knew I had met you before. Haven't you got a brother working with Golovin at the Mariinsky Theater? A tall, dark young man with intense eyes, a lazy voice, and the most beautiful hands an artist was ever cursed with? I always felt they should be kept under glass. And they are always dirty — he has a habit of wiping his brushes on them."

"You mean Boris Almedingen. He is my cousin! But I don't remember having ever met you."

"I am Sonia," she said simply. "Once I had a surname, but I never use it now. I am a mosaicist. I know Boris. We were in Rome together. You have an aunt there. She wrote to Prince Massimo about us, and Boris did some fresco studies at the palace. Those were gorgeous days, centuries before this wretched war. And now I am miserable because the people for whom I have begun a life-size St. Michael have just told me that nobody in this country would ever want mosaics again, and would I please stop the work! So I bought some apples and decided to have a walk in the cemetery. But what is the matter with you?"

"Nothing!" I was curt to rudeness, but Sonia remained unruffled.

"You don't tell fibs very well," she commented. "I believe you had better begin talking. There may be impiety in words, but it sometimes pays to be impious. Nobody in the world has the right to look so miserable. Look at me — my lifework gone, and I can still eat apples. By the way, have an apple —"

I muttered that I never ate between meals.

"Of course, you are no pure Russian. I forgot. I never

[103]

have proper meals. Well, if you won't talk, you might let me see your hand." She seized it even as she spoke, and I let her have her way. "What a jumble! Your heart seems quite ousted by the mind. Please don't grow into an academic fossil. . . . There is something *manqué* about you. . . . It won't be your work. It might be people —"

"You caught me talking to myself," I accused her, but she answered quite indifferently that she had already forgotten all about it.

"I can see you have no use for people. When I was your age, I thought so too. I imagined that I could drink my soup alone, but I soon found that the world is not big enough for such lordly isolation. It always keeps round the corner. . . . Some people will never share their soup . . . they hug it so jealously that they forget to drink it, and the soup gets spilled, and nobody ever refills your bowl. It is rather unpleasant to sit in front of an empty bowl." She let go of my hand and leant back. "I wonder if you have ever thought that people might have some use for you."

"I know they haven't."

"Rubbish!" So vehemently did she clasp her hands that the skin of her knuckles went blue. "I am certain you have never given them a chance. You have merely sat still, neither drinking out of your bowl nor sharing the soup. I should say that hoarding is worse than spilling."

She had spoken strangely, almost wildly, but then she was a stranger; I could not remember having ever met her anywhere. In an ordered and orderly environment I might have dismissed her as a tiresome crank. But at that time everybody was either a crank or a fool. Few were soberly wise — like my own mother. The brooding temper of life was drifting towards a dark-cliffed island on an uncharted sea.

I glanced at her, black and white and pink, her small hands engaged in polishing yet another apple. Some unaccountable impulse stirred in me. Without much further reflection I laid my small life's mosaic before that strangely spoken mosaicist, who had no longer any use for her surname. The narrative must have been incoherent enough, but she never interrupted. The apple forgotten, her hands were comfortingly still, and her black eyes stared at the dreadfully mournful sarcophagus opposite the bench. I guessed that the whole of her mind was listening, and words kept coming with a vigor I had never suspected I could use. My early life, Father, Gay, Mother, Cyril, Xénia, men at the Obuchovskaya, Petrograd and Finland, dreams, moods, ambitions and preferences, all in untidy bits and pieces, slipped into the story. When I had done, I felt as though I had drunk some cooling draught. At the same time, a corner of my mind hoped that I might never meet her again.

"Well, yes, I see it all . . . at least, you are so terribly alive," she said slowly. "If you were not, things would not trouble you. If you were not, you'd take it all for granted. But evidently you can't. It is all the travail of growth. It has been a patchy process in your case — too early in some things, unpardonably late in others. Hence the confusion."

"I want to do," I said passionately. "I want to be by doing."

"You are. Read Descartes for comfort. Thought is the kernel of being, and thought is action. Advice and comment are the shoddiest alms imaginable, but I should say that the shabbiest bit in your picture is that dreadful sense of superiority. Yet it looks as if you were growing out of it. . . . You never knew the lovely, leveling influence of comparisons. Don't keep aloof from your kind . . . think of your bowl of soup . . . don't grip it too hard." And she got up so abruptly that I stammered, "You are not going?"

"Of course I am, you silly child. I don't believe you'd like me to stay, either. You are being lamely polite. Well, I am glad I have met you. Now I have made up my mind about the future. I shall sell my mother's emerald earrings and a few other things today, and leave for Japan tomorrow morning. I might learn something new out there. Russia is no place for artists. Good-bye." She moved away, not offering to shake hands. "I am sorry you never eat between meals. Those apples were good." And she was gone.

I went home and told Mother about her. My description of Sonia, who had once had a surname, bewildered her. But she said she rather liked the strange parable, and added: "I have some news for you. How would you like to carry your little bowl to England?"

5

THE Norwegian wife of an American engineer was going back to the States in February 1917. She had just had a baby, and the long journey across Finland

and Sweden to Bergen, not to mention the crossing to Hull, terrified her. She was looking for someone to accompany her as far as England. "Her child never lived," explained Mother. "She is very depressed. I hope you will be able to cheer her up. I don't think she will want much else. If only you could go with her as far as London."

Feet winged, heart beating high, I went to see the young Norwegian. I found a slip of a girl with enormous gray eyes which looked as though they would never recognize any joy again. In almost unbroken English she said she hoped to leave for England in February 1917; she could offer me my fare and a very small salary, but figures meant nothing to me. In a moment a map leapt into my mind; I could see myself across Finland and Norway, down at Bergen, crossing the North Sea, in England. The delirium of wildly glad hopes must have come out in my face because something like a smile softened her mouth. "You seem keen on going?" I nodded, but the word she used could not express it. If anyone had offered me the whole riches of the Imperial Library, I would not have thought as much of such an offer. This was like a gate into Damascus.

Yet a war was on, and getting out of Russia meant walking through the tangled shrubbery of police regulations. They used to be stringent enough in the past. Now they resembled so many knots tied together. In the eyes of my kin and acquaintance I may have been an inconsequential human atom, given to reverie and not much else. From the police point of view, I may have been a potential "political suspect."

That evening the *starshy dvornik* (head porter) came to interview me. His fat, red, bearded face was familiar enough, but, seated at the edge of the table and chewing the stump of a pencil, he seemed almost omnipotent in the dim candlelight. The *starshy dvornik* had direct dealings with the police; all the tenants of the house were duly registered at the local station, and the *starshy dvornik* probably knew more about me than I did myself. Certainly he tried to impress on me that the coveted foreign passport would be issued through his good offices and his alone. He was maddeningly slow, but I dared not hurry him.

"I shall want two copies of this paper, *baryshna*, six photographs, and twenty rubles. It may take something like two months to get your passport. Those important people at the Gorochovoya are very busy just at the moment, and you cannot worry important people." He had said it about seven times before he produced a greasy, crumpled form out of the depths of his blue overcoat, and, from her chair by the window, my mother suggested that we might promise him five rubles more. "It might be done quicker if we did," and the sound of English speech made him fidget and clear his throat.

"Yes, *baryshna*, it is unwise to worry important people. Passports are hard to get nowadays with the war going on. I shall have to go to the Gorochovoya by tram, and fares cost money."

I said that we would not let him be out of pocket. He sighed profoundly and pushed the paper towards me, a broken, dirty nail marking the place allotted for my signature. "Please, *baryshna*, write it all in ink. And don't spoil the form, they cost money. The job is expensive as it is. I will see what I can do. But thirty rubles is no joke." I broke in, "But you said twenty a minute ago?"

He sucked in his red cheeks, and into the fat-ringed eyes

stole genuine and hurt astonishment. He had meant thirty
rubles all the time. He could never remember figures, mis-
takes were common to all mortals, and he was certain he
meant thirty even if he said twenty. At last Mother suggested that we had better offer him his thirty rubles and so
get rid of him. The room was small enough, and the windows had long since been "sealed" for the winter, double
panes protecting the walls from the frost. The *starshy
dvornik* had brought in the rich aroma of his lodge. Hurriedly I began putting down my name on the allotted line.
He had not brought a duplicate form: my hand shook like
an aspen leaf, and the inkstand threatened to topple over.
At last it was done. A crumpled red note, ten rubles in
advance, was slipped into the large hairy hand. My application for a foreign passport stowed in his pocket, the *starshy
dvornik* left us in peace. But I sat at the table, staring past
the flickering candles into a world beyond the frost-fretted
windowpanes, a world of normal gestures and sanely
ordered behavior, where a *starshy dvornik* would be an un-
desirable curiosity, and where no policeman assumed the
role of bogey. Yet I could not see my England clearly. . . .
Through the mist of my thoughts I heard Mother mention
a house off the Strand with a beautiful winding staircase
and exceptionally good mantelpieces. But England was not
a house to me, nor a field or a wood. It had no familiar
form as yet, though I remembered a sunrise seen once near
Loksarjarvi when the lake shimmered in silver cleanliness,
the pines looked as though they had been born anew over-
night, and even the lonely, stern juniper trees were clad in
a beauty all their own. I remembered a forester's boy running up with a small plaited basket of button mushrooms,

and his large freckled face seemed washed with the same
light of renewal. And I knew that higher up north there
were innumerable lakes and forests I should probably never
see in my life, that there were rocks whose shape I should
never learn, and yet I knew that I knew them. This is
expressed with a lamentable crudity, but it does reflect more
or less what I felt about England, known from books only.
Formless and vast in my imagination, she yet seemed intimate, familiar, worthy of loyalty and devotion. The plain
seed cake of the Southee world seemed far more necessary,
attractive, and nourishing than the gorgeously iced con-
fection raised in the Poltoratzky legend.

My mother was saying in her quiet voice, "And you
might go to Clifton where I was at school, kept by Miss
Cheshire at White Ladies. She lost her fiancé in the Crimea.
. . . I suppose Clifton is a large and busy place now."
She paused. "I hope you will love it all." And I replied just
as quietly, "But I love it all now."

6

∽∾∾∾∾∾∾∾∾∾∾∾∾∾∾∾∽

YOU must not leave without seeing Grandmamma. You have not been there since the summer. Things
are uncertain, and she is getting old."

Of course I must go and see Grandmamma. The journey
was not very comfortable in the winter, but Grandmamma

was worth any sacrifices. One blue, frosty December morning I took the orange tram to the Finland Station. I felt
cold. I had forgotten to put on my gaiters and my scarf,
but there was no time to turn back. I caught the train by
the skin of my teeth. I went on through Wiborg, changed,
and at last came to Loksarjarvi. I felt frozen to the marrow by the time I reached the white-timbered house on the
little island. She expected me, and hot coffee and saffron
cakes were ready in the small parlor, where she sat erect in
a hard-backed chair, a white shawl over her shoulders, her
slate silk dress shining in the firelight, her few rings spar-
kling against the old ivory of her fingers. Within those
walls, time lay motionless, and I could see myself waking up
in a tiny blue and white room upstairs and shouting, "Oh,
was it all a dream?" As I sat eating the saffron buns, I did
not know that I sat there for the last time, that never again
would anyone of her flesh and blood cross over the low-
linteled door, that the next time I was to hear about her
would be through a dry official channel informing me of
her death.

Of course, I had to burst forth with my news. Her finely
seamed face looked pleased. "I will tell you something. I had
little love for England in my youth. My father remembered
the bombardment of Copenhagen all too well. But I have
changed my views since your mother's coming. England
bred her and shaped her, in spite of all the Poltoratzky
leaven, and a country which could produce such a woman
deserves respect."

In the morning I awoke to the old remembered feeling
that the lake had been merely "thought of" in a fairy tale,
and, almost unconsciously, I cried, "Oh, was it all a dream?"

when Grandmamma came into my room and sat on the edge of the bed.

"I have not had you here as often as I should have liked. There were so many of you. . . . I don't know what you are going to be, but I should like to tell you one thing — don't run after fame. It is nothing but a will-o'-the-wisp. You might paint a picture, and people might start making comparisons with old masters, and the picture might be good enough, but the Lapps in the North would stare at it and dismiss it for a daub which tells them nothing at all. Fame is so relative."

Within a few brief hours it was time for me to go. The house could not say good-bye in a lighthearted fashion: it had begun snowing, the clouds looked heavy purple and gray. The wonder of all remembered corners was curtained off. In that strange, woolen world I could see the sledge man waiting, a smudgy dark blur against the wet gray-white murkiness. Grandmamma stood, swathed in furs and shawls, her brown eyes steady enough. "You must hurry. Arni is waiting. God bless you."

She turned back and I hurried away. But the snowstorm had wrought havoc with the train from the north. I had several hours' wait at the station; there was a very good fire, but no warmth could unfreeze me. . . . The train came. It was well heated, but the carriage became a furnace for me long before we reached Wiborg. Somehow I got back to the Finland Station, jumped into a droshky and drove to the Bolshoy Prospect. Once home, I tumbled into bed. I never left it till the end of January.

The foreign passport was ready. The thirty rubles, since grown into forty, had been paid. The young Norwegian was leaving early in February. My slender suitcases were packed, but the anxiety lest I should not be strong enough to go could not help my convalescence. I tried to prove my fitness, crawled out of bed, and collapsed at its very edge. I had had influenza, and the doctor had prescribed butter, milk, and cod-liver oil. We had forgotten the taste of butter. What milk came our way looked and smelt like watered chalk, and cod-liver oil, which, my aversion notwithstanding, I would have swallowed by the gallon, could not be obtained for gold.

I was back in bed when the Norwegian came to say good-bye. I knew she could not put off her own going, but my dreams were wounded unto death, and I was glad to see her leave the room: I wanted to slip into the dark, be alone, my face buried in the pillows.

7

THE Mochovaya Street was fairly distant from the Bolshoy Prospect, but I had a friend there, one Gabrielle. I had met her at Wolf's; we both wanted to buy Carlyle's *French Revolution*. Wolf's had a single copy left. I had hoarded the money for months, but I drew back. The tall, spare woman in a shabby fur coat pulled out her hand and made me come back to the counter. "Oh please, you seem so keen on having it. I can easily borrow a copy from the library." So Carlyle was mine. I stammered my thanks, and she asked my name. She appeared to know it, having met my Uncle Alexis. She gave me her card. "Come and see me — if only to talk about Carlyle."

I went. Soon we were friends.

She was about forty, and she taught modern languages at a high school. She should have had a Chair at the University, but she said that comparatively easy work at such a school left her with adequate leisure for private study. She was certainly erudite, but it was not her learning that had first attracted me to her. She had traveled from one part of the world to another, absorbing vision and beauty of all the countries. She also had the happy gift of bringing out the best in all whom she met. When you were with Gabrielle, you imagined yourself on a mountain top. Her presence would have turned a tramcar, crowded with people in sodden clothes, their bodies flabby and their faces sour, into a Greek chariot full of athletes, their prowess fitly proved and as fitly recognized. She lent me books and got me a few pupils for French and English. She did far more: unlike the lady of the Smolensky Cemetery, Gabrielle neither counseled nor preached, nor yet wove exotic parables for my benefit. She talked about ordinary people and things in such a vivid, extraordinary way that she roused my curiosity to learn a little about those same ordinary people and things.

One day in early March I went to see her. The brief winter day was near its dying, the snow rang hard and sharp underfoot, and the air was tinged with fugitive lilac-silver. A crowded tram carried me down the Nevsky. There were groups of policemen strolling up and down its broad face. Here and there, mounted gendarmes sat stiffly on their great horses, the saddles covered with thick gray blankets. A pink-golden spear of the dying sunlight caught at a gendarme's lance and, for a short second, he looked like a sculptured medieval knight, ready for the fray.

The presence of the police was so usual that one almost failed to notice it. Earlier in the week there had been a number of food riots. I should never have seen that particular gendarme but for the fact that the sunset chose to stamp his lance with incredible beauty.

I reached Gabrielle's house. I found her in a strangely sober mood. The girls at her school had been told to keep away. She had heard that the military were being entrained for the capital. "Another food riot?" I asked, and she replied abruptly, "Well, let's hope it is nothing worse."

Dasha, her shriveled old maid, called us in to supper. I believe we talked about Anaxagoras and his school, as we ate a savory enough mess of dried vegetables, mushrooms, and potatoes. Gabrielle had a small hoard of coffee, and we spent a happy hour over it. She told me the story of a marriage offer she had had from a French skipper somewhere in the seas of Indo-China. "We'd had such rough weather, and I was the only passenger aboard who simply would not get sick. He proposed to me on the strength of it — after a few days' acquaintance," she laughed, suddenly a very young girl again, in her neat blue serge dress, touches of white embroidery at throat and wrists, young in spite of iron-gray hair brushed well away from her beautifully shaped forehead.

But the coffee had gone cold. The bellrope was by the

window. Gabrielle went towards it when a sudden noise outside made her pull apart the dark red curtains. She could not open the window because of the double window frame sealed up for the winter, but, tall as she was, she reached the small square opening always left free in the upper pane. She raised the latch and a sharp blade of frosty wind cut across the warm room. Candles flickered. One of them went out.

"Sorry!" She spoke with her back to me. "Did I freeze you out?"

I had an idea something might be happening in the street. I suggested that she keep it open, and we heard the sharp dry sound of hoofs hammering against the hard beaten snow. Gabrielle pushed a footstool to the window, jumped, and leaned her head out of the *fortochka*. In a hoarse voice she complained that she could not see anything. "The street lamps seem to have gone out."

Here the door was flung open. Dasha, her shabby green shawl flung on anyhow, her eyes enormous, burst into the room and screamed at Gabrielle to shut the window.

"For pity's sake, pull the curtains, *baryna!* The Cossacks are tearing down the street. The *dvornik* says it is the revolution. They are burning down houses, palaces . . . there is not a train running anywhere . . . they'll starve us . . . they'll burn us to death, antichrists. . . ."

Gabrielle went towards her.

"Nonsense, Dasha! Why shouldn't the Cossacks come down the Mochovaya if they want to? Leave them to their business and they won't meddle with yours. Tell Feodor he is a stupid gossip-monger. You have had fires on the brain ever since that towel in the bathroom caught fire.

. . . You should be ashamed of yourself. Look at the young lady's face — you have scared her to death."

"It's Mother," I stammered — "she will be out. She is at my aunt's house."

"Are they on the telephone?"

"Yes — 45–46."

The polished receiver in her hand, Gabrielle stood, waiting calmly. Dasha remained by the door, twisting and untwisting the frayed ends of her green shawl. Presently my Aunt Catherine answered. I rushed to the telephone. Was Mother with them?

"No," came her metallic, precise voice, "she left quite an hour ago. Boris went with her. He is not back yet, and now I am worried about him. Where are you?"

"In the Mochovaya."

"Well, get home as soon as you can."

"What is happening?"

"Nobody knows really. But girls of your age should not be out at a time like this. For heaven's sake don't try to walk home. Take a cab. There are no trams, and — " Here the line gave a prolonged, agonized wail and died off. I turned to Gabrielle.

"My aunt says I am not to walk home."

"Did you imagine you could?" she asked almost ironically. "Oh, child, if only you had got out of the country in February." She spoke so gravely that I tried to laugh it off.

"Gabrielle, this is so unlike you! Just because trams aren't running and they have got a few extra policemen out because of the food riots."

She stopped me vehemently.

[117]

"Food riots! Is that all you think it is? Can't you see this is not going to be a rehearsal of another tuppenny-ha'penny barricade business? This country is like a big wooden house, rotten in every beam and joist, and it is bound to crash; and you talk about food riots — "

Dasha chimed in: —

"Now there you are, *baryna!* Scolding me for a gossip-monger, and here you are yourself going hard at it!" She mimicked, "Look at the young lady's face — please do — you have scared her to death," and Gabrielle's eyes and lips softened.

"Revolution or no revolution, old Dashinka, you and I have been good friends. We have made a mess of it together. Go and get us some tea, and we will all drink it here. Make plenty of it, dear soul."

Dasha went. Gabrielle put her hands on my shoulders.

"I can't tell you what is going to happen to any of us. But tiny separate atoms always have to suffer in an upheaval. . . . Whatever comes along, don't get frightened. Years later, you might meet people who would tell you that you never had any youth because of all this. Don't believe it. Thrust the idea out of your mind. Learn to do without anyone's pity."

There was something almost sibylline about Gabrielle at that moment. She finished, I was silent, and the room stood eerily quiet.

My interest in politics had always been very thin. Our position was too unimportant to justify our being in the swim of reliable knowledge about "inside" affairs. What I knew of the war as such came to me through the jealously censored pages of the *Novoye Vremia*. Of course, I had

long suspected that food shortage would end in the bitter
impasse of absolute famine. I had known sharp hunger
in the days of ubiquitous plenty in the land. This did not
frighten me. Yet I knew, too, that Gabrielle was not merely
referring to unbuttered bread and frozen potatoes for dinner.

The very next moment the grave comfort of her counsel
slipped out of my consciousness. Time was not. The future
itself was divorced from it, became a desert without light,
form, space, and meaning. I saw that, before another year
was out, what faint semblance of home life I had ever had
would be uprooted and destroyed by a force no single individual effort could stave off. "Why," I thought wildly,
"why is it that, having known so little of the comfortable,
ordinary ways of life, why is it that this 'I' should have
been born in time for chaos and havoc?"

The moment came, and its sharp claw bit into me. I
turned my back to Gabrielle, afraid lest she read the trace
of that dark mood in my face. I peered through the chink
of the curtains. The street lay quiet. The Cossacks had
ridden past. Much was happening elsewhere, as I came
to learn later, but all the mad sound, all the diabolic fury
of that March evening in 1917, were far away from the
faintly aristocratic Mochovaya Street. The outside quiet
depressed me far more than any deafening noise could
have done. Once again I was in the grip of a mood when
premonition, horrible because of its vagueness, got hold
of me and would not let me go. Something in my mind
was, as it were, striding across the five stormy years to
come. Detail was mercifully blurred, but the faint outline
of those years stood out, clawing at me, casting one shadow

after another across that impassable, spaceless space. From the heart of those shadows a whisper mocked softly: —

"Don't believe this woman, she is a foolish dreamer. You may be young, but such as you, stranded here, shall never know youth. It is going already, don't run after it, you'll never catch up with it. It is running away downhill, as swiftly as death," and with hideous selfishness I forgot all about Mother's possible anxiety on my behalf. There was one possible panacea for such moods — a good long tramp. I said aloud, my eyes away from Gabrielle's intent face, "I ought to go, I'm going to tramp it home."

She did not smile.

"Dasha and I will find a cab. You must crouch under the seat if you see anything happening. I would come with you myself but I don't suppose your mother would want any visitors tonight."

I did not argue. I felt certain there would be no cab. Dasha thought so, too. And go and look for one she would not. She grew magnificently voluble. No decent, God-fearing mistress could expect her to sally forth and search for a cab and court death. She well remembered 1905. There had been plenty of shooting, and wise folk had stayed indoors. Gabrielle merely told her to fetch her *shuba*. I struggled into my coat and pulled the little fur cap well over my forehead. Dasha, the shawl half covering her face, started another lamentation by the front door.

"*Baryna, baryna.* . . . I am old, but I am fond of life. The Cossacks will murder you, *baryna.*" But Gabrielle refused to listen.

We went out into the yard. The *dvornik's* stuffy cubbyhole was dark and apparently untenanted. The great yard gates were shut and bolted. Dasha muttered that even *dvorniks* were wise enough not to run risks, but Gabrielle retorted that the Petrograd *dvorniks* were well known for their ability to scurry away at the very first thunderclap, and Dasha must fumble with the big bolt. As soon as we got out, we heard a sledge coming from down the Quay. I knew then that I could never have tramped it home: I felt wrung out like a useless old sponge.

Gabrielle hailed the driver. He drew level with the pavement. Out of the tangled beard came hoarse sounds of protest. He did not want to take a fare. The Vassily Island lay too far off.

"Had you started such an argument this morning, I would have called a policeman." Gabrielle was firm but polite. "I have no idea where the police are tonight, and I don't much care. But I do care as to what might happen to this young lady. You look old enough to be her grandfather. She must go home. Her mother is anxious. For Christ's sake, will you drive her home?"

"H—m—, I might — for Christ's sake," he muttered, and flipped back the coarse fur rug.

I shook hands with Gabrielle. The old man brandished his whip in the frosty air, the sleigh creaked, and in a few moments the quiet of the Mochovaya lay behind us.

The street lamps were still burning. When we reached the Palace Quay the old man urged his horse to go faster. The little sledge lurched, bumped, and swerved. I could see to my left the massive outline of the Winter Palace, dark and brooding. Later, I knew that, at that very hour, the Central Criminal Court buildings on the Liteyny Prospect were being set ablaze. But the Palace Quay looked

ordinary enough, and so we came to the Senate Square.
There, lorries, never before allowed on the Quays, stampeded past, crammed with armed soldiers and civilians who
seemed to be brandishing most extraordinary weapons.
Untidy red rags waved violently here and there. Hurrying
women ran along the pavements. At the corner of the
Nicholas Bridge stood a group of "black" people. The lamp
burned brightly enough. I saw a man dart a sudden glance
at the sledge; he looked neither terrifying nor overpower-
ing, just a feeble-bodied, weedy man from some factory or
other, but there seemed a strange hunger in his face. I felt
fear creep into me as the sledge swung onto the bridge. The
old man turned halfway round in his box and spoke for
the first time: "Revolution — that is what it is." The foreign
word came startlingly from the peasant lips. "Well, well,
come on, old lady . . ." and down the great slope of the
Nicholas Square we careered at a breathless pace. Soon the
Bolshoy Prospect, flanked by gaunt tree trunks, loomed
ahead, I leaned forward and gave him the number of the
house.

"No use going there," he mumbled a few seconds later,
"it's on fire. Look, *baryshna*, burning nicely, isn't it?" He
cracked his whip above the mare's ears, and for a moment
I wondered if I was mad. Sheets of flame, almost metal-blue
in the frosty air, seemed spread all over the end of the
street. The sledge raced on, and I peered ahead. "No," —
I can't remember hearing my own voice, — "it is the police
station opposite."

"Ah, they have got at them," he said quite noncom-
mittally, and halted his horse.

I paid him, the money almost slipping out of my fingers.

The lift was out of order, the *dvornik* nowhere to be seen. I rushed up the stairs to the sixth floor where we had two rooms for a home. I forgot that I had a latchkey in my pocket, and banged on the door. Mother opened it. "I am glad to see you," she said, just as if I were returning home from an ordinary occasion. "Boris brought me back. This floor seems strangely silent. The floor maid has taken French leave and all her belongings as well. They are burning houses already."

"Yes."

Together, in silence, we stood by the window. Across the wide street the great pile of the police station was a roaring inferno of red, orange, and violet flames, shooting upwards to a sky which reflected the blazing colors in low-hanging cloudy drifts. Below, black dots of figures could be seen bustling round the pyre. There were no firemen anywhere; the building was meant to burn, and burn it did.

Few, if any, people went to bed that night.

Next morning there was no water to be had in the whole vast building, and never again in Russia was I to see water running from a tap in any house I lived in. The food store on the ground floor was shuttered, and people said that it was no use expecting anything from ration cards. The Vassily Island markets were all looted, and some of the tenants brought grim stories about lampposts in the Maly Prospect and elsewhere "decorated with policemen and gendarmes." Much later, from books, I learned a good deal of what was happening. From our own small niche little could be seen except a few separate crimson details of communal frenzy — sniping in the streets, the sprawled body of a police inspector, shot through the face. "Death can be vile," I thought. But seldom enough did we venture out of doors.

That morning I stepped across the threshold of dear and familiar precincts. I found that beyond their boundary nobody walked softly, nobody troubled about anything abstract, and it soon became impossible — not to say grotesque — to theorize about death because of its shocking, terribly clothed frequency. The Mochovaya was in a different world. Later, in the spring, I heard that Gabrielle had managed to escape to the south of Russia. Indeed, most people found nothing else to do but prepare for running away. "We are so unimportant that it does not matter whether we stay or not," decided my mother. There was only one terrible urgency — food. Rent had ceased. Mother's small income, which came from the Imperial Chancery, had also ceased the very first day of the Revolution. We had nothing else. Some fortunate ones, their bank resources denied them, could fall back on what valuable things they had within their homes. We had the slenderest possessions imaginable, and their total worth was insignificant enough. The remembered privations of the summer of 1909 seemed a pleasant pastime on occasions. Life was raw, shapeless, sometimes fantastically horrible, but always urgent. Repeated metaphysical excursions were now about as useful as a sieve held under a running tap. I sold buns in the streets, worked in an engineering company whose foreign correspondents had fled the country, was a porter at the Zarskoselsky Station . . . it was a chain of sudden jobs, begun in a whirl and finished in another.

The Vassily Island became a closed-in universe. It teemed

with half-starved, frightened, ragged men and women. They were shadows. Mother alone was real. All the social links were snapped by the ubiquitous frenzy; relations and friends, even if still living in St. Petersburg, were distant, themselves absorbed in the ever-growing task of keeping themselves away from the brink of a hungry death. Food of a kind did seep into some households, spared the initial looting and ravage of the early days. But money joined in the whirl. We came to count in millions, and the dizziness of mere figures made one sick with fatigue. Gabrielle had been right: rotten in every beam and joist, the house of the country collapsed with a crash. Am I wrong in saying that the unnoticed, unhunted people suffered worse than dying? They were allowed to live . . . but life was dark in both senses. The house on the Bolshoy Prospect had neither lamps nor candles, and the sixth floor must now be reached by slow and patient groping. Within our two rooms we guarded jealously a small store of cheap stearin candles. But there were days when we wished we might have none, days when we drank water, imagining it to be tea, and also pretended that we had no use for food.

Chapter Five

MAD MUSIC

1

PAPER is soft and ink is fluid; it might be better if some pages of this chronicle could be written on chips of granite at the point of steel.

The great block on the Bolshoy Prospect was intact: neither flames nor bullets had come near it. Yet, in spite of its inviolate bricks, it was a shell, and no more. Lack of central heating, water, and light contributed to its desolation. It was a huge warren, inhabited by furtive, frightened ants. Unlike ants, they labored but little. The entire meaning of existence was centered round food, food, and food again. People killed and stole for food in the darkened city; they did worse things, and nobody could have condemned them.

The Brest-Litovsk Treaty was signed: we heard of it through a sequence of rumors. Peace bells rang in Europe: we knew nothing of their peal until a long time after. Our newspaper was the tongue of the bread queue, our frontier the granite girdle of the Nicholas Quay. We lived on the Vassily Island, and the outside world was too threatening for us to undertake lighthearted excursions. Even bridges and outlying streets were not safe. The dreadful music of machine guns had long been stilled; not so the occasional shot in the dark. They had opened prisons and asylums in the early days of the Revolution; their tenants hid in the cemeteries by day and had the freedom of streets by night-time.

But I could not stay at home. Even in the chaos, work of a kind continued being done somewhere, and it was possible to search for it and imperative to find it. People of the *ancien régime* bought expensive food by selling furs, plate, and jewels. Our few silver spoons and our pathetically slender hoard of trinkets would not have supported us for a month and, moreover, we were never *au courant* of the intricate business of selling and barter. Others spent time and substance in devising means of escape. Such a venture was beyond us: sums quoted by occasional acquaintances made us feel dizzy. They were not the millions of the then current exchange. They hinted at the solid fortunes of the vanished days — fortunes extracted from bank deposits and kept under mattresses. "We can't escape," said my mother, "we must see it through"; and she added, "I am not being heroic. There is nothing else for us to do."

The summer, with its precious mercy of light, flew on wings, and the winter closed in, an angrily snarling animal. Time for work became brief, since dark spelt danger, and the present war blackout is nothing compared with the darkness of those days. I searched for work daily. Sometimes I found it. Jobs were brief-lived but varied. A Dutchman, stranded in the North with his shy South American bride, wanted to perfect his English. A moribund electrical company desired an Anglo-French correspondent. Everything for a few weeks, everything coming and going with the breath of the wind. There were dull jobs, mildly exciting jobs, exasperating jobs. At last they ceased, and we took stock of our humble possessions. The inventory took a bare half hour. Most of the house linen had been patched and darned. But we had heard people say that everything had its market value since nothing was being produced. Down the Bolshoy Prospect was a market place, and there, my arms laden with funnily shaped bundles, I crept at dawn. The bundles could be neither unwrapped nor exhibited: all private trading was taboo, and raids happened with a deadly monotony; you heard a whistle at the fringe of the market square, you gathered all you had, and you ran for it, hoping that luck would be on your side. Sometimes, it was not: you found yourself dumbly staring at the rusty bayonet of a Red Guard, your arms forgot what strength they ever had, you dropped everything, and you were lucky if you ran away again, empty-handed, the last shreds of your miserable possessions left to the raiders. Raids apart, the business was brisk and amusing. The least likely things fetched most. Once I brought an ancient photograph album, bound in faded crimson leather. A peasant gaped at its tarnished silver clasps. He stroked the leather reverently. "From a palace?" he inquired, and I disillusioned him. "From a very humble private home." "It does not look humble to me," he muttered. It probably did not, and my candor about its provenance did not make him haggle about the price: he parted with a week's food for the privilege of taking it to his home far away from St. Petersburg.

All the same, we were not as badly off as so many others: our pre-Revolution poverty certainly stood us in good stead. We lived in two humble rooms, and we had not been evicted from any house. Nobody could come and sequestrate things which we did not possess. Nobody troubled us with midnight searches. So Mother reminded me, and she always succeeded in finding honey among bare stones. I had forgotten about Oxford and history by that time; I had forgotten that a daily paper used to be a pleasant thing to see in the morning. I had then forgotten most things except God, who had given me a mother to learn from. She never preached; she lived, and from her I was now learning day by day that life could be not merely possible but even worth-while in spite of cold, darkness, hunger, and inevitable dirt.

In my childhood she had been everything to me — in a vast, inexplicable, warm way. I could not always understand all she did. This did not matter; trust and love seemed to fill all the gaps. Now, in the dark and slimy horror of communal life, her little-understood virtue became light.

I had always suspected that some of my father's people thought her rigid. She never shifted from a once-recognized principle. Out of a very misty past I can see a small, modestly furnished drawing room. A door opened, and George, my eldest brother, stood there. I heard his voice — "Mother, may I bring in my wife? She is outside." And both the question and my mother's unhurried, quiet reply came to be graven in the memory even though, at the time, the mind could not, naturally, grasp their import — "She shall be my daughter when she is your wife." I can see the door closing suddenly, violently. It had so closed on her pride, her first-born, one who, more than any other of her children, had inherited her own father's fine mind, who had won himself an honorable niche at the University before he was thirty, a scholar and a poet. It would have been easy enough to keep the door ajar, but Mother's code of morality, whether for good or otherwise, was too definite and honest for any such evasions. Not until I grew up did I realize what the closing of that door must have meant to her, but she would not have remained herself had she hesitated and bargained. It may have been a crude and ancient fashion to prefer black and white in their separate worlds instead of mingling them together and finding ease and comfort in the furtively born gray. . . . I don't know, but the sorry stuff of makeshifts and compromises was not in her, and certainly such things would have led to a mental and moral suicide in those dark months of 1918 and 1919. On her strength I built my own feeble effort, and from her lovely candle I lit my own fitful, flickering taper.

Nobody molested us in the one-windowed room with two iron bedsteads, trunks, and a great padlock on the door. Midnight searches, "legally" organized by the Red Guards, passed us by. But the porter had long since gone from his lodge, the great block was open to all and any marauders, and an ordinary key would not have been enough to check them. The door had a fairly wide clearance. Sometime late in 1918 the electric light was restored from about nine in the evening till midnight. Huddled in bed, under what blankets were so far spared the market, I heard her urgent whisper — "Darling, switch the light off." Her hearing was so much finer than mine, and she had already heard the tramp of boots on the staircase.

The room dark, we sat still, close to each other. The hobnailed boots came nearer and drew level with the door. A bang followed. We never knew who the visitors were: Red Guards, Tcheka (forerunners of the OGPU), or simply those "knights of the night" who pestered the city all through the dark hours. If the Tcheka men met the knights, they were invariably worsted, but the aim of the Tcheka was to hunt down the counter-revolution — not to protect the citizens from any such depredations. The bang followed by a coarse mutter, the hobnailed boots tramped further down the passage. "Anna Feodorovna," whispered Mother, "she does not hear well. What if her door were unlocked . . ." and we sat, full of anguish for our only friend in the block, but it would have been worse than useless to venture into the passage until the visitors had gone.

Anna Feodorovna, fat, florid, fifty, and nice, was a midwife who had her room further down the passage. She was a peasant woman, unlettered, rough, and slightly too communicative about her work, but we should have had many more hungry days had it not been for her clumsy kindness. She fetched water up the six flights whenever I happened to be out at work. She taught Mother an ingenious method of lengthening the life of a tallow candle. She was the proud possessor of a "double-barreled" oil stove, and my mother's food must be cooked on it. She worked at a hospital and received more or less proper rations, but her natural appetite mysteriously dwindled on the days when our own larder resembled that of Mother Hubbard. "My stomach is upset," she would say almost angrily, pushing a large chunk of bacon through the door.

"I have nowhere to keep this food. It is sure to go bad. Now then — let me hear no more of it."

Now men were tramping down the passage. We sat in the dark, waiting, praying for Anna Feodorovna's safety. She had a sharp way of silencing the Tcheka men. But the "knights" had their own manner of dealing with those who did not welcome them. Finally, the noise died away. We struggled with the padlock. We tiptoed down the dim passage, reached Anna Feodorovna's door, and knocked. Her large fat face peered cautiously. "Don't worry. I am all right. By the mercy of God, I heard them just in time. Come in, I have a kettle boiling" — she seemed to spend all her scant leisure in putting kettles on to boil. "Now then, dear," she fussed over my mother, "here is a cabbage pasty. . . . I have something to tell you. . . . Such a day I have had. . . . Seventy-eight hours the poor body took. . . . Just imagine — seventy-eight hours — "

Anna Feodorovna had a passion for her job. She must have shocked my mother often enough, but certainly, some of her views were philosophical rather than crudely gynecological. "It makes me feel all queer whenever a child leaves its mother's body. . . . Holy and marvelous, that's what it is, but you can't really feel queer — that's the worst of it, you have to get on with the job and think afterwards. . . . Life — there is prayer and worship for you, that's what I say. A woman said to me the other day, 'Anna Feodorovna, is it alive?' I ask you — a lively, kicking boy he was! 'Of course it is,' I soothed her. 'What did you think would happen?' 'Well,' she sighed, as feeble as a mouse in a cat's mouth. 'Too much death around. . . . Why should life come — anywhere?' Of course, her being feeble and all that, I could not tick her off properly, but I did the job as soon as she rallied. 'Why should life come, indeed?' I asked her. 'Because life is of God and death is of man — at least, the kind we see thudding down everywhere.' She said afterwards I kind of helped her."

That was Anna Feodorovna, holding forth in her one-roomed home, a bit smaller than ours, full of cardboard boxes, baskets, bits of linen, dusty jars, and pillows. Pillows seemed to be her only furniture. But tonight she did not discourse on the seventy-eight hours of labor. She turned to me and said she had heard of a job for me.

"My niece scrubs in a house on the Nevsky. Kind of a bookshop — I don't rightly know, I am not educated. But she said they are looking for someone with foreign languages. I told her to tell them about you. I said you knew them all — "

"Anna Feodorovna!"

"Well, one or all — it is the same to me. It should be the same to them." She clinched the argument by offering strawberry-leaf tea and another large cabbage pasty.

Anna Feodorovna, apart from her professional pursuits, was indeed uneducated. Her carroty-haired niece knew scrubbing, cooking, and sewing, and little else. But between them they succeeded in placing my first literary job in my hands. The carroty hair did not char in a bookshop, as I found the next day. That place housed a publishing firm. A few were still left in St. Petersburg, though the one I went to was a new one, fired by a novel and grandiose ambition to acquaint the Russian masses with European classics in "proletarian dress." The offices were in the back-yard of an extremely ancient building. I opened the door, and found myself in a room packed with paper and humanity. The carroty hair had mentioned a name to her aunt. I repeated the name to a sandy-mustached irritable little man who stared at me blankly as though I had come from a world he had decided to ignore. "Introductions? We have no use for them," he said so curtly that I all but turned away, when he tugged at my sleeve. Did I know any English? They wanted several poems translated verbatim since their own people knew no English. Would I do the work? Would I not! He told me to follow him into another drab room also packed with papers, books, and people. A man stood by the window, reading a proof. The sandy mustache grew voluble. "She can do it . . . Splendid!" "Splendid," rejoined the proofreader without a glance at me. "Tell her the rates and give her the books. Is she going to do the Persian stuff?" But the sandy mustache was feverishly piling one slim book on top of another. "Sign for these. You won't be long?" I brushed the titles with a cautious glance. "All these . . . Yes, but —" I saw myself buried in them for months, if not years . . . Coleridge, Swinburne, something of Byron, and Macaulay's *Lays of Ancient Rome*. The sandy mustache realized that he had been talking in the fog. "You'll have to put the Russian equivalent under the English words — in pencil, please, but legibly — we'll pay you . . . " It worked out at something like a farthing for six lines, but it sounded wealth to me. "Sign for them." He thrust a narrow paper slip under my nose. I signed. He barely looked at the signature. "You'll be paid as soon as these are brought back. Siemen Ignatiewitch, ah Comrade Siemen," he shouted at the proofreader, but nobody answered, and he pushed me towards the door. "We are all so busy, so busy, and nobody seems to be where they are wanted — " They had not asked for my address, and I ran down the Nevsky, the volumes in my arms.

In the evening Anna Feodorovna came to learn the result of her niece's intercession. I flung myself on her neck. "Now then," she said severely, "when do you begin? What hours?" I pointed at the books. "Straight away. I am going to work at home."

"But these are books," she said in a flat voice.

I explained what was wanted of me, and Anna Feodorovna spat on the floor.

"Take a book and make two of them! Well, well, there may be some sense to it — I reckon I am too blind to see it, but you look happy enough! Bless you!"

It was a bitingly cold February. I worked mostly in bed, my hands wrapped in odds and ends of wool and rug to make up for the gloves we owned no longer. "Write in pencil — but legibly." A pencil was something dearer than flour. I had a few left from those remote pre-1917 days. But as I came to the end of Swinburne's *Songs before Sunrise* I knew that pencils used themselves up with a ruthless rapidity.

Wasn't the work good! We had no clock, and I knew it was midnight by the sudden rush of darkness. I groped round my bed, depositing pencils and books in safety. I fell asleep, imagining another day among lovely words and great ideas. At last, the volumes were done. The journey to the Nevsky was repeated. The sandy mustache furnished me with another gray slip for the cashier. I had some money and more books. But the third expedition was shorn of all that glory. The sandy mustache was nowhere to be seen. Those who rushed about, proofs and manuscripts in their hands, ignored me. I found the cashier's warren and handed over the finished work. He almost swept the books aside. "You mustn't come here, you mustn't come here." He sounded fussy and annoyed. "I have not been paid for these," I ventured to insist, and he measured me with an ironical look. "Well, what about coming tomorrow? Leave these here. Nobody will gobble them up." I came the next day and once more — at my third visit I found the door boarded up, and a brief notice announced that the publishing firm had closed down.

"Never mind, little pigeon." Anna Feodorovna refused to see any calamity in my experience. "Something will turn up." She thought for a moment. "Come to the hospital. I could wangle it for you. We want a lot of writing done in the office. I heard the almoner was leaving for the South — escaping — that is what she is bent on." Anna Feodorovna lowered her voice: "It would be easier for her to vanish if she got someone straight into her shoes."

I went to see the almoner "bent on escaping." I sent my application to the hospital board. In spite of the chaos prevailing in all administrative quarters, even Anna Feodorovna could not interfere there. They took about a fortnight to consider my application. It seemed life or death to me — because of my mother.

It was late April, the winter had gone, a winter of cold, dark, and hunger. Pack ice had vanished from the face of the Neva, and I could see young grass pushing up here and there between the cracks in the pavements. The old trees down the length of the Bolshoy Prospect were breaking into leaf, and it seemed almost easy to glean new hope and strength from all the beauty waking up from the soil. But the winter had been such a thief. It had stolen things that spring seemed unable to bring back — strength and health of so many people in the city. This may have been kind: the winter to come was to bring thicker shadows and sharper hunger. Yet in the spring of 1919 I knew nothing of this. I only knew that stairs seemed so much to her, that tiny efforts brought more and more exhaustion, that the worn, sapped flesh seemed more and more in the ascendant where once the spirit had moved so firmly and triumphantly.

At last I received word that they had approved my application. I found myself almoner at the Stock Exchange Hospital. I knew little about my duties, but the matron, obviously tired of considering an endless queue of applicants, said that it would be a blessing to find someone who could read and write. The pay was slender, but in those days nobody gauged a job in directly monetary terms. There were generous food rations — millet, flour, condensed milk, and even sugar on occasions. I began my work the day after one such distribution. The matron tried to get me my share in advance, but she failed, and I had something like thirteen days to wait for the next "food day." Some dates become graven in the memory — nineteenth of April to the second of May.

I had my work to take my mind away from the dread I could no longer escape at home. Also our life was rudely interrupted by the sudden going of Anna Feodorovna: her sister having been taken ill in Moscow, she wangled a railway ticket and left. The block on the Bolshoy Prospect held no more friends. But, "On the second of May," I kept repeating to myself, "I will see Mother eating properly, and then it will be summer, and things must get better next winter: nothing could be worse than the last one."

Early in the morning of the second of May I left her in bed by the opened window; the lilac tree in the courtyard was in breaking bud. "When the lilac is in bloom, I always wish we lived on the ground floor," I said to her. An indeterminate old body on the floor below would, I knew, look after her few wants during the day — a good third of my rations had already been mortgaged that way. And I went to work, an empty sack slung over my shoulder.

It was a very busy day. I got off about seven in the evening, and then there was the distribution of food. I came back to the house of the Bolshoy Prospect. The chairman of the house committee met me in the doorway. He stopped.

"Two whole rooms, haven't you? Well, you'll have to look for smaller quarters now that your mother is dead."

"I must go upstairs." I must have said something of the kind when he checked me.

"We have had her taken away. The Stock Exchange Hospital mortuary. . . . Aren't you working there? I might have remembered and sent word to you."

I spent that night on a bench in a consulting room at the hospital, the useless food bundles lying on the floor beside me. The matron knew and would not object. People were all the kinder because I could not respond to any kindness.

2

∽∾∿∽∾∿∽∾∿∽∾∿∽∾∿∽∾∿∽∾∿

I HAD a decent job and enough food, but I had no home. About a week later a thin, sallow-faced patient, wife of a chemist, came up to my desk and whispered that she had a room to spare. I went to them, and in their poky flat I stayed till July. Their kindness would have beggared all description. They refused to accept either money or food for rent.

The room gave out onto a dark chute of a backyard. It looked west, but no sunset ever came to invade it, and to provide a bit of color, as she said, the chemist's wife parted with her only handsome possession, a gorgeously colored Persian shawl. A dome-topped trunk, the last relic of home, served me for a chair. A bed and a table were provided by my new friends, and the bed certainly looked beautiful with the green, gold, and scarlet shawl spread over it. In the late evenings I got back, cooked what supper I had on a tiny rusty oil stove, and spent something like an hour with them. He was a Baltic German by origin, unfortunately born at Pskov. His people were still at Riga, but he could not get his Latvian papers. She had been a well-known dressmaker in her day, and now added to the family exchequer by making clothes for commissars' wives, about the only people able to afford new frocks in those days. She had a keen sense of humor, and often amused us by describing the materials she was working on. Silk, brocade, and velvet curtains, looted from palaces, were among them.

Later in the evening I fetched a pail of water from the pump in the yard, went to my room, had a cold bath, and went to bed. I had to be up at six: we were allowed to cook our breakfast in the hospital kitchen till seven. I got there soon after half-past six, boiled some water, drank my ersatz tea out of a tin mug, ate whatever I had, — either rye bread or a rusk, — and then went to my almoner's cubbyhole behind the white screen — almost an hour before I was due to start my work.

The duties were simple enough. Each outpatient had a card, kept in the files in alphabetical order. On his or her coming, the card had to be taken out of the files and slipped into the appropriate pigeonhole on my desk. There were several of them, each neatly labeled "Lungs," "Skin," "Oculist," "Dentist," and so on. When the doctors arrived, the sister-in-charge came to my desk, grabbed the cards, and the patients were called up in their turn. The ambulatory closed at six, but the day's report had to be made out of the remarks scribbled on the cards by the doctors. Sometimes those reports took two or three hours.

The duties were simple, and I worked singlehanded except for a raw underling whose ideas about alphabet were rather hazy. In the early mornings I had a crowd some sixty or seventy strong waiting round the desk. I had to put the day's date on each card before pushing it into the pigeonhole. That card had to be found in the file, dated, and pigeonholed as quickly as was humanly possible. True that the men and women who came before me moved more or less like soulless automatons, yet any delay chafed them. Some benches were provided in the body of the room, and I knew that the least I could do was not to keep them standing longer than was absolutely necessary.

For something like three months they were cards and voices to me. I worked like fury, but I was unaware of them as separate individuals. Any lull in that feverish momentum spelt a threat. I liked getting tired. I might easily have worked sitting in the chair. I preferred to remain on my feet through most of the day. When the matron suggested that the daily report might be changed to a weekly one, which could be easily done on Saturday afternoons, when the number of patients was always negligible, I begged of her not to introduce such a change: the daily report made for more work in the evenings, and it was negatively good to come to a day's end almost spent in body. My mind was more or less numb.

The daily ebb and flow of that crowd was outside my world. I heard the sound of their voices above the tall edge of my desk. I learned to distinguish their various smells. There was a herring woman, and a scavenger, and a girl who obviously worked in a soap factory. I preferred to take them as cards, voices, and smells. White, yellow, pink, gray, blue, and green, they were just cards and no more. When their voices faltered and trembled, I sometimes raised mine in an irritable hurry to have done with one card because of so many others waiting for their turn. When my clumsy, red-cheeked underling, having first searched among the *S*'s for a name beginning with an *E*, shrilly piped that a card was lost, I just as irritably gestured her away and rummaged myself among the *E*'s. The people outside my cubbyhole were so many multicolored cards,

[144]

and she, my assistant, nothing but a clumsy cog in an alphabetical machine.

But one morning a fussy sister chose to clean and wash a very dusty mirror hanging on the wall behind my desk. I came in. I saw my face reflected in it. It made me furiously angry for the space of one morning, but very likely the washing of a mirror ended by waking me up. I was not yet twenty-one, and it was a shock to find myself staring at a set and hardened face, and to know it for my own. "And this face," I thought vaguely, "looks out on what?" "On a room full of brooding, smelly, grumbling men and women, who had better remain so many differently colored cards," suggested my impatient, benumbed, and hardened self, as reflected in the mirror. Or else that face looked at a room full of patient and uncomplaining folk who had long ago learned to endure without saying much about it and who had turned their very endurance into something rare and precious, suggested another, barely awakened self, of whose very existence I was still unaware.

I could no longer think of them as cards.

3

THAT night I heard that the chemist and his wife were about to leave. He had been appointed to a job in the South of Russia, and he dared not refuse to go. He had about forty-eight hours given him to get ready.

His wife cried and wanted me to keep her Persian shawl. Their modest quarters had already been commandeered by the house committee, "and now you'll have to go and search for another home," she said tearfully.

For the next forty-eight hours, having obtained temporary leave, I hunted up and down the Island in search of a room. I roamed the whole length of the once-despised Maly Prospect, hoping for a possible perch in what looked like anything but possible houses. Yet, apparently, even a slip of a room could not be had for the asking. There were no private landlords, and my search always ended in the dingy offices of a house committee, with a blank form in my hands and the blank face of a house commandant telling me that "the local Soviet might take a month to consider my application" and that, "anyway, it was not much good sending it in since they had no vacant rooms to allot." "Houses are tumbling down everywhere," one of them said, trying to be helpful. "No repairs made anywhere. Where is the material? And all those buildings burnt down in 1917." "But one must live under a roof," I murmured, and he nodded. "Never a truer word spoken. Well, citizen, I hope you may have better luck elsewhere. . . ."

There were the consulting rooms. The matron said very kindly that she could raise no objection to my sleeping there — for a time. But the nights spent there were not exactly comfortable. A few shell-shock and incipient lunacy cases were admitted into the Stock Exchange Hospital. The amount of vigilance was negligible, and none of the doors had keys to them. One day a sister had talked rather too much about a homicidal case being sent in. I barricaded the door with lockers and a ladder. But I could not sleep much that night: the room was on the ground floor, and the window had no latch to it.

4

As a mere onlooker, away from the people "in the know" and still farther apart from those whose "in the know" was a glib and comical pretense, I was in no position to form any opinion as to what was happening in Petrograd, still less so in the rest of the country, let alone the outer world. There were no papers, and even the inland post functioned erratically. For human pebbles on the national beach (and I was one of them), the only channel of information was the interchange of rumors in the food queues. Those queues had an element of infernal eternity about them; on certain days they started shortly before dawn, and ended somewhere near midnight. Since we were all registered at the same communal food depot, we got to know one another by sight, if not by name. Those were the only clubs left in the city. The snakelike pattern of a queue was broken up more often than not, an interesting bit of gossip made knots and bunches in that mass of half-starved men and women, but the rigid sense of honor among them held one's turn to be sacrosanct. You simply marked your place by a couple of human landmarks, you wandered up and down at your leisure, you even absconded for a time, but your place was there when you came back.

It had thundered that Saturday afternoon. The sky hung low and leaden. The storm, which had gone as quickly as it had come, did nothing to cleanse the hot, sultry air. That particular queue was in curious harmony with the weather: in cautiously subdued voices they discussed someone's offensive, the fighting supposed to be going on round one of the suburbs, and the possibility of the White Army capturing the city. For once I kept aside. My mind was absorbed in a scene witnessed early in the morning, as I was hurrying along to the hospital. That picture was embedded all the more disturbingly in my mind since, some two or three days before, I had overheard the matron discuss the probable cutting down of the staff with a stranger from the Health Commissariat, and I was not at all sure whether my underling, who had by now learned to be more or less at home in the alphabet, might not be found suitable to take my own place.

In the old days, grocers, bakers, and fruiterers of St. Petersburg used to have painted signs inset between their windows. The poorer the neighborhood, the humbler the shop, the louder were the colors used for those signs. A third-rate baker would not be content with anything less than an enormous canary-colored cottage loaf, surmounted by some ocher-tinted French rolls, the whole crowned by a profusion of bright orange *baranki*, a kind of cracknel once very popular in Russia. A grocer insisted on some design which usually incorporated a huge jar of strawberry jam, each berry the size of a florin, placed side by side with a snaky, magenta-painted sausage and an equally gigantic currant cake.

In 1919 bakers and grocers had long since closed their shutters. But the loudly shrieking signs remained, their colors grown somewhat paler from a succession of rainy and foggy days. In the days when jam had been forgotten and a white loaf seemed as accessible as a lake in the moon, those signs were admittedly provocative. More than that, they almost maddened the senses. But nobody thought of giving a wholesale order for having them whitewashed, and they stayed in their places, glaringly unashamed of their wicked incongruity in a city slashed and darkened by almost ubiquitous hunger.

There was one such sign at the corner of the street leading to the Stock Exchange Hospital. The luscious purple ham, reinforced by twin coils of fat crimson sausages, made me wonder occasionally if the appropriate use of a sharp-bladed knife, strong enough to deal with three-ply wood, would be a real offense against the community. I usually hurried past the crimson-purple mockery, my eyes purposely turned away.

But that morning I saw a cluster of people in front of the deserted shop and, coming nearer, I saw a frail, gray-haired man, his thin hands coming out of the sleeves of a very shabby overcoat. Those hands clawed at the gaily painted sign. An old lady, a torn black lace scarf over her gray hair, was trying to wrench him away. Yet, though obviously feeble, he resisted her efforts, and there was something of a nightmare about those thin, blue-veined hands clinging to the painted wood. I heard a tremulous voice: "No, my dear. I simply must have another slice of that ham. I wish you would be a little more patient. See if I don't cut it off neatly. If we were to leave it here, somebody else would get it, and nobody could be as

hungry as you and I are," and the thin hands went on clawing away, until blood began trickling from under the nails,
and the painted wood showed white where the knuckle of
the ham had been scratched. Someone behind me tittered,
and a young girl's laughter was like a wound. I turned on
my heel and ran away.

Now, standing in the queue, waiting for the few weekly
ounces of bread, I could still see those bruised hands across
the painted ham. Then someone tugged at my sleeve. It
was a blind woman I had often seen before. She held her
own bread under her arm, and she was asking me to take
her home. She was alone, her granddaughter had gone to
get fish and oil at another depot. She lived a bare couple
of streets away.

The day before I would have found a very glib excuse.
The pavement was hot, and my ill-shod feet hurt me. The
old woman wore tattered clothes which smelled worse than
any dustbin. There was a running sore on her cheek, and
the hand which tugged at my sleeve was covered with
unwholesome red blotches. Yet the scene witnessed earlier
in the morning must have turned me into an embryo
masochist: I took that dreadful hand into mine and piloted
her away.

Those two streets, however, proved unaccountably long.
She walked slowly. At the door of her tenement she mumbled something about the dangerous stairs, and I must
needs take her to the top where she lived. I did not wait to
hear her thanks, which I had not deserved, and tore myself
away, running back as fast as I could. But the depot doors
were being bolted just as I was turning the last corner.
Panting, hot and angry, I pummeled the door with my fists.

A gruff voice from within told me that the day's business was over. They would have me arrested if I went on making such a nuisance of myself. As a dubious afterthought, the voice added that, anyhow, the bread supply had given out long before the end of the queue had come into the shop.

Now bread at that time was issued about once or twice a week, and the sudden, bitter injustice of it made me sit down on the dusty pavement — not in sorrow, but in fury. Cold salt fish would be my supper, but I did not yearn for bread as such: I felt ousted of my rights and injured by the whole world. As was usual on such occasions, my mind grew busy in adding up the list of my misfortunes. I had no home and no family. I held a very precarious job, and my slender wardrobe was falling to pieces. Everybody predicted an exceptionally harsh winter: I possessed neither a fur cap nor snow boots. Above all, I had no bread for the rest of the week.

I got up and turned back, my head hung low, my temper burning high. Round the corner I collided with somebody and drew aside impatiently, angrily, not a word of apology on my lips. Then I heard a voice say very softly: "I was coming to see if you had got your bread after all."

I felt like a dog robbed of a choice bone. Reluctantly I halted and raised my head. I saw a girl of about twenty-five, tall and slim, rather plain except for her large eyes, the color of cornflowers just washed with rain. Her exquisite manners put my boorishness to shame. The sadly belated grace of an apology came rather awkwardly.

"So you know me?"

"Yes, I have seen you here in the queue . . . and at the

hospital. . . . I had a very bad turn there a little while ago . . . all the benches were full . . . you got me behind the screen and gave me a glass of milk."

I remembered none of it, and I said nothing. She began twisting the fringe of her gray shawl with nervous red fingers.

"I have heard it said that you have no home. My husband, thank God, is in work. We have two rooms and a kitchen. We may have to go away, but just for a little while — if you did not mind — " I must have stared at her because she blushed and added in a stammer, "Pay us something if you feel that way. It is only a tiny room, partitioned from the other one. I could make you a nice bed on a trunk."

Then I knew that we were standing level with a long since deserted public house, a *traktyr* of old St. Petersburg. There must have been a wooden bench placed under the broken windows. Hazily, uncertainly, I groped towards it. The girl must have thought me mad: for something like ten minutes I sobbed, my head on her shoulder.

5

THEY were Poles, now waiting daily for their repatriation papers. He was a small, taciturn man of about thirty, almost eaten away by consumption. He was foreman at some chemical works. Skilled labor was rare to find in those days, and he had kept his post through the very worst times. Yet he knew he could not hold out much longer, and Zosia told me that unless their papers arrived soon he would never see Poland again. She told it quietly enough, even her lips did not shake, but her eyes looked as though they were already learning to get accustomed to the darkness beyond.

One night, through the matchboarding partition, I heard him talk to her about the things he wished done when she (he never mentioned himself) was back in Poland. He had an uncle farming not far from Zakopanie. She was to go there, and he knew they would welcome her. He was Warsaw-bred, and he wished to be buried in a churchyard not far from the village of Wilanowa. "You have never been there, Zosia, but you will know it. There are elms leading to the village, a narrow rutted lane. . . . I was born in the small hamlet just beyond. I want two Masses said each year — one in Lent and the other on the anniversary. You must not forget, Zosia."

Uncomfortably enough, I heard it all, and wondered if those cornflower eyes were moist. But her voice rang as steady as ever. "Yes, Jan. Of course I shall not forget. It will all be done as you wish, Jan."

They gave me the room and took no money from me. Zosia had one passion, however: she loved gauze swabs and bandages. I had no idea what she wanted them for, but I used to bring them from the hospital, and her blue eyes looked so pleased that I asked her once, "What in the world do you do with them?"

"Oh, *panenka* dear, they may come in useful some day. Anyway, they are clean and white — like snow."

I was at the hospital by daytime, but in the evenings

Zosia invited me into the kitchen. There were two hard-backed chairs and a bench. Jan lay on the bench, his eyes closed, his thin body covered with a red and blue rug. Zosia, like everybody else, economized on candles, and often we sat in the dark. She and I talked, and sometimes she sang mournful Polish songs, her head with its knot of copper-brown hair leaned against the faint gray wall, her hands clasped on her knee. I could see her eyes until twilight thickened into dark: there was something tenacious in her look, as though her whole will were concentrated on making daylight linger a little longer.

A candle was lit, and Zosia "gathered" supper. Uncarpeted boards never creaked under her light tread. She handled crockery and cutlery without the least noise. Her whispered grace was a fragment of music.

"Now, *panenka*, please break bread with us."

Sometimes the environment seemed unreal enough. I had come to them as a stranger. With the innate breeding of their people they accepted me as a guest, and guests are not pestered with questions in any Polish household. They asked for no information from me, and I knew little about them until the day when Zosia answered my idle question as to whether she had any people in Poland with a brief chapter of her own history: —

"My two brothers were killed early in 1914. My mother worked in the laundry of the Vladimir Military School. A bullet got her in those November days of 1917. She was trying to drag one of the young gentlemen down into the basement. You see, he had been badly wounded in the street. But the Reds were swarming all over the place, and one of them pounced on her. I was in the basement." She paused briefly and added, "It is late, *panenka*, you look tired."

The autumn came, and Zosia sacrificed two warm blankets and made three pairs of gaiters. She handed me one pair without a word, and my thanks rang wooden because I felt too grateful for mere words. In the hospital, behind my tall white screen, I tried hard to bring something of Zosia's spirit into my own manner of dealing with all those patient folk. I no longer considered them as cards, but I was too shy and awkward for anything like really intimate approach.

One morning a nurse strode up to my desk. I knew her well. She was a violent Communist, untidy and unpunctual; she broke nearly all the rules, was an ever-present thorn in the matron's flesh, but, by virtue of her membership in the Party, she sat on the hospital committee, had a vote in all medical and clerical appointments, and could not be dismissed from her post under any pretext whatsoever.

You could not buy cosmetics anywhere, but that girl might have had a wholesome enough complexion were it not for the slightly yellowish powder caked all over her face. Her hands were always far too dirty for a nurse. She introduced innumerable scarlet touches into her white uniform: a bandana kerchief, a scarf, a ribbon casually tied round her bare forearm. She disliked me, and had been rude on several occasions. Now she elbowed her way through the crowd waiting round the screen, put her arms on the edge of the desk, and demanded to be put down for the dentist. "First turn, mind, I am busy today."

A man on crutches was standing before me, and I was hurrying over his card. A few seconds slipped by, and the girl banged her fist on the desk. Two or three patients looked frightened. A card file clattered to the floor. My assistant stooped to pick it up. Blood leapt to my face.

"Ivanoff, done! Next, please."

"Put me down for the dentist." This time she strung an unprintable word to her request, and I had to say something. My head over a card box, I snapped that I would ring for the Commandant if she did not move away instantly.

"Ah, you will, will you? Here is sabotage! I am on duty the whole day and I can't suit your convenience. Put me down at once — for the dentist."

Next to her stood a quiet elderly woman with her arm in a sling. The girl raised her hand to bang the desk once again. She brought down her fist so suddenly that it missed the desk and fell on the other's bandaged arm. I heard something like a hurriedly muffled groan, and the girl shouted: —

"What are you making faces for? Think yourself a heroine with all those bandages on? A softie, that is what you are." And she stopped because, leaning across the desk, I raised my own arm and hit her on the thickly powdered cheek. She staggered back for a second, then, one hand to her flaming cheek, she rushed out of the room screaming "Murder" with all her lung power, which was considerable.

Hot with fury and shame, I turned to the card files. My hands were trembling. The room was oddly still. It was hard to believe that some fifty or sixty people were in it. But the silence was soon broken by the Commandant, a fussy, stout woman, who ran in. "Now what is the trouble?" she shouted from the door. "Oh goodness, she's screaming for the committee to be summoned at once. Surely you never hit her?"

The crowd kept still, though they might have so easily chorused "Oh yes, she did," and so put themselves into the good graces of both Commandant and Communist. But they kept silent. I found a shred of courage to answer: —

"I did. She was so insolent and used foul language. That did not matter to me. But she hurt one of my patients, an old woman at that, and she was beastly about it afterwards. Let her go to the dentist if she wants to. . . . I'd much rather she never came to me again."

Then the crowd came to life. They mumbled, muttered, grew louder and louder: —

"Haven't we got any rights? That nurse is a wildcat, she is! You never hear a rude word from her behind the desk, and that fiend went for her hammer and tongs. We have seen it. Shame, shame!"

The committee was summoned. Having refused to apologize "for the assault," I was fined. "The wildcat," however, decided to keep away from the ambulatory. A sister arranged for her appointment with the dentist. That no longer concerned me. But the people in the room would not let me forget them long after the last patient had walked through the swinging white doors.

I had tried to forget them as multicolored cards, to learn them as so many men and women, but I had not progressed very far, and all my attempts were crippled by shyness. Yet they evidently saw in me a friend, though I had never earned their friendship. Perplexed, I went home to Zosia. I found her alone in the kitchen. I told her the story. A thin wraith of a smile broke on her lips. "The world is like that, *panenka*. The harder the life, the softer the heart. Now I have got some hot soup and a pancake for your supper."

"Where is Jan?"

"Don't make me cry." Her voice went hollow. "He coughed blood this morning. He is in the Marines' Hospital. They said I might come and be with him all the evening," and she vanished.

I sat and waited for her till midnight. She got back in the small hours. Those blue eyes were leaden, washed of all joy. But her mouth would not shake. They were so kind at the hospital. They were letting her stay there with him. "They say it won't be long, *panenka*."

Jan died within two days. At the end of the week I followed Zosia to a remote Roman Catholic cemetery in one of the suburbs. Hundreds of miles from the narrow, rutted lane near Warsaw with old elms overshadowing it, and the white palace of Wilanowa half hidden behind the tall poplars, they laid him. I went with Zosia to a Requiem Mass, and nothing except the words of the Preface seemed likely to afford comfort: "*Tuis enim fidelibus, Domine, vita mutatur, non tollitur —*" But Zosia was so still, so far away that I dared not let a single word of mine intrude upon her.

Soon after she began packing. She told me she was not going to wait for the papers. She sat no more in the kitchen, nor did she sing. She moved from one room into the other, folding and putting away her small, modest belongings. She gave me the pair of gaiters she had made for Jan. She never mentioned him. She said she meant to go to Zakopanie, the last evening we were together in the friendly kitchen. She had a permit for a train journey southwestwards and "God would take care of the rest." But she also said that she had tried hard to make the house committee allow me to stay on in the flat. They had refused because a single person was not entitled to so much floor space owing to the housing shortage. She still hoped I might be able to keep on my room after the next tenants had moved in.

We had finished our supper, and she stood up.

"Zosia," I faltered, "I shall see you in the morning. Dear, dear Zosia — "

"Go to sleep, *panenka*." She put her thin arms round my shoulders and kissed my forehead. "God will take care of you. Go to sleep now. . . . Morning is wiser than evening."

I never saw her in the morning. She must have slipped away in the small hours. I dressed and rushed to the Warsaw Station, but I had neither permit nor ticket, and found myself checked at the first barrier, guarded by sullen, armed sentries.

The house-committee people were not quite inhuman. They let me stay on for about a month. Then a family of four were put into possession. I found them installed with all their goods and chattels on my return from the hospital one sleety and cold November evening. The woman seemed kind enough, but her husband, a suspicious and sullen railway workman, grumbled at his wife for the pity she dared show to an obvious *bourjouyka*. In the early morning he came into my room, insisted on my packing all I had into a bundle, and told me that I would find the door locked

[159]

if I ventured to go back in the evening. My worldly goods under my arm, I went to the hospital to learn that my world had collapsed indeed.

I had heard vague rumors about the coming changes. I found a burly nurse installed behind my desk. She was there instead of me, she said, and I went to see the matron.

"I have to do what I am told," she sniffed into her handkerchief. "There will be a fortnight's rations in advance. I feel sure you will find something else. Of course, if things went too badly, I might be able to manage a pound of bread for you now and again. You will let me know, won't you?" She whisked out her handkerchief again, and I knew that if she had had her will, I should never have lost that job. So I thanked her warmly and went out.

6

ABOUT six hours of daylight were left. It meant that I had six hours to find a home. I had enough food for about a fortnight, but a fortnight in those days meant something like eternity. It was November, however, and vagrancy, so much of a picnic through the summer months, could no longer be accepted as such. "I am homeless," I said to myself, as I stalked along, hands deep in the pockets of my coat; "I must find a home before it gets dark. I have just six hours left," and, unaccountably, I wasted one of those hours on a visit to the housing committee of the local commissariat. They were neither rude nor unkind, but they had no home to offer me. "What about the place you are working at?" suggested a mild-faced clerk. "They should be able to provide for you." When I mentioned having lost my job, he shook his head. The unemployed, it seemed, had to shift for themselves. The housing committee were hard put to it to find shelter for those who worked. . . .

I went out. Habit, more than intention, led me towards the Quay. It was not as I had once known it: many houses stood in charred ruins, snow lay in untidy heaps all over the middle of the road, the wide pavement gaped with holes, half-buried under snowdrifts. The Quay was deserted and gloomy, but the wind still came from the sea, and my eyes looked at the same river which had nursed and cradled all my dreams.

That day I knew how much alone I was. My eldest brother may have been still in the city, but we were strangers and, had I known of his address, I might have gone to him with the story of some triumph, certainly not with the broken narrative of a plight. Aunt Catherine and Uncle Alexis's children were still there, but they lived near the Taurida Palace, a world away from the Vassily Island, and I had seen nothing of them since 1917. There were no trams in those days, and my strength was not equal to a tramp which so easily might have ended in a cul-de-sac. All the others had either escaped or left the city for some other part of Russia. The few intimates of my world were not there. Wistfully, I remembered Sonia of the forgotten surname. Was she in Japan, working at her mosaics?

I halted at the buildings of the ex-Imperial Institute of Mines, "Gorny Institute," at the end of the Nicholas Quay. I stared at its enormous, ocher-painted face. I kept still.

It was a mere wisp of a rather problematic straw, but my memory clutched at it. I remembered that my father had once been connected with the Institute. Also at Xénia we had the daughter of a professor who lived there. The girl was not in my form, and I had to make an effort before I could remember her name. At last it came. I went through the great gaping mouth of the porch. The place seemed empty and quiet, and no uniformed porter came out to pepper me with inquiries. I went on through the huge, untidy courtyard. Myriads of grimy windowpanes looked at me blindly from the four sides of the building. The place seemed inhuman, deserted, as frozen as a lump of quartz in prehistoric ice. "I wonder if anyone is still living here," I thought, when I saw a woman come out from one of the apparently dead doorways.

She was of middle height with a broad pale face. Over a loose fur coat she wore a thick gray shawl, and yards of bright yellow stuff were swathed round her head. She shuffled along, her hands stuffed into a shabby astrakhan muff. She took no notice of me, but I ran up to her.

"I am sorry. Could you tell me please if Madame X still lives here?"

I might have asked her whether she carried dangerous explosives in her muff. She dropped it in the snow, she staggered back, her blue-veined hands raised to her face.

"I am Madame X," she said thickly. "What can you want with me?"

I had never met her before. Now the yellow turban, the

pale gray eyes, the thick voice, and the abrupt gesture with which she seized my wrist, made me feel frightened. Haltingly I told her who I was, and she listened, her face unchanged. Then she let go of my hand, and picked up the muff.

"Why didn't you say so at once?" She dropped into rapid, nervous French. "You frightened a poor old woman out of her wits. I thought you were one of the enemies. . . . Of course I remember your father. He was a great friend of my poor husband. How sad life is! You look rather like your father. Where are you living now?"

The question fanned the ashes of hope into a faint flame. I told her about my plight.

"Of course you are coming here. It is very providential. I am all alone in an enormous flat. There are twelve rooms and no servants to keep anything tidy. My poor boy is dead and my daughter is away. I believe she got married. Yes, come at once."

I followed her shuffling steps through one of the gaping doorways up a staircase which could not have been swept since the beginning of the chaos.

The flat had twelve big rooms. Some were still furnished, others stood bleak and bare — except for a profusion of dust and cobwebs. In the drawing room was a small tin stove, its clumsy funnel thrust through a broken window-pane. The stove had been lit in the morning, so she told me, but the great room was cold and damp. The smoke almost stifled me at first. I rubbed it out of my eyes. I could see little else than dust. Velvet-covered chairs and sofas, tables and whatnots, floor boards, were all coated with it. Pictures and mirrors were daubs of yellow gray.

A big table was littered with saucepans, cups and plates, and several chipped teapots. Everything was soiled. Each teacup had a generous coating of dark brown sediment at the bottom. A heel of a rye loaf had grown green with mildew. But I stood under a roof; dust and dirt could be remedied in time. So I left Madame X alone in her dusty kingdom, ran back to the hospital, and told the matron of my good fortune. In less than an hour I returned, pushing a sledge piled high with my belongings and rations. Through the thick curtain of smoke in the drawing room I saw Madame X get up and come forward, and I thought, "She is certainly queer, but she has a kind heart."

I laid my bundles on the least littered table. She had got "tea" ready for me, and, sipping the weak strawberry-leaf concoction out of a Dresden cup, I told her that I was looking for a job.

"There will be plenty of time to arrange everything." Her manner suggested that she had a thousand jobs to bestow on any deserving candidate.

She was not very talkative, yet prolonged silence seemed to add to the dust of the room, and I murmured that it seemed wonderful to see her living unmolested in such a great flat at a time when most people were denied even a slip of a room. Over the cup her gray eyes widened in mysterious triumph. Nobody dared trouble her, she said; they were all afraid of her because they knew she could harm them once they began interfering with her. Such a statement was oddly at variance with the obvious panic she had shown on meeting me in the yard, but I realized quickly enough that a great many things warred against one another in Madame X's mind.

Soon after she went out, making some misty allusion to very important business. I put on my coat and meandered about the vast, icy flat. In the enormous dining room the table stood, thick layers of undisturbed dust covering it from end to end. In some of the bedrooms the dressing tables were still there with their silver-backed brushes and cut-glass bottles, but the silver was tarnished to the tint of ebony and the cut glass looked dirty brown in the winter light. A few rooms had no furniture at all, and they appeared all the vaster for their bleak emptiness. There was no water running anywhere, and the kitchen taps were encrusted in ice. The bath itself was stacked with roughly hacked kitchen furniture, which Madame X had apparently been using for fuel.

But daylight was dying, and I found my way back to the drawing room and unearthed a candle from under the litter on the big table. Presently, Madame X returned. Her pale cheeks were flushed, her eyes shone as if something very pleasant had happened on her excursion, and when she had unwound the yellow cashmere scarf off her head, she seemed almost presentable.

"It is good not to be alone." She threw a wistful glance at the untidy table. "Such dreadful disorder, but, my dear, I am not used to keeping things tidy. I had six people to run this flat. I am so stupid about housework. No sooner do you get rid of one heap of dust than two more appear in quite different places. It is not worth cleaning up, I have more important things to do. We'd better eat now."

There was no food on the table — except for the mildewed loaf. So I unpacked some of my rations and Madame X boiled a pannikin of water. We ate the improvised meal

[165]

in silence. Then she rummaged in a chest and produced two clean blankets. She was sorry but she had no sheets to offer me.

The next morning she vanished early enough, and I found a couple of darned dusters, some brooms, and a pail, and set to work. I had no ambitions beyond cleaning the room we were using. I knew that the rest of the flat would defeat me. As soon as I started, dust rose up to challenge my efforts. It whirled, it curled, it spiraled, it tickled my throat and made my eyes smart, but in the end I succeeded in giving the room a more or less tidy face. The mildewed loaf was by no means the only example of wastage: in chests, table drawers, lockers, and cupboards I found things which had once been eatable; their appearance, however, was somewhat hard to recognize. There was a dustbin in the kitchen and, wandering about the yard, I stumbled on an evil-smelling dust heap in the farthest corner. I dumped about five dustbin loads in succession. But away from the living room I found things which needed tidying up, and there was "rubbish" in the flat which must needs remain unspecified. By the time I had done with it, I felt rather sick. It was afternoon, and I had had no food since early morning, but the mere idea of a meal seemed unthinkable. I decided to wait for Madame X's return. She came, looked round, and almost snapped: "You should have left things as they were. There is no point in tidying things up when I hope to leave quite soon."

My heart sank.

"But didn't you say nobody would turn you out?"

"Nobody could. I am going away because I want to. Perhaps you might go with me. I'll tell you all about it.

Let us eat first. Keep your rations. I have brought a few buns." We munched in silence until I said: —

"I must begin looking for a job tomorrow." The innocent remark annoyed Madame X. The whole world, she said acidly, was either looking for a job or else doing one. Most jobs were quite futile. Hers, of course, differed from all the others.

"It is most providential that you should have come here. Now we can begin working together and, between us, we shall put the devil under our feet. I saw you say your prayers last night, therefore I take it that you are not on the devil's side." She rapidly dispatched the last of the buns and looked at me with something like strange satisfaction. I had a curious fleeting feeling as though she were seeing a blank wall in me and preparing to start her own picture on it. I said nothing. I knew that she was mad, but since everybody seemed more or less insane in those days, there was no point in getting frightened until I had learned a little more about her particular mania. Unprompted, Madame X proceeded to enlighten me.

"The devil has so many children. At first I quite thought you might be one of them. Of course, you are not. My son-in-law is, most decidedly. And many others. Look, look." She swung round and reached for a shabby leather box on the table behind her. "My dear father was a doctor. This used to belong to him. It is full of most lovely poisons, I am fighting the devil with them," and she snapped the lid open. I saw row upon row of grayish glass bottles, filled with tablets of different shapes and colors. For all I knew, they might have been dangerous poison. Again, they might have been harmless enough, but I judged it wiser not to

[167]

offer immediate comment. Madame X picked up one of the little bottles and fondled it lovingly.

"They dissolve so beautifully," she crooned. "Even in cold water. Listen. My methods are simple enough, inspired though they are. I go to a commissariat. I insist on seeing some official brute or other. I beg him to sign a paper for me, a permit to leave the city for a week or even three days. I say that my poor daughter is in Orel. Sometimes I make it Perm or Riazan. You understand that I have no idea where she is. Well, all those beasts misspend their time drinking tea, real tea, mind you, with lemon and sugar, greedy brutes that they are! I come in to beg for my permit. The devil sits there, sipping his tea. He begins hunting for a blank form. They are all so untidy — most of their papers lie on the floor. He must stoop. I never waste a single opportunity. I slip one of my tablets into his glass. They are all tasteless. He either gives me the permit or else refuses it — neither matters much to me. Then, his back to me, he picks up the glass, drinks the tea, and, soon after, he goes to the devil. This is my work. Isn't it simple and grand?"

The flush had gone from her cheeks, the usual yellowish pallor lay on them, her eyes had gone dull and dim, nor was there any color in her voice. She might have been rattling off an unusually lengthy order to her grocer, and I shivered.

She stretched her hand for another of the dusty bottles, stroked it, and continued in the same wooden voice: —

"My little daughter was seventeen when he came. A gross creature, old enough to be her father. Perhaps even older. I never asked him about his age. If I had, he would have

lied. He was a prince among liars. You could not even ask
him a simple question about the weather. If he were to tell
you that it was raining, you would have been wise to go
out and have a look for yourself. Yet he dares call himself
my son-in-law! No law in the world would recognize him
as my son. He just came into this flat. I forget what he
wanted here in the first place. He, too, forgot all about it
when he saw her. He looked at her in such a way that I felt
sorry she ever came to be born. The day he stood here
something lovely was killed in the world. He stayed here,
and soon afterwards they went off together. I never said
good-bye to her when she was leaving: she had really gone
long before, and a stranger, who could kiss that foul mouth,
remained in her place. Of course, it was all his work. He
turned her into the devil's daughter. Then I knew what my
work would be like. Now — have a lump of sugar. I can
spare it. I stole about four lumps today whilst I was at
work."

I accepted the lump of sugar. The colorless voice went
on. She knew that the heart of all devilry was in Moscow.
Anyway, her work would soon be finished in Petrograd.
At first there had been about four hundred devils at large.
She had dispatched almost all of them. It was obvious the
angels were on her side. Still, she was getting a bit tired.
There were no trams, some of the commissariats were so
distant, and often enough she had to tramp home, nothing
to show for the day's labors. She had to use great cunning
in her work, crude measures were out of the question, and,
whenever she felt weary, she wished she might push the
tablets down the brutes' throats instead of slipping them
into the glasses of tea. If ever she did anything so stupid,

she might be discovered, and the devil would laugh in triumph. So my coming was most providential. She paused and stared hard at me through those eyes which were as dim as her poor mind.

"You are not on the side of the devil. Will you help me?"

Her eyes held me in their cold, colorless stare. I knew I must answer and answer quickly. I also knew that if I showed myself lukewarm about her scheme she would have no hesitation in turning me away from her door. The fierce wind moaned and wailed outside, whirling round and round the four walls of the courtyard. Within, the room was thick with smoke, but the tin stove certainly yielded some warmth, and the thick walls afforded good shelter from the bitter mercy of a November blizzard. I thought rapidly, and I saw she was getting restive. Hurriedly I assured her that I was not on the side of the devil. I promised all the help I could give her. I added that I thought I would have more opportunities to help if I held a job of my own elsewhere. "If you and I went together on such expeditions, we might run risks. I could not be as clever as you are."

Madame X looked doubtful, but the hour was late, and the discussion died a more or less natural death.

Well, that phase of her malaise continued for something like a fortnight. Then she grew tired of trekking round, a gray glass bottle concealed in her shabby muff. I knew already that the dusty fragile phials contained no poison. One evening she had a violent headache, and she helped herself to some three or four tablets out of the same bottle she had carried in her muff during the day. With those very tablets, as she had admitted on her return, she had been able to "dispatch" no fewer than seven "devils" in a few hours.

She swallowed the tablets. Fascinated, I watched her from my corner. But nothing happened — except that the headache left her in a short while.

7

A ROOF I had, whatever the peculiarities of my hostess. But a job would not come my way. The hospital rations, however carefully managed, were running out. Madame X's own budget was balanced most precariously. Sometimes she left the flat, a towel or a rug under her arm, and returned with a few buns, a bottle of saccharine, some frozen potatoes, or a pound of salt fish. The Sixth Line market still functioned spasmodically. But I had no more possessions to sell.

I went on tramping in search of a job. Most official avenues seemed barred. My labor book was in order, but the gentlemen in commissariats took a sudden dislike to the name on the front page. "*Bourjouy*, aren't you? One of your name shot a while ago?" and could I stand there and explain that I had never really known that first cousin of mine? "Yes," I stuttered, since a denial would have been useless, and the labor book was pushed off the desk. "No

job for you here, citizen." Once a hostile remark followed
on the heels of the formal refusal — "Thank your stars you
are still alive," and I very nearly retorted, "Well, it doesn't
look like going on much longer," but caution got the
better of temper.

8

T HE official channels remained closed. But
odd jobs began trickling down my way. I was lucky
enough to find a two days' employment by sweeping the
snow in front of a house in one of the Lines on the Vassily
Island. The man who should have done the job absconded
on an illegal excursion into the country "to get hold of
some victuals." He was a Communist, a member of the
house committee, and in order to avoid any unpleasantness
with the heads of the local party headquarters, the house
committee gladly gave the job to the first applicant, who
happened to be myself. The work was hard enough, but
it left me all the richer for three pounds of bread and a
lot of *wobla*, salted dry fish of unspecified variety, eu-
phemistically known as the Soviet ham.

Visits to the local labor exchange proved barren. I looked
elsewhere for further opportunities. I cut bread one day
for the local store, the bread man having hurt his thumb
with a ten-pound weight. I minded a house for a few

nights when the man assigned for the job had to go to a hospital. There was also an unpleasant scavenging job which gave me a thick wad of pale pink paper. I could hardly count "the millions," but they enabled me to spend about four days in comparative luxury.

Yet all those were so many stopgaps, maddening in their brief insecurity. There seemed nothing permanent left in the world.

Meanwhile, at the Mines Institute, Madame X kept on swinging from one startling extreme to another. The "poison" campaign came to an end the day she dropped a bottle out of her muff and a street urchin picked it up and ran away with it. She immediately decided that the boy meant to carry on her work, and she spent about four days in trying to trace his whereabouts so as to supply him with more bottles. When she failed to find him, she gloomily decided that the devil himself had trespassed on her preserves, and she talked no more of poisons. That evening she kept silent. My own suggestions of help were met by a stony stare, and, under the avalanche of rough, tickling blankets, I spent a broken night, wondering about the immediate future.

For days she sat, hands folded in her lap, pale eyes staring at the smoking, spluttering fire. My presence seemed no longer any concern of hers. She would get up, ransack a cupboard for food, bring it to the stove, and eat slowly with a peculiar sucking noise. I kept alone in my corner, trying to stay silent and still and to fight down my fear.

I certainly was afraid of her. Covertly I tried to scan her face, to read in those broad, ungainly features some portent of the storm gathering within. But her face was like a slate wiped clean. Those sullen pale eyes revealed nothing at all.

One afternoon in December I came back after several hours of fruitless search for work. I had not had even a casual job for more than a week. It was a day when the frost all but killed the birds in the air, and I found the little stove had nearly burned itself out. My stupidly benumbed fingers proved clumsy with logs and matches. The wood was damp. The matches were pitifully few, and I had to use them very sparingly. But at last one of the sticks caught fire. The mere sight of that slender orange-blue tongue shooting upwards brought on a foolishly emotional reaction.

I nursed the fire, squatted in front of the stove, and I indulged in a reckless outburst of self-pity. It was all coming to an end, I said to myself. If you did no work, you starved, and there was no work to be had. I had offered my services as charwoman at one of the commissariats, but I must have looked too much of a weak reed: they merely shrugged and said they knew I could not possibly cope with the work. Yet I knew I could do anything because I wanted to live with all the passion in me, and it looked as though nobody else wanted me to go on. At twenty-one tears are sometimes good. They were certainly good then. I cried until I felt that nothing could be either worse or better: I found myself groping in a shadowy no-man's land where little mattered at all. . . . I devoted myself to the fire, and presently warmth began creeping into my half-frozen fingers. My toes reminded me of their existence with a sharp, exquisite ache. I unbuttoned my coat and unwound the scarf. It was very dirty, but hot water was beyond the price of a pearl necklace, and it would have been sinful to waste even a cupful of it on such a luxury as the laundering of a scarf.

The room was peopled by the sizzling and crackling of the damp logs. It had long since stopped snowing outside. Through the dark blue square of the uncurtained window, I saw whimsical traceries of the ice and snow grow into gold and rose from the flame of the stove. Those delicate, fantastically textured patterns were about the only lovely thing left in the world, as I saw it that night. I went on staring at them until my tired eyes took their fugitive shapes and translated them into something different, according to the sudden dictate of the imagination which I had long since dismissed as dead. The gold began muting with entirely imagined green, crimson, purple, and deep orange. I lulled myself into thinking that I was staring at the east window of some great cathedral: Salisbury, Rheims, Chartres, Louvain, Cologne, Strasbourg, Milan, Canterbury, Durham, Toledo, Burgos. . . . The mere names were singing, dancing, painting in my mind. They crept away and danced nearer again, a glittering garland of names, weaving a curious mood in which neither envy, nor regret, nor yet self-pity, had any room allotted to it, but only a strange, inarticulate conviction that all the sculptured, graven loveliness and my own tiny, squalid life in a dusty room, made all the more sinister by a madwoman's presence, a gray, bedraggled feather and a shining white plume together, were in the same world, and that world was made by one God.

The mood fostered no desire for prayer. I had nothing left to pray for, so I thought, since I wanted everything, and nothing seemed to come my way. Nor could I pray for others: the harrowing emergencies of the moment loomed so disproportionately big that they somehow eschewed the vaster reaches of charity. Still, there remained a dim and flickering recognition of a world which need not grow remote because of the immediacy of squalor, penury, and the grim clutches of misery. The winter day had freely used a windowpane for its canvas. I kept staring at it, and knew myself determined more than ever to keep on trying to preserve some foothold on life. . . .

But Madame X was back in the room. I looked up. She shuffled no longer but walked, her head erect.

"Thank heaven — I have caught him at last," she cried, clapping her hands. "Just imagine — he is in the dining room. I have locked the door on him, but, of course, anything might happen in a moment. We must act at once. Get up and don't look stupid. I have no time to explain. He is far more cunning than we know. Come on — "

I jumped to my feet, conscious that another bat had invaded Madame X's belfry.

"Yes," I agreed so faintly that she broke in: —

"Haven't you heard me? The devil has got into the furniture in the dining room. Something dreadful will happen unless we act at once. We must take everything out of the room and dump it somewhere in the yard. I don't care who finds the things. They will be welcome to the devil in them. I refuse to harbor him under my roof."

I remembered that the table was enormous and that the chairs numbered about a dozen. But Madame X was already pushing me down the passage. Outside the door she halted. "Keep still. . . . Can't you hear him? He will not be quiet — " I heard nothing except the chattering of my own teeth.

Meanwhile Madame X was lighting candles and dumping them all over the place. I wondered if they were meant for the devil's requiem, but it seemed prudent to ask no questions. Presently, the stairs were all lit, and then we came back to the passage. She opened the dining-room door with a broad gesture which spoke of martyrdom and bravado at once. "You must be quiet. If you say nothing, he will never guess why we are here," and we started on the work.

That table took us something like an hour. The six heavy legs were unscrewed after a succession of futile efforts, made all the more difficult by Madame X's admonitory whispers about silence. The legs, however, had to be detached; even Madame X could see that otherwise we should never have got the table down the none too wide stairs. The broad polished leaves clattered on the floor boards. At last we heaved it on the landing. I was hoping that the dreadful noise we made might attract someone's attention, but the block seemed to be untenanted. People must have heard us, but probably they had long since decided not to interfere with Madame X.

Slowly, gasping at each step, we dragged that enormous sheet of mahogany down the stairs. Nothing but the middle of the yard would satisfy Madame X, and to the middle of the yard we transplanted the devil's portable habitat, sweat beading our faces in spite of the frost. Then back to the flat for the chairs! After the sixth had been taken to join the table, something began stitching in my side. Madame X grumbled but accomplished the work alone, and came back to the drawing room panting, sweating, and triumphant.

"It came to me quite suddenly as I was opening the front door." She spoke conversationally. "He is in the dining room, in the table and the chairs. Put him outside. You will die if you refuse. . . . Sure enough, as soon as I got near the door, I heard him roar just like a lion. You never heard it? You must be deaf. Isn't that what the Scripture says — roaring like a lion?"

Within the next few days the devil chose to spread his fleeting perch all over the flat. The whole furniture of a bedroom went one evening, but the pile in the yard kept getting smaller and smaller, whatever we dumped on it. In those days some people reaped vast profits out of the madness of others. Furniture, even if useless as such, was always good for fuel.

Having played his pranks about the flat and laid bare almost every room, the devil decided to invade the drawing room. His activities had perforce to cease on the evening when we sat on suitcases and my pile of blankets was spread on bare floor boards. My sofa and her bed had gone earlier in the afternoon. But Madame X was exultant.

"I think we have got the place clean now. It does not matter that the silly furniture had to go. I am resolved to fight the fiend down to my last possession, why, to the last drop of my blood, if that should be necessary. Besides, it is time I moved away from here," and, trying to keep my legs away from the draft of the door, I silently agreed with her.

9

❧❧❧❧❧❧❧❧❧❧❧❧❧

I BELIEVE Christmas was coming near. I
had spent something like five weeks with Madame X. I
was not sure if I could pass another week under her roof.
It seemed almost imperative to start looking for another
perch as well as for a job. The next morning I woke early,
and she was still asleep when I tiptoed out of the room. In
the gray yard, the brown golden velvet of the sofa, on
which I might have slept, gleamed grotesquely, the only
bit of furniture left from the enormous pile we had dumped
the evening before. I suppose the thieves must have thought
the sofa too heavy.

I tramped towards the Quay, dimly thinking of a certain
commissariat I had so far left untried. Suddenly I heard
a gruff voice behind me: "Can you use one of those machines for writing on?"

I swung round and answered without thinking: —

"You mean a typewriter? Of course I can." I suppose I
would have given the same answer if asked whether I
could build bridges.

"Then come along and help me. I am like a bear in a
bog — "

He did not suggest a bear: rather an ape. He was small,
wizened, middle-aged, a hunchback, with a thin, earthen-
colored face, a mop of red hair, and a straggling, flaming

beard. His long arms dangled up and down rather alarmingly. He wore a sheepskin coat. I noticed the edge of a dirty blue shirt and a gleam of something metallic stuck into his leather belt. He looked a "chance" man, a peasant washed on the urban shore by the tide of the new regime. But his eyes were not hostile, and I followed him to the basement of a house in the Eighth Line. The room was apparently used as an office and a living room. From its gloomy depths an untidy woman emerged, stifling a yawn. Her waxen face looked a mask in the shadows. She said nothing, but stood, arms akimbo, challenging me with a piercing look from her small eyes. But the hunchback paid no attention to her. He hurried me to the end of the room, to a table facing a grimy square apology of a window, where a rusty typewriter lorded it over an ocean of ledgers, papers, envelopes, ink bottles, and innumerable scraps of soiled pink blotting paper. It was so noisy at the office, he muttered, that he preferred working at home. He had held his present job for about a fortnight, and had the machine brought over a few days ago, and then found he could do nothing with it.

He talked on, tugging at his unkempt beard, and I tried to gather my wits together. The typewriter spoke of years of neglect and ill-usage. There was no ribbon. The type was worked by a pad, gone bone-dry, as I discovered after a casual glance. I extricated the pad from its dusty moorings, soaked it in ink, wildly praying that some sixth sense would tell me how to put it back. The little odds and ends of metal clips which had held it in place seemed to have vanished. I tried once, twice, but the pad remained loose, and a great deal of the ink it had drunk removed itself to my

[180]

fingers. At last I pushed it in rather blindly, and it fell between the clips. Nonchalantly, I snatched at the nearest sheet of paper, slipped it in, and struck one of the very dirty keys. The thing worked. I could hear the man's labored breathing down my neck, I knew that the woman was watching me, but I had scored the first innings, and could afford to raise my head.

"It is all right. The type needs cleaning. I can manage it easily."

He spat, swore something inaudible, and demanded my labor book.

"Unemployed, are you? Well, I can't give you a state job, this is something private — see? Will you work here from nine till four? There will be victuals and a bit of money now and again — "

From behind us the woman's voice rose in a shrill plaint: —

"Victuals, indeed? Are you mad, Stepan?"

"You leave it to me," he shrugged. "Well, what of it, comrade?"

I pretended to hesitate. Was it a safe job? Could I have something in writing? He exploded.

"None of that, citizen. . . . Private, I told you. . . . Take it or leave it — "

I took it.

It was rather unfair. The authorities should have allowed him enough for a private secretary; Stepan could hardly wield a pen to scrawl his own signature, let alone work a typewriter. His wife was quite illiterate and regarded any paper covered with writing with the gravest suspicion. But her bark was far worse than her bite. As soon as she saw that I did not prowl about the basement, rummaging in chests and lockers, she offered me a glass of well-sugared real tea, a buttered roll, and a thick slice of sausage. I wolfed the food, not having seen anything like it for about two years, and she moved away from the desk, telling me kindly enough that I had no need to go hungry so long as I remained with them.

"It is cruel what this life does to young people. Saps all their strength, it does. Why, you are nothing but a reed to look at — "

Stepan had vanished. I set to clearing up the desk. Agafia ensconced herself at the opposite end of the room. She had some mending in her lap, and she never ceased munching. In about an hour she offered me another "snack." When an old rheumatic clock announced the noon hour, she bestirred herself to get the dinner ready. We sat down to an incredible meal of cabbage soup, sausages, potatoes, and walnut cheese, *halva*, all of it washed down by several glasses of tea.

The meal made them both much more real. They proved themselves to be pleasant enough people of the smaller shopkeeper class, slightly on the defensive, an attitude engendered by their environment far more than any innate tendencies. The skeleton of their life story was built to the rhythmic accompaniment of the samovar's steam song. He had had a small grocer's shop in a tiny townlet somewhere in the Pskov government. A cousin of his wife's was an important person in the Kremlin in the early days of 1918. The whole family were sent for to bask in the reflected glory of the important cousin. Stepan had had many an administrative plum tossed to him. This was one of the juiciest he had ever had.

In those days delicacies like wheaten flour, eggs, butter, sardines, jam, even cocoa and chocolate, were still to be had in the city, but people had to get doctors' prescriptions to receive them from a special depot. If a doctor certified that you were suffering from, say, acute appendicitis, some liver disorder, or even gout, you might be solaced with a tin of Norwegian sardines or else a slab of German chocolate. The prescription, issued by specially appointed doctors, had to be countersigned by officials detailed to deal with such matters. Each district had its own "prescription" store, guarded day and night by armed sentries. Stepan was managing one such store on the Vassily Island.

Of course, he stole from the store. They all did. Some doctors plied a successful trade in issuing prescriptions; no price could have been considered too high for soap or chocolate, and there was no other way of obtaining them — unless people belonged to the privileged party circle. Stepan stole as much as and sometimes more than he needed. But he hardly ever made any bones about it. Once, giving me a cake of Sunlight soap, he said by way of a polite explanation: —

"If I hadn't clapped my eyes on it, that devil Vanka would have grabbed it. And why should he have had it? He got a lion's share the last time we had soap in. I said to him my turn must come round sometimes. No, he did not argue. . . . Thieves we all are, and thieves should not quarrel. . . ."

The work proved monotonous. A list of supplies was sent over from the headquarters, and I had to make about seven copies of each such list. At the end of the day Stepan returned with the chits about supplies distributed during the day, and he made it plain that all embezzled things were to be entered as "loss in transit and error in stock taking at headquarters." The seven copies meant typing every list seven times over — Stepan's stock of stationery included no carbon paper. But such details were unimportant. I worked in luxurious warmth and I fed like an Andersen princess. At the end of the week Agafia had compassion over my poorly shod feet, the big toe of my left foot having gone nearly black with several near frostbites.

"I shall give you a pound of butter for the New Year. You can exchange it for a pair of good felt boots. But if there should be a raid and you get caught, mind, don't say where the butter comes from. You would not like to have my husband stood against the wall, would you?"

I gave my address to Stepan, but I volunteered little information about my hostess. I said that Madame X was very poor and lived all alone — except for me. Stepan warned me against saying too much about "the office." I assured him that she had no clear idea about my work.

No more she had. Having successfully expelled the devil and all her furniture from the flat, Madame X fell into absolute inertia. For days she remained unaware of my presence. She crouched on the floor, her pale eyes fixed on the oil stove. She took what food I brought in, and ate it like an automaton. The victuals were varied, plentiful, and good, but Madame X's face grew pinched and angular. Her chin jutted out till she ended by resembling a witch out of an old engraving. Her dirty hands went pitifully thin. Obviously she could no longer be left to shift by herself. Yet I could not help her very much. She took no notice of me. I decided that I had better consult my new employers. I did not expect any padded sympathy from Stepan, but Agafia, I felt certain, would help. She was a thief and a thief's wife, but I had seen her furtively feeding some tattered hungry waifs she found meandering down the street, and I had read the simple lettering of her kind heart.

It was the last day of 1919. I found a lot of work on my desk. There were ten copies of a report to be made. Stepan had left when I came. I discovered a sheaf of untidy "service" chits left on the desk as the material for the report. Somehow I hammered it into shape, and not till dinner did I notice that Agafia was in a disturbed mood. She kept shuffling up and down the room, unable to settle down even to her usual munching. I dared not ask her questions. I began wondering whether I had not made a dire mistake about some items "lost in transit," when Stepan arrived in time for dinner. I saw them exchange glances, and her face looked brighter when he said — "Don't you worry, old woman. It is all over — not a chance of any trouble ahead!"

They said no more. In the evening Agafia handed me the pound of butter and a stick of chocolate. "Happy New Year to you"; she gestured away my awkward thanks.

I found Madame X sitting on the pile of dirty, dusty rugs which now served her for a bed. She was shaking from head to foot, clenching and unclenching her fists and repeating that, once again, she had found the devil in the flat. I heated some water and handed her half of the chocolate slab. She took it without a word. She ate it, darting quick glances in my direction. I heard her mutter: "I am ready to act, yes, I am quite ready to act. . . . Would you believe it — the devil daring to come here again?" I carried some tea near her improvised bed; she unclenched her fists and took it, something like a furtive smile curving her mouth. "You are good, you are good," she mumbled, getting hold of my hand. "You are patient, I know, and you must be sorry to hear about the devil getting into the flat again."

I was sorry indeed — not about the devil, but for her. And I suppose that pity drove out all fear that night, otherwise I doubt if I could have stayed in that room. Madame X never stopped mumbling. The candle guttered at last. The stove went cold. A day's hard work sent me to sleep. It was still dark when I woke to hear Madame X's wooden voice mumbling quite close to me: —

"I am going to act now. The devil is in you. Out you go — this very instant — " She dropped her voice to a whisper which made me go wild with fear. "I picked up my muff yesterday, I heard the words quite clearly: 'Get rid of that girl, you'll score a great victory.' . . . Most providential . . . I am sorry — I was not told to kill you — but out you go." She stopped, and I knew that her bony hand was clenching my right shoulder, and it hurt.

Later, I blessed the darkness around me. Had I seen her face at that moment, I might have fainted, and the devil might have ordered her to kill me then and there. As it was, I leapt and felt that she was staggering back. Somehow I wriggled myself free. We did not undress for bed in those days, and, of course, I never stopped to gather my few belongings. Somehow I groped towards the door. In a few minutes I must have been racing across the yard. The dawn was coming, its timid gray fingers beginning to pattern the tall, bleak walls.

The bitter blades of the wind from the Quay made me

halt for a second. Where could I go? I don't suppose I could think clearly that morning because it was some time before I remembered Stepan and Agafia. Yes, I would go there and ask them to see that something was done for poor Madame X. She could not be left alone for another night.

Soon I was knocking at the familiar door. For several minutes I heard no sound from within. I began wondering whether they were still asleep when I heard the cautious shuffle of slippered feet. A bolt was drawn and the key grated in the lock. The door opened an inch, and a voice I could hardly recognize as Agafia's muttered, "Go away. . . . What do you want here? Go away," and, my teeth chattering, I pleaded with her to let me in.

She breathed heavily. I could not see her face, but I knew she was hesitating. At last she opened the door just widely enough for me to squeeze through. As soon as I was inside, she bolted and locked the door. I looked round and wondered if my own wits had vanished that night.

The room suggested that a herd of frenzied elephants had stampeded up and down its whole length. Chairs and tables were upside down, most of them splintered. Floor boards were ripped up here and there. All the doors of Agafia's food cupboards were hanging loose on their hinges, their shelves swept bare. There was no Stepan. I stared at her, and her mouth twitched.

"They came, the fiends. . . . Soon after midnight. . . . They took him away. A thief they called him, and is there one honest man among them, I ask you? Not a single crumb, not a single thing did they leave behind! Well, I must save Stepan. I am going to Moscow, Feodor will show them what it means interfering with Stepan. They think

[187]

Moscow is far away. . . . They'll see, antichrists." Suddenly she thrust a couple of bread cards into my hand. "Go
to the store, there's a dear, and get me the day's rations —
else I shall have no food for the journey. You may keep
them for yourself. . . . Those are January cards, good for
the whole month. But you must not stay here. . . . It
might be dangerous. . . . You never can tell — those fiends
might be back today. . . . It is all right with me here,
though. . . . The store does not open till eight." She kept
chattering away as though the mere words were bringing
her solace she might not seek elsewhere. "Oh, Queen of
Heaven, what a calamity! And what has he done that they
had not done? There is not a single straight man in the
whole damned bunch of them, all are thieving and looting as
fast as they can." Here she suddenly realized that I had
turned up at an unearthly hour. "And what is the matter?
There is no blood in your face. . . . Feeling ill?"

"Nothing." I spoke woodenly. "Just nothing at all."

"Yes," she hurried on, "this job is lost for you. . . .
That's no joke in these hungry days. . . . Listen, you go to
Number 79, Bolshoy Prospect, Petrograd Side, and ask for
Elena Semenovna Vlagina. She is an old Pskov friend of
ours. She is the manageress of the bread store there. Stepan
got her the job, and she is a grand woman, never forgets
any kindness done to her. Say nothing about Stepan being
taken away — just tell her that we are sending you along
on the chance of a job. She is a kind woman and will fix
you all right, don't worry."

We sat there in the dismantled room waiting for the
clock to strike eight. Then I got up. The store was a good
ten minutes' walk from their house. Agafia begged me to

be quick. The soles of my worn boots slipped on the snow once or twice as I ran.

My mind was no longer in a tumult. I could not return to Madame X, that much I knew. The lady who lived on the Bolshoy Prospect, Petrograd Side, might prove her reputed kindness by offering me a job. But a home was a different matter. I wondered if I had better return to Agafia's basement and stay there. If the "fiends" returned for another search they would arrest me, but at least a prison was a house — not a street, open to snow and wind.

The morning's frost lay lightly on the snow-caked pavement. The pale northern sun came out and graced the first day of the year. But the snow underfoot was treacherously slippery, and once or twice I all but lost my balance.

There was nearly an hour to wait for my turn at the store. I grew restive, thinking of Agafia's probable anxiety over the delay. At last I seized the enormous chunks of rough, gray-brown bread — quite obviously those rations must have been very special ones — and I started running back to the Eighth Line.

Rounding a corner, I slipped off the pavement onto the road. I lost my balance and fell, the bread still clutched in my arms. There may have been a shout, but I heard it come from a remote distance, and I felt that it did not concern me. Something jingling and very cold was over me. But my eyes were shut, and I had never seen it come.

Chapter Six

BACK TO THE MIDDLE AGES

1

ABOUT three centuries earlier, I had made my first acquaintance with hospital life. The experience had been at once bewildering and salutary; all I met there brought a sharp reminder that there was greater pain in the world than the doubtful luxury of self-shapen loneliness. I dared not offer those men even a crumb of sympathy; its least expression would have amounted to an insult. My foolish arrogance was humbled and my heart knew strange pity in those days, yet it was always with a definite sense of relief that I came to the last ward on my list and murmured polite thanks to the chaperoning sister. Inside those dirty, ocher-painted walls, I had gone as an onlooker. There could be no question of my ever sharing that life of yellow cotton bedclothes, chipped enameled ware, and the ubiquitous smell of iodine, chloroform, and suffering human flesh.

Three centuries earlier, I thought, my head lying on a pillow which was neither cool nor comfortable. A tickling blanket covered me, and the naked light of several electric bulbs streamed on rows of narrow beds. "The ugliest shade in the world, colored beads and shirred pink silk, would be a thing of beauty." But was I thinking of shades? I saw heads, all marked with a peculiar, unkempt wispiness, dark heads, fair heads, red heads, flaxen heads. In front of me were very tall windows, innocent of all curtains. The bare electric light exposed their griminess. Someone coughed and someone moaned, and I recognized the smell.

I was in a hospital, and I had no business to be there. Where were Agafia's bread cards? She had no other food for the journey to Moscow. And there was Madame X, convinced of the devil's presence in her flat. And I was lying in a warm bed, whilst Agafia thought me a common thief and Madame X was left uncared for and alone. I remembered falling in the street, but the recollection came in a very muddled fashion, something wholly disconnected from the earlier happenings of the day.

The heads on the pillows around lay quite still, but a nurse passed by. Under the lamp her broad red face looked friendly enough. I called to her, and she spoke with an astonishing brusqueness. There was water by my bed if I wanted a drink.

"I want to go," I said, "at once. I've got a lot of work to do."

She stopped and gasped.

"Go? Are you raving? You were knocked down by a horse cart this morning. You could not move if you wanted to. They are taking you to another hospital as soon as the ambulance is free." And she clopped away on her heavily shod feet.

Alone, I moved my hands under the blanket. My body

[194]

seemed whole enough, but I found something strange about
my left foot. It seemed rather too big, something that had
never before belonged to the rest of my body, and I
guessed that I must have broken my ankle. This comforted
me. A few broken bones meant staying on in the hospital.
By virtue of an accident, home and food of a kind would
be mine for several weeks. Yet the question of Agafia and
Madame X remained unsolved. Agafia's affair touched my
sense of honor. Madame X was more or less a responsibility,
but neither could be profitably discussed with strangers, and
I was in a world of strangers. The worry kept me awake
until the ambulance came, and they moved me away from
the ward.

It was hardly a comfortable journey. The horse must
have been very near the end of his own tether: he lurched,
lagged, and stopped with a jerk every few yards. The ambulance had no rubber tires. There was a thin blanket over
the wooden seat, and the nurse decided it would be much
easier for me if she held my foot between her hands. She
meant well, but her hands were rough and clumsy. Somehow, that journey ended, naked lights and the strong smells
of antiseptics broke again on me, but this time I was soon
past all caring — even about Agafia and Madame X.

"I am glad they brought you here. But please go to sleep
again."

She should not have spoken in English if she meant me
to go to sleep. My eyes opened wide. I saw a vaguely familiar face, its color something come out of a rose garden.
"Scilla Siberica," I thought, staring at the blue-gray eyes,
"and ripening wheat," when a loose strand of hair peeped
from under the white veil. But the name eluded me.

[195]

"We have met," I whispered very slowly, "but where?"

"You must promise to sleep if I tell you. I used to nurse at the Anglo-Russian Hospital. We met there often enough. Once you told me all about the history of some imaginary country you wanted to write. But I thought you were British and had gone with the rest of them."

"You are Sister Esther."

"Yes. There will be plenty of time to talk later on. You must sleep."

She vanished. I lay with my eyes closed. But sleep was impossible. The world had changed again: it held a friend whom I could tell about Agafia and Madame X. But Sister Esther must not vanish; I opened my eyes and saw her at the end of the long room. I slept.

I woke to see her again. I told her about my two friends, and I knew I could trust her brief promise to go and find out about them. So I could afford to lie quietly. The bed felt hard and lumpy. Drafts came from every door and window. But life was glory because of Sister Esther and the food wagon wheeled into the ward three times a day. Vegetable soup, fish, and tea for dinner, tea and bread for supper, rusks and tea for breakfast. . . . The fare was frugal enough, but the wheel wagon worked as regularly as the clock. The coarse white plate, the tin bowl and mug, came to your bed, you did not have to stand in a queue for hours to get the food, and you ate gratefully.

In the evening, when half the naked lights were put out and someone had begun snoring in a corner, Esther tiptoed near me. She had found Agafia gone and the house shut up, but a neighbor said that Agafia had heard about the accident. "So that's over," whispered Esther. "The old

[196]

woman said she was dreadfully sorry to hear of your
mishap, and she also left a message for you to be sure and
go to see someone in Petrograd Side."

"I am glad," I whispered back. "And Madame X?"

"I've been to see about her, too. You need not worry
about her. She is all right."

"Does she still think I have got the devil in me?"

"No, not in the least."

"Something must be done about her."

"Yes," said Esther. "Please believe me," she added very
earnestly, "Madame X is not miserable any more."

"Have you been able to arrange anything?"

"It was done before I got there."

Much later I learned the end of the story. Poor Madame
X! Late in the morning of that day she came out into the
yard and told a tenant she met that she was quite convinced
the devil had found a home in herself. It was "most providential" that she had discovered it in time, and now she
was ready to act. The tenant, aware of Madame X's illness, did not think much of it. She left the yard and
turned back to the house. She must have climbed the stairs
to the very top because, a few minutes later, someone saw
her wrench open a window on the fourth floor. They
thought nothing of it, and there was nobody to argue with
her, nobody to pull her back from the window ledge.
Mercifully, she was killed outright.

But this was not a story that Esther could have told me
at the time. She said things had been arranged for Madame
X, and I knew I could trust her. So I lay there, basking
in the peace and the warmth.

Early in February they decided I was fit to be discharged. Esther was not on duty that morning. Another sister brought the news to me, a fussy, black-browed woman with mind and manner tied up in tidy knots of red tape. The surgeon said I was ready to go, and the hospital would lend me a crutch. There was a long waiting list, and they had no room for purely convalescent cases. I asked dully: "When is Sister Esther coming on duty?"

"I am not talking about any sister," she snapped, "I was saying that the nurse will bring your clothes in an hour. You may stay till dinner, but we must have the bed ready by one o'clock," and she marched away, formal, fussy, and starchy.

My clothes were brought in, and I dressed myself very slowly. Then I ambled towards the nearest chair. The crutch proved rather too small and the floor of the ward was slippery. At last I managed to reach the big table standing in the middle of the ward. Someone had brought a flat bowl of delicate pink and violet moss, and it stood on the table, but I dared not look at it too much: it was a piece torn off the Finnish soil, and Finland was walled off by the impassable barrier of frontiers. Spring would be there soon enough, I remembered, with little rills breaking between tall, lichen-coated boulders. Little rills, surely, it was not hard to imagine their music. But I strove to imagine a clump of primroses, peeping out among slender fern fronds, in a pallid stain on the wall where a patient had long since spilt a mug of thick brown tea. Rills, boulders, primroses, crags, and pines! I turned my eyes away from the bowl filled with pink and violet moss.

All too soon, the food wagon was wheeled in. I received

my portion and ate it at the table. Immediately afterwards the black-browed sister sailed up to me. "Finished?" she asserted rather than asked. "You are not a patient now, and visitors are not allowed in today. You must go. You will sign for the crutch and bring it back later on."

"Yes, I will sign for the crutch and bring it back later on," answered my voice.

Could I really hobble all the long way to the Petrograd Side? That grand woman, called Elena something Vlagina, might give me a job or again she might not. Perhaps Sister Esther might think of something. Surely not! Sister Esther had done so much. I could not worry her about anything else. It was more than enough that she had come in, a friend, a human being, a wonder, and . . . "Splendid, *Liebchen*, I am just in time to take you home." Esther, unfamiliar in a rough tweed coat, was by the table.

"But I have no home," I answered in English, and the starchy sister snapped again, "Now then, are you ready?" and I murmured, looking away from Esther, "I have no home — but, of course, I'll manage somehow. You see, winter is over."

The next moment that bleak, ocher-painted ward was turned into an anteroom of some fairy palace. There was the sun, of course, and it rioted all over the plain deal table, the chipped enameled plate, and the tin mug, and the softly violet moss shone and gleamed with purple and gold. The sun and the moss were real because Esther was saying, "Don't be silly. Of course you have a home. It's only a very small room, but there is enough space for a second bed. I'd have told you before, but I'd no chance of talking it over with Mrs. Strauss till this morning."

The black-browed sister frowned in disgust.

"She must go this very instant, Sister Esther. If the doctor were to come in . . . I really can't have people crying in the ward," and I never heard Esther's reply.

2

IT was a small enough room in an ordinary flat, its walls were covered with bookshelves, and its furniture looked very modest, but it was paradise to me: I went there to share it with a friend, and the drab courtyard outside the solitary window seemed vested with a glory all its own.

I went there still a cripple, and for about a week I did little more than browse about the books. I could not really read them. My mind seemed wrapped in a thick rough rug. But it was good to rest and to feel the incredible quiet of the little place. Nearly a fortnight passed, and one evening Esther found me reading Mommsen's *Roman History*, and she smiled.

"I was afraid you had forgotten all your German."

"Not quite," but I shut the book almost guiltily. "All the same, this is waste of time. I must start looking for a job — and at once."

"And I must talk to you, and you mustn't mind what I say. Listen, when I found you at that hospital, you were down and out. You must stop drifting once and for all."

"Of course." Blood rushed to my face. "I tell you I must find a job."

"I am coming to that," she murmured, but instead she began talking about apparently irrelevant things. She said that in all social upheavals it was always the comparatively unimportant people who came off worst. Terror swooped down on those who mattered and, in most cases, destroyed them. But it hardly ever destroyed people like her and myself. "It cuts us off our moorings," she said, "it robs us of the little we possess, but we are not big enough to get killed. We are allowed to live, which is probably much more difficult. Now I know I am far luckier than you are. No nurse need beg her bread as yet. But I have heard things about you. Your people may not have been important socially, but some of your connections were, and you never led the ordinary life of the rank and file, for all your poverty. Also you are not practical. In this chaos, unpractical people might find it easiest to turn their faces to the wall and die. This is cowardice, and you are no coward. You must live and *be*. You have not *been* for some time."

"No," I admitted grudgingly enough, "but is there room for people like myself and so many others?" and Esther's face looked happy, as if I had brought a candle into a darkened room.

"I'm so glad to hear you mention those 'others.' Don't laugh at the platitude — but there's room for just anybody. And you've got something to give, but you'll never be able to give anything by running from one casual job to another. There's one place in this city where you belong, and you are going there."

I read her meaning in the look she gave to the book on my knees, and I shook my head.

"The University? You are right — I have not *been* for a long time. How could I study? They wouldn't admit me."

"You told me you got yourself enrolled some four years ago. Well, in a sense you're there already."

"I've hardly ever been inside since 1916. I tell you," my voice was almost shrill, "I couldn't even dream of it."

"Go on with the *Roman History*," Esther said suddenly. "I'd better get that fish fried."

For a week she kept silence about it. In my own mind the idea lay like a wounding thorn, and I, too, said nothing. I would pick up one book after another and put it down. Neither reading nor clear thinking seemed possible. I did not feel merely stupid but a changeling: the "I" who had read Spinoza and reveled in the Mozarabic Liturgy was dead. The new self had an intellectual range which could venture no farther than filling in Stepan's chits about cocoa and soap.

At last Esther said casually: —

"Why, your limp's nearly gone! Now when are you going to the University?"

I said nothing. My head was bent over a book. She put her hands on my shoulders.

"*Liebchen,* I must be a terrible nuisance, but if you don't do it now when you know how difficult it is, you'll never do it at all. Then you'll be wasted. You've had no training of any kind. Your health is so badly undermined that all manual labor is out of the question. Get your mind back. It's the richest part of you. You must do it. We'll rub along somehow once you've taken the plunge. Students do get some rations, you know. Now I must be off to the hospital. When are you going?"

"This morning," I stammered, and was glad when Esther left the room without a single word of comment.

But I was afraid. My mind seemed a blunted and rusty blade, and I hated the very idea of anyone else telling me about it. For more than three years I had neither read nor thought, and I wished I had not committed myself to an adventure as futile as it would be painful. "If only it were anything except history. I wouldn't mind being told that all my languages had gone rusty, but history's always been such a sanctuary," I thought, limping along the Nicholas Quay.

Nonetheless I reached the University, and at last came to a brief halt at the Chancery door. There an old, kindly man welcomed me in a manner which somehow allayed my fear.

"I joined the college in 1916," I mumbled. "I am afraid I have not done any work at all."

He got up, found my name in a ledger and smiled, stroking his short gray beard.

"Well, you needn't have kept away all these years. We've carried on — in spite of everything. Now don't you think you'd better start with an individual plan straight away?" I looked so bewildered that he explained without any preface.

"There are two alternatives for you. Either you come in and run the usual course for about three years, or else you could start with medieval history at once. You will, of course, have to pass the usual curriculum examinations, but they can be spread over the next two years. The second alternative has this much against it — you'll have to pass a stiff preliminary examination before any professor accepts you for the seminar work. It's hard, but at least you'll have the satisfaction of knowing that for the next three years you'll be doing real work — not just listening to compulsory lectures."

My face fell, and he added kindly: —

"There's no disgrace in choosing the easier way."

I almost replied, "Of course, I must choose the easier way," when I remembered Esther and her strange faith in me. It was so extraordinary and flaming, and I felt that my own effort, whatever the outcome, should not be cheapened by anything even remotely suggesting a compromise. So I said, "Do I have to ask for an interview with the professor?"

"Which one?" I liked his lack of commenting on apparently extraordinary decisions. "Dr. Dobiash is in college now. Professor Greaves is ill, and Professor Karsavin will be away till the end of the month. Would you rather wait for either of them?"

"May I go and see Dr. Dobiash?"

He bent his gray head over the desk and wrote out a chit. When I was at the very door, he said quietly: —

"Best of luck to you."

In a big study behind the cloisters Dr. Dobiash, thin, grave, but kindly, talked Life rather than history. Within a few minutes my dread had gone. I answered her questions and wondered, "Why hadn't I thought of it before? Of course, I do belong here," but, having got a certain idea of my background into her mind, Dr. Dobiash became very much a professor of history, and my heart thudded again.

"Now I should like you to come in about three weeks." She bent her small, neat head over a notebook. "You can get all the books you want in the College Library. I should also like you to read this" — she handed me a heavy German book, Euken's *Weltanschauung im Mittelalter*. "I want to see how your mind can handle a 'heavy' book. The rest please use to refresh your general knowledge."

She saw me out with an encouraging smile, but I went home, bitter ashes in my heart.

"She said all these are to refresh my general knowledge. Esther, I keep telling you I've forgotten it all."

"All of it can't possibly have gone."

The three weeks began. The mornings were spent in the old Imperial Library off the Nevsky Prospect, a good long tramp from my home. Afternoons, evenings, and large "nightly" chunks were given over to the study of the college books. I worked among an avalanche of notes, and those grew more and more crabbed, illegible, and disjointed as each day slipped by. They were all written on blank temperature charts brought by Esther from her hospital.

The muddle grew apace. Dynasties, battles, peace treaties, a maddening chaplet of dates and names, economic conditions, the shaping of boundaries, treaties again, racial developments, Roman, Frank, Barbarian, Arab, Norman. My mind, as I thought, was being rapidly filled with all kinds of historical lumber, none of which, I felt certain, would pass the examiner's scrutiny, let alone win her approval. Once or twice, when calling at the College Library, I heard someone mention Dr. Dobiash. "Thorough, isn't she? And what a teacher!" "Yes," replied someone else, "but doesn't she just grill you?" And my heart sank below all conceivable depths.

The day came. I woke with a very natural headache. I saw that the great table was swept bare of all books and notes. "I've put it all away," said Esther, and I knew it did not matter: I could not have grappled with another printed line.

Her own plans were ready and I acquiesced in them woodenly. We went to the little pier on the Nicholas Quay, where we tendered a few bits of dirty pink paper and so secured deck seats on board a tiny steamer which carried us to the Summer Gardens. There we sprawled under an old lime tree, and the cool shade brought my headache to an end. Presently, Esther untied a bundle she had brought, and we lunched off rye bread, hard-boiled eggs, and a cake of potato flour and pressed strawberries. The milk bottle looked like a gigantic pearl thrown on the grass. I stared at it until I fell asleep to be woken by Esther. She said that, whatever happened, we must not miss the next steamer. I scrambled to my feet and shook the creases out of a coat Esther had made for me out of an old sheet. The terror of the humiliation so soon to break upon me seized me again, and I sank back on the grass. I knew I was a failure, but I had no wish for Dr. Dobiash to find it out.

"I've never yet disgraced myself in such a way. Is there any reason why I should start now?" I demanded of Esther, who retorted: —

"Indeed, there is not. But do get up. I am getting really anxious about the steamer."

[206]

We caught the steamer, and the return trip was uncannily quick. My mind seemed an utter blank. I watched the water and the clouds.

It took us something like ten minutes from the pier to the college gates. Once there, Esther stopped and held out her hand. She would wait in the cloisters, she said. She had brought a book to while the time away. I shook my head feebly. All articulacy seemed to have left me.

Somehow I found my way to a door at the end of the great courtyard. There was one flight of stairs to climb, a bell to ring, a dim passage to go through. A great part of my body was a jelly, and my mind became a slab of suet pudding. At the end of the passage another door loomed before me. My clammy fingers struggled with the handle.

"How punctual you are! And what about some tea before we begin?" invited Dr. Dobiash.

3

MORE than two hours later I limped towards the bench and Esther. She never asked a single question. She got up and spoke briskly: —

"Well, now we are going home, and you *shall* go to bed tonight."

But I groped towards the bench, and for a few moments the red wall of the cloister became pitch-black.

"*Liebchen.*" From somewhere in the clouds Esther's voice reached me. "Never mind! You've made the effort. They'll let you try again, sometime in the autumn, perhaps. It isn't a failure, *Liebchen*. You've won. Don't you see you've won, even if you do have to try again?"

I knew I must speak.

"But I've passed," I whispered. "She said so. I can't remember much else of what she said. Yes, perhaps I do, but it might sound conceited. Esther, I've passed. Is it a dream?"

"You are going to dream tonight," she said.

Much later I lay in bed. The curtain was pulled apart. From the window I could see the grim outline of the ruined Litowsky Castle, once a prison, burnt down in 1917 — just the edge of the tower, the uneven, blurred line of a shattered wall, imprinting its blackness against the soft blue sky of a May night. Very occasional horse traffic rumbled over the cobbles of a near-by bridge. I lay, my mind refusing to recognize the fatigue of the flesh. The dark ruin, the gold-studded sky, the wind, and the faint street noises, all of them slipped into something ordered and whole, at one with the book-lined walls of the room, the bed I lay on, and my own body. All grew into a satisfying whole, and in it my own "I" moved freely, no longer either tethered or afraid.

It was Esther's achievement, not mine. Without the fire of her endless persuasions I should have gone treading my way among dusty streets, paved with alien cobbles. The exterior structure of the examination, for all its stiffness, was not so very important. What mattered most was the inner texture, the ensuing flooding of the mind with ideas as such, the weaving of a surprisingly colored picture on an all but shattered loom. At the time I knew nothing about the details of the process, nor did I stop to analyze it immediately afterwards. I set to work instead and, once within its walls, I found that the University lived a life apart. There were hardly any political discussions, and what spasmodic arguments broke out among us were always colored by the endless, petty economic problems of the day. There continued a grim shortage of most necessary commodities, and sometimes the shortage reached a still grimmer cul-de-sac of absolute dearth. By dint of teaching the French alphabet to the little daughter of a co-operative store manager, I succeeded in laying in a good supply of brown-yellow paper, some of it in the shape of stickily gummed bags. My essays on the medieval routes of the Northmen and the definition of time in the Middle Ages were written on that elegant stationery, which, when exhibited for the first time, roused envy among my colleagues.

Our life was spent mainly within the four walls of the seminar room. There were a long table, about two dozen rush-buttomed chairs, something of a stove in the corner, and books all over the place. Often enough the meager ration of electricity gave out, and we must work by candle-light. In that room we had our formal seminar studies with Dr. Dobiash in the mornings. In that room we also did our private work, and briefly we spent all our time there with but occasional excursions into bleak and dusty auditoriums, where we picked up crumbs of logic and political economy and other "essentials." Anything was grist to the mental mill in those days.

"How selfish you must have been," said a plump and wealthy lady I was to meet a long time afterwards — I don't remember whether in Berlin or Rome. "You lived in the midst of terror. You saw starvation and misery all round you. Yet, from your own description, one might imagine that you were quite comfortable, almost smug."

Well, we were not smug and, certainly, life was not very comfortable. The lady whose pearls and furs I still remember might have recoiled from the environment which was ours. It meant doing homework in rooms with no fires to sit by, trapesing to lectures without having a proper breakfast — except a glass of tepid water and a rye rusk. It sometimes meant an hour's work under the solitary gas jet in an icy cloister, for the simple reason that the seminar room was closed for the night, and one knew that at home the last stump of the last candle had been burned the previous night. It often meant tramping eight or ten weary miles for the monthly potato rations only to find at the end of the trek that the university clerk had put the wrong date on the potato chit. "Why have you come today? Your turn comes on Friday, and today is Tuesday. Sorry, we haven't got anything."

No, we were neither comfortable nor smug. How could we be? We made jokes about our ersatz clothes and ersatz menus, but jokes seem preferable to a scream over some poignantly remembered scene of starvation. We eschewed politics and incautious comment on the Government ways, but we never forgot the Gorochovoya, the Schpalernaya, the lorries, speeding through the streets at night, carrying loads nobody dared mention. We lived in a separate world, created by the selfless effort of those who guided our studies, but we never imagined we were living in safety.

There were about ten girls and eight young men in my

seminar, all in their early twenties. We were close comrades and no more. We spent a lot of time together, discussing most things under the sun. Splendidly productive
friendships were formed, but they must always rely on a
more or less constant interchange of severely objective
thought for their continuance. Most likely, this would appear sterile to some people. Yet, if any personal emotions
had been unleashed, the result might have been devastating.
This was no normal condition of life. Of warm, intimate
feelings we had none to show. Our individual experience
of life in the raw — I speak for the whole body of us, not
of any isolated case — had been such that all the fierce and
lovely crimsons of youth had to be put under lock and
key, as a crude measure of self-defense against all further
tarnishing. In a sense none of us were quite alive, and how
could we be? Our reticences were almost cloister-bred, our
sense of distance well-nigh fetishistic.

4

It was winter once again, and the work was
cut short by an attack of pneumonia. They sent me to the
T.B. Hospital. My convalescence over, I was allowed to
stay on there and continue to work at college. Yet this ar-
rangement was not a success. In spite of the chaotic conditions at the hospital, certain hours were still being kept,

and once or twice evening lectures delayed me so long that, on returning, I found the gates barred and locked. I finally succeeded in rousing a porter, who came to open the gates, but I saw that it was hardly fair to go on giving trouble every time I happened to be late.

Just at that time, Esther heard of a possible future home. The one room was really too small for the two of us, and besides, my night work often kept her awake. By sheer chance we heard of some friends of hers who were leaving for Sweden. They had a big flat on the Moyka Quay in an enormous house, one side of which faced the Mariinsky Place. The flat had seven rooms, a bathroom, a long corridor, and a spacious kitchen, but two rooms only were available for us: a big bedroom at one end of the corridor and the old drawing room which opened out into the hall. In between those rooms there were two smaller ones, now occupied by a workman and his wife. A sailor and his lady were installed in the old dining room, and yet another small room was tenanted by an ancient, dirty, shiftless female, who answered to the name of Grannie, and whose antecedents and occupation remained abysmally mysterious. She wore rags and carried rags, and the little one could see of her room — she never opened the door more than a couple of inches — was a profusion of dirty lumber, indeterminate pieces of scrap iron, and rags again.

Those five tenants, including Grannie, had been allotted rooms in the flat by order of the house committee, and it took Esther and me something like a fortnight to get a room warrant from the local Soviet. This was by no means an easy job, but we got the warrant in the end.

The doors of our two rooms had heavy padlocks, and

we were warned never to leave the flat without locking up. Kitchen and bathroom were, of course, communal property. The bathroom was of no use, since the pipes had burst long ago and no water came from the taps. The kitchen range could still be used, but we were advised to invest in a small oil stove of our own. The sailor's lady spent all her time idling in the kitchen. If she saw anything lying about, were it a match, a drop of milk in a jug, an empty saucepan, or a teacup, she instantly appropriated it.

The front door of the flat had no key, nor was there a hall porter left in the building. The flat, most fortunately, was on the first floor. We were warned that queer tenants, to say the very least, had been installed in flats above. There were no lights on the stairs, which were very narrow and steep. It was suggested that, after dark, we had better go up and down together, and always carrying a candle. There had been a few cases of people who had ostensibly missed their foothold on the slippery steps.

The building, an immense stone warren of flats, was once eminently respectable and quite expensive. Now the great hive seethed and teemed with the most weird human riff-raff imaginable. In the winter evenings it looked especially bleak. Its several courtyards were great dark cavities. The pronouncedly defective drains made themselves felt everywhere.

Despite all warnings, it happened on several occasions that, hurrying back from college, I would find myself with neither matches nor a stump of candle in my pockets, and so must grope up the stairs, my fingers running along the wall. Of banisters there were just a few perilously unreliable fragments. More than once my fingers ran into something warm and soft, plastered against the wall. "Who are you? Please let me pass," I would say, and there would be no answer at all, merely a furtive movement aside, guessed at but never seen, and I was thankful to have learned the steps by heart. I vaulted them to the next landing, conscious of loud breathing in the darkness left behind.

Our two rooms were spacious and comparatively well furnished. The very first morning Grannie shuffled out of her den, filled the small hall with her peculiar odor, and politely inquired whether we would like her "to oblige" us with cleaning. But dusters and brooms, we felt, would not go well in her company, and besides we had been warned about her light-fingered propensities. We thanked her just as politely and said we would prefer to manage on our own. She bowed and shuffled away, an unpleasant smile crooking her toothless mouth. Soon after we discovered a mysteriously emptied pail, the dirty water from which had flooded the hall and was trickling through the wide clearance into my room. The connection was rather obvious, but we mopped up the water and said nothing about it.

Those were minor unpleasantnesses. The sailor's lady was to become a very real thorn in our flesh. She was a slatternly lump of fat, her pale face had no intelligence in it, but she could and did devise endless annoyances. She thieved, spied and eavesdropped, she used kitchen, hall, and corridor as though they were her own premises. She and the workman's wife, both seated at the kitchen table, talked together — and always about us. "What was it you said the other day, dear? Of course, both of them are spies, or else counterrevolutionaries. Each with a foreign name, what good can you expect of them?" And the workman's wife nodded.

"Never mind, dear," said the lump of pallid fat, pouring out her tenth glass of tea, "it won't last long. When those two *bourjouy* pigs are dead, you shall have the big bedroom and I will go into the old drawing room."

Esther and I were chopping our meager supply of firewood in one corner of the kitchen. Esther saw my face go crimson, and she said in English that it was no use taking any notice of them.

Sometimes the sailor got what his wife called "a couple of bottles" (three or four dozen of them judging by the empties which littered the kitchen floor the following morning), and they gave a party which began any time in the afternoon and finished in the small hours. On such occasions they left the dining room and took possession of the kitchen and the hall. The party enjoyed themselves lustily by eating a little, drinking a lot, and roaring at the top of their voices all the time. Sometimes they came out into the hall and glued their drunken faces against the keyhole of my room. They could see nothing: the key having vanished, I bolted the door with a latch, and had the keyhole stuffed with thick paper. But they liked to pretend they were invading my privacy. They invented marvelously. "There is the *bourjouy* for you! Wasting time over a book and an oil lamp burning." I trimmed my solitary candle and tried not to laugh on hearing that I "was sitting there in idleness, wearing a velvet frock and all! What is the house Soviet doing, allowing people to live like that? Dirty shame, comrades." After that, the comparatively sober fiction of a book and a velvet frock vanished in the richer haze of cigar smoke, bottles of champagne, palms in pots, and boxes of chocolates. Those entertainments were usually brought to an end by someone's vicious kick at my door, when the merry company trooped back to the kitchen and finished their modest "couple of bottles" to the accompaniment of singing and playing an old concertina.

Such parties, however, did not happen every evening, and, on the whole, barring the sailor's lady and her viciousness, we were more or less immune from real annoyances. Our two rooms were always locked — either from within or from without. Still we had a roof over our heads, and we also had each other. We spent but little time together — my work at the University and Esther's at her hospital made large inroads into our time. Yet, within a few brief months we had, as it were, learned each other; our friendship did not need to be fed by a constant interchange of purely trivial, everyday impressions. Often enough, of an evening, both of us were too spent to talk, but I soon knew that with Esther one word answered where twenty might not have been enough in the case of someone hungering after the obvious surface of things.

We had been at the Moyka place for some time when one evening she came to tell me she thought she should go away and "do something." She said they were cutting down staff expenses at her hospital. She added quietly enough that she had lost her job. The wages, as such, were less than a pittance, but her rations were gone.

I heard and looked at her in silence. The idea that she was to go away and "do something" was more than preposterous. My own work, once she was gone, would lose both purpose and savor. I said that we would manage all right, there were my student's rations, and other openings might come later. "You need all you get," she protested, "and what you do get is not enough for you alone."

This was true. But I knew that it would be useless to argue on such lines. Our larder had to be supplemented; I had a few free hours every day; were I to use such leisure in a profitable way, the comparative sanity of our days need not be shattered. I had already heard about a pupil at the Conservatoire who was looking for an English teacher. I made up my mind then and there. But I had no intention of telling Esther anything about it.

"We'll manage — somehow," I repeated stubbornly.

She seemed just as obstinate. She was not going to be a burden to me, and I retorted that if she went elsewhere, looking for probably ephemeral opportunities outside Petrograd, I, too, would chuck my work at the University, and all her efforts would be undone. "You would hate that, wouldn't you? You see, this cuts both ways. We swim or sink together."

"That's madness."

I shouted at her: —

"And wasn't it madness my trying to get into the University? You urged me to do it. I've got there. Well, I suppose this is madness, too, the whole of life is mad — except that you and I are friends. You talk as though the whole world has come to an end because you've lost a nursing job. What about your painting? You can get yourself enrolled as a student at the Art Academy if you are so desperately keen on having your own rations." Here I picked up my book. "This is the last candle in the house, and I must work."

5

THE student at the Conservatoire had talked a lot about her English lessons, but she never made up her mind. Nonetheless, I had a pupil who paid in kind, though not too lavishly. She wanted to be taught French as well as English. She lived in surroundings whose barbaric luxury was sickening in those days of almost ubiquitous squalor and want.

A fat, khaki-clad commissar had very thoroughly got tired of his lawful wife, a plain, illiterate peasant woman. The commissar, when very young, had lived in White-chapel and also in some slum of New York. Those were rather embarrassing days, now happily remote, and he never referred to them. But he could speak oddly accented English, and he nursed hopes of an eventual foreign appointment. His lawful spouse, in such a case, would have done him little credit. She never unlearned the art of drinking tea out of the saucer, of scratching her head whenever she felt like it — and that happened often enough. She could never remember that handkerchiefs were, presumably, carried for a definite purpose. Still, even if crude, she was genuine enough. A peasant she was born, and a peasant she remained; no vestige of any "class" could have ever been grafted on that peasant consciousness. She would have disgraced her husband at any modest Communist meeting in New York.

My pupil was different. She never talked about her beginnings, and I readily understood that nobody could have waxed eloquent over a gutter. She thought herself to be "unusual," and was convinced that her very manner of entering a room startled everybody out of their senses, and, to give her justice, she was not wrong there. Not too tall, but extremely corpulent, she frizzed her thick dark hair into some semblance of a Papuan coiffure, preferred loud yellow and shrieking red to any other colors, and appeared in any doorway, including her own, her face generously caked with very pink powder, her big black eyes rolling, and her plump, heavily beringed hands clasped to her prominent bosom.

So I met her in an airless room, crowded with badly polished rosewood furniture, obviously looted from some palace or other, heavy blue velvet curtains screening off the lovely and delicate December sunshine.

"You are the teacher," she minced, carefully sitting down in her bright yellow knitted suit, obviously much too tight for her. "Well, sit down. We are all equals nowadays. I had better tell you what I want." And for something like half an hour she instructed me in the way I was to instruct her. She rolled her eyes and confided that her dear "husband" thought that she had brilliant conversational gifts. She paused and added that, unfortunately, her education had been cut short. "You can imagine why."

I really had no manners. I could not imagine why her

education should have begun at all, and so said nothing. Offended, she pursed her lips and ended brusquely: —

"To come to my terms. I shall want you for four hours a week. I can give you a pound of black bread per lesson. I have heard that this is extremely generous."

On the table before her stood the remains of a meal. Bones of a chicken leg, a broken white roll, butter in a dish, caviare in a china pot. Of course, I accepted the pound of bread without any argument. This pleased the lady, and she became chatty.

"Isn't it bitter weather? Your hands must be cold. Haven't you got any gloves at all?"

My gloves were lying in my lap. They were funny, shapeless things, cut out from an old red tablecloth. But they were warm enough. Esther had used an old woolen stocking for the lining, and I loved them for their warmth as well as for the fact that they were made by her one evening when our fuel had given out, and her own hands were nearly frozen as she sat there, trying to finish gloves for me to wear. So I replied frigidly that my gloves were all right and held them up for her to see. She clasped her fat hands and remarked that they looked worse than "those awful gauntlets worn by peasants. Look here, I received two pairs from Berlin the other day, such nice leather gloves, all lined with fur. I could give you one pair" — she paused, calculating carefully — "for, say, twelve lessons in advance. I can afford to be generous in my position."

I thanked her politely and said I preferred the bread. Then I glanced at her unshapely ankles, sheathed in flesh-colored silk stockings, also presumably sent from Berlin. My last pair of "real" hose had gone the way of all worn-out tatters more than a year before, and so had nearly every-body's, but the lady who sat before me belonged to the privileged class, unconcerned about shortage and untouched by privation. There was some food for reflection in that, about forty years earlier, her forebears would not have known the luxury of fur-lined gloves and would most likely never have tasted a wheaten roll, yet I felt that it would have been much easier for me to accept such a comparison had she herself been ready to admit her real antecedents.

She appeared pleased with my prompt refusal.

"Well, perhaps you are right. They might have thought you were one of those speculators, and, of course, I could never admit having given them to you."

Well, I tried to teach her for about six or seven weeks, but her accent, both in English and in French, defeated all my efforts. Also she proved evasive about payment. The pound of bread per lesson soon dwindled to a pound and a half for two hours, and when I tried to tell her that it was not fair, she became unpleasant.

"Indeed? Don't you know that any private occupation is illegal? Private lessons certainly are. You should be grateful for what I choose to give you as a favor, and not quibble about a pound more or less. Unfair, indeed!"

On several occasions she had tea brought into the room whilst I was trying to make her understand the difference between *le* and *la* and the varying sound of *th* as in *tooth* and in *though*. Once a plate of obviously English biscuits appeared on the tray. But she always ate and drank in regal solitude. I carried on, trying not to hear her munching. At last I decided to break off with her. She kept forgetting to have the bread ready for me, excusing herself under the pretext that she never ate it herself, and, naturally, it was something of an effort for her to have it ready for someone else when it never appeared either on her table or in her kitchen. The little rosewood table was nearly always laden with food, but she never suggested any substitute for the rye bread that was not there. At last this wearied me and, having found another pupil, I forsook the commissar's lady.

My second pupil was a young, hard-working scientist, a charming girl with not a trace of any pretensions about her. To her little poky flat off the First Line on the Vassily Island I went three times a week, and I began looking forward to those lessons. She had studied English before, and could speak it quite fluently. She was very keen to get on with it, so as to be able to read English books on chemistry and allied sciences. She paid me generously enough, sometimes in kind, oftener in money. I told her the story of the commissar's lady and her gloves, silk hose, caviare, and English biscuits, and the girl, herself a Communist, was furious.

"I see you'd rather not mention names. All right, I won't press you, but people like her ought to be shot."

"She may end that way."

"Not too soon," insisted my chemical engineer. "She is doing harm in this country, and she'd do much more abroad if they ever send her man out. A commissar's wife aping a lady! It's disgusting. He ought to be thrown out of the party."

"She is not the only one," I said boldly. "Do they live on *wobla* and rye rusks at the Kremlin? It has nothing to do with your party — it is merely a question of social and economic redistribution. The thing that does sicken me is — " I stopped, but she prompted me.

"I'd rather not say it — you might be hurt."

She urged me until I said: —

"The sickening thing is that there is so much talk about equality. There was enough cruelty, God knows, in the old days, but at least nobody prattled about everybody being equal."

We had had many arguments before, none as sharp-edged as this one, and I quite expected her to be furious, but she laughed it off.

"I can't quarrel with you. Why should we agree? I am a thorough Communist and I'll stand by the Soviet to my dying day. You couldn't. I don't for a moment suppose you could be an active counterrevolutionary. If you were, I'd denounce you at once. But you are not. You wouldn't talk about the old days so critically. Really, politics mean nothing to you. You are not as bad as some of your people — "

I parried the compliment by telling her that she was not as bad as some of her brethren, and she pretended to be shocked.

"That sounds like high treason. I ought to sit down and report it to the Sovnarkom. Wait, there is something I have been meaning to ask you for ages. I hope you won't think me impertinent. You must have had a very rough time of it, and you look as though you were still having a bad spell. Why in the world didn't you go to pieces" — she paused — "like so many of your own brethren, for instance? . . . But I should not have said it. . . . It's unkind — forgive me — "

"I did go to pieces," I admitted after a pause, "but it all got patched up in time."

"By whom?"

This was an awkward question, and I parried it by asking whether she belonged to the Atheists' Union.

"I do — with reservations. I mean all that sort of thing is nothing to me, but I quite allow that it does mean a lot to others — "

"Surely, you don't defend the persecutions?"

"I do — in a sense. You see, when the Soviet took power, official religion certainly represented something inimical — "

"How in the world could it?"

"It did. Tell me, can you reconcile Communism and religion?"

"Of course not — "

"Well, that answers your own question rather neatly, doesn't it?"

"That's not the issue at stake," I said stubbornly — "you just cannot oust God — "

"I agree with you — from a different point of view. You cannot oust what does not exist. We are not trying to do that. We are being practical. We are out to crush the external form, and the inner conviction will go of itself. We don't wage war against abstract faith. We don't meddle with abstruse metaphysics or even theology. We are out to fight the outward expression, we find it cumbersome to our own acceptance of life, also it might impede our schemes for the future. You've admitted it already — Communism and religion could never walk together."

"Do you know — " I ventured, "I feel rather sorry for you all. You seem so terribly keen on a cause which is doomed to be defeated."

"But I have already told you — "

"I know you have — but what I know is — "

"You know? You mean what you believe — "

"No, no, it is more than that." I clasped my hands together. "Didn't this argument start by your asking what or who patched up the broken pieces? Well, you see, it is something like this — God isn't there because we believe Him to be there but just because He *is*."

My chemical engineer smiled.

"I should say that is an admirable theological phrase, but it says nothing whatever to me."

So we talked, argued, differed, and never came within sight of the ugly frontiers of an unmannerly quarrel. She and I could never have become genuinely intimate friends, far too many barriers stood between us, but there ran a definite current of sympathy in all our differences. That girl was indeed an honorable enemy, and though I abhorred her party and its teachings, I could not but wish that there might have been more like her in its ranks. Unfairness seemed alien to her, and even the inevitably wild frenzy of circumstances seemed to revolt her. She knew how to marshal her arguments with a perfectly detached clarity decidedly worthy of a better cause, and, disagreeing and differing, I came to respect her. For the rest, she was a quick and intelligent pupil. I enjoyed my work for about four months when the Chemical Trust, where she worked, sent her out to the Ural country on a three years' contract. A useful oil stove was her parting present to me.

I looked round for other pupils. There were none to be found. We just jogged on, day in, day out. "Sufficient unto the day be the evil thereof" was the text woven into every thread of our life. Esther received her meager rations from the Academy of Arts. On occasions, the University deities awoke to the fact that brains could not thrive on black bread and frozen potatoes alone, and chits for butter and fish would be issued.

6

⚙∽⚙∽⚙∽⚙∽⚙∽⚙∽⚙∽⚙∽⚙∽⚙∽

IT had been a hard enough winter, but Easter came round again to break the ice on the river and the buds on the trees. Young grass dared greatly and ventured to find a home among the charred ruins of the Litowsky Castle opposite our house. We wrenched the windows open and filled the room with fresh air. I don't remember flowers, but pussywillows, in a chipped white water jug, brought the country into the room. It was more than pleasant to sit and work, one's body unencumbered by layers of blankets and rugs.

"Anyway," I said to Esther, "the ink won't freeze for a great many months. . . . Oh, what a winter. . . . Three more of them, and I suppose I'll have done with the University. . . . Think of it, Esther. In a few years I'll be a Doctor of History, and it'll be your doing. They should give you a special degree — for valor and heroic counsel."

She sat still in the chair. I wondered if I imagined a shadow which came, danced across her eyes, and went before I knew much about it.

[226]

"I wonder . . ."

"What is there to wonder about? Neither of us must go under — "

"Yes, you are right." The shadow had gone, and she was laughing. "Now you'll need another skirt, and I do wish I could get hold of some stockings for you. Those carpet leggings are so uncomfortable."

I looked at her searchingly. Her laughter had rung an unfamiliar forced note. She sat there, examining a table-cloth, her lap covered with folds of heavy maroon stuff, but I knew that her thoughts were worlds away from the tablecloth.

"Esther — "

"Well," — she raised her head. "Yes, if you must have it. Things don't easily upset me, but Grannie came in this morning, her arms full of children's clothes. She looked dreadfully pleased with herself. She said she'd be able to sell them all very quickly — "

"But that's nothing to brood about — "

"Wait . . . She said that this morning she found two small children, a boy and a girl, lying on the pavement on that little bridge — what's its name — she said they must have died of hunger — they were nothing but skin and bones, and so she stripped them."

"She must have invented the whole thing — "

"She looked so ghoulishly convincing when she told me. Besides, people do die of hunger — every day. No use pretending it doesn't happen. *Liebchen*," — the maroon cloth slid off her knees, — "you see, I have told you because I know she'll tell you herself. . . . It would have been worse to hear it from her: she has that dreadful way with her lips. . . . What was I saying? Oh, yes, work as hard as you can, *Liebchen*, don't think too much, and never look back."

"I only look back on what you have done for me."

"I've done nothing at all. You must not look back — for a long time — and then, perhaps, something will come out of all this, something to be really grateful for. I don't really know what I'm talking about. Come on, it's time we ate and went to bed."

"Never look back. . . ." Had I kept any diary in those days, its pages would not have made cheerful reading. Esther was right: you had to hold on, almost unfeelingly. Yet you lived nonetheless. You lived in a strange world, crowded with unrecorded acts of high courage, of humbly made heroic decisions, of courage again, which had once known the stark nakedness of fear and had not shrunk from its desolation. There were people who cheated and lived lives of crude immorality, and people who had seen their homes uprooted without any regret. There were people who loved to scaremonger and those who, on seeing one dead body in the street, came back and said they had seen twenty, and wallowed in the very occasional scenes of horror their eyes may indeed have looked upon.

There were people, their inmost hearts wounded, who kept silent and withdrew themselves from the outside world, like a medieval anchorite to his cell; there were those who died — without the swift mercy of a bullet; died, and went on living after their death. And there were also those whose sanity could not withstand the shock, who invented a world out of the tissue of their madness, and lived in it, swayed by moods, now bright and again gloomy, now stonily indifferent. For some, madness proved a rare mercy of God. Also in that checkered, ever-shifting world there were countless others, puzzled, buffeted by their own thought as well as by external circumstances, muddled and tired in spirit as well as in body. But were it not for something higher and stabler than reality, as perceived by the senses, that ubiquitous grimness might have ended either in despair or in madness for them all. It did not. The city was no aslyum. Nor was it one huge graveyard — in spite of silence, grief, and horror.

"We are running short of everything," said the sailor's wife. "It's famine, famine, famine, everywhere. . . . Have you seen? Have you heard?" And she started telling one gruesome story after another, her yellow teeth crunching, crunching, crunching.

"No bread will be given out this week," roared the manager of the local food store. "Here is dried fish — if you like."

"Students' ration to be cut down by half from next week onwards," the notice on the Chancery door said tersely enough.

"We shall all be dead in the winter," croaked Grannie, the door of her den opened its customary inch. "Man must eat to be alive. Last night I saw — "

"They are giving nothing but potatoes," said the prefect at our seminar. "It's miles away, and only ten pounds per head, but I suggest you all go and fetch it. Goodness knows where the next lot is to come from."

Potato peelings were saved and used for making funny flat cakes. Queer herbs were infused in fond pretense of

[229]

tea. Grass in public gardens was gathered for soups. Some-body argued that bark could be edible. On the way to the University, I saw several tattered women stripping the bark off the old trees in the Roumiantzeff Square on the Quay. They said that all our earlier experiences of hunger would be as nothing compared with the coming scourge.

Chapter Seven

THE CRUMBLING
OF THE WALLS

1

∾∾∾∾∾∾∾∾∾∾∾∾∾∾∾∾∾∾∾∾

B Y the end of 1918, a Chinese wall had come to be built between us and the outside world. There were no letters from abroad, and the burden of general conversation, mostly carried on in bread queues, dealt with the thrills of "escapes." "She got across the Gulf of Finland, a revolver in each hand, and broke down completely as soon as she was over," or else, "It cost them two million rubles to bribe a guide, and even then something got muddled, and they had to spend three nights in a hut just off Bieloostrov. If any of the frontier guards had caught them, it would have been all over in less than five minutes. They shoot anybody without trial. . . ."

Naturally, not all those escapes were successful. Detailed results of such as were could not be known to anyone: people who did escape could not get in touch with those left behind, who, in their turn, were completely cut off from their more fortunate brethren. Yet marvelous stories, largely mythical, went on growing in volume and in number, and at least they relieved the tedium of a great many people to whom the very meaning of adventure would have ceased to convey anything, were it not for epics of this kind.

But by the beginning of 1921 things were changing. The Chinese wall began showing a fissure here and there. The "escaping" business had lost its earlier novelty, and the outside world was remembered from a different angle. The very bread, eaten, say, in Sweden or in Germany, was unlike any loaf eaten by a mere mortal. A knitted jumper that somebody's aunt's cousin had contrived to send to Petrograd from some place abroad was like a garment made for fairy folk. A letter with a foreign stamp was received with as much awe as though its contents had been taken out of some book of revelation. Those apparently trivial things were all the more important because, to a great many among us, the things which were at the time going on in the country where we lived were so many mysteries.

Several years later, I happened to read a very able history of the Russian Revolution. A great many facts and, most of all, their chronology, took me completely by surprise. "Why, this and this and that must have happened while I was still in Petrograd," I kept saying to myself as I read on. The man wrote authoritatively, there was no reason either to question his facts or to doubt his findings, but it was something of an effort to realize that, while those very things were in the process of happening, we, living in their midst, were ignorant of them.

Probably this was due to our subconscious reluctance to be aware of a great many such things. Too much was just thrust upon us. The governing practice of the Soviet reached us through maddening, irritatingly narrow channels of decrees, through just as irritating and probably more obvious curtailments of personal liberty, through countless regulations which interfered with the food we ate, the clothes we wore, the use we made of our time, and the manner and scope of our work. Of the broader political principles, as laid down by the Sovnarkom, a great many among us preferred to know nothing. Discussions in public were prohibited. Even private critical outbursts were not always safe. The skeleton of the governing system came to be learned through a series of obvious landmarks, and in this particular knowledge an illiterate peasant stood on the same level with an erudite university professor.

Sovnarkom ruled from the Kremlin. The Smolny was its Petrograd offshoot. When people got arrested they were sent in the first place to the Gorochovoya branch of the Tcheka, and later to the Shpalernaya. The grim house in the Shpalernaya was to us what the Inquisition headquarters in Seville must have been to a timorous Protestant. Filtering through the tall barred gates of the Shpalernaya house came stories, one more bloodcurdling than another: they did not just shoot prisoners at the Shpalernaya, they did far worse things to them. It is quite likely that some of those things did happen, but their actuality never came to light — at least, not within the circles I knew. The only example of such practices I ever heard of came to me from a reliable enough source, though I never learned all the details. Our Vice-Rector, a prominent lawyer, was arrested sometime in 1921 and condemned to death. By some mistake, his body was delivered to his widow, and the sight of that body turned her mad. All I knew was that he had not been shot.

A somewhat milder edition of the Shpalernaya prison

was the old König sugar factory in the Wiborg Side, a place kept apart for "minor offenses." There I once spent a bleak and extremely tedious day. It happened in the middle of a particularly severe winter, and I had forgotten to take my turn in sweeping the snow in front of the house. The local commissariat arrested me, confiscated my labor book, a somewhat sorry equivalent of a civilized passport, and pronounced no sentence, saying that this did not lie within their province. I was merely told that my labor book would be sent to the proper quarters — together with the dossier of my offense. For two days, no summons arriving for me, I walked in fear and trembling: the confiscation of a labor book amounted to the medieval oubliette. You were beyond the communal pale in the most rigid sense. Food cards could not be issued to you, no shelter could be given you, no official job could be offered to you. Without your labor book you were virtually condemned to civic annihilation, in some cases a far more bitter fate than that imposed by a straightforward death warrant. Yet, incongruously, a labor book was usually confiscated for a minor offense.

The summons arrived, however, and to the König factory I tramped, paid a fine, and retrieved my precious book. The offense should have been endorsed in its blank pages, but the lady clerk was busily telephoning to a "Sasha, my angel," and she forgot the endorsement. Of course, I would not have dreamed of reminding her!

This is a minor digression, but what I meant to say was that, speaking from a communal point of view, the selfsame Chinese wall which cut us off from the outside world curved inwards in a few places and isolated us from the main pulses of national life. The Soviet Press was then in existence, but we bought and read no papers. Our organ and our post office, all in one, was usually the bread queue. At the University, most Government topics were tacitly taboo.

2

ᴏ~ᴏᴇ~ᴏᴇ~ᴏᴇ~ᴏᴇ~ᴏᴇ~ᴏᴇ~ᴏᴇ~ᴏ

So there had been fissures in the wall, and in the spring of 1921 quite a large window was opened, and we could remember the remote outer world.

One late afternoon I was walking home from the University. I lingered on the Nicholas Bridge. The ice had gone, and it was good to watch the river running below. Such symbols of freedom as were still left to us could be summed up in the running water, the wind, and the ever-moving processional of cloud.

The river was running on towards the sea which I had not seen for something like four years, and, as I leaned my elbows on the rusty parapet, I knew myself homesick for a country I had never seen but had loved from my childhood. Something had happened in the seminar that morning, such a very trivial thing, caused by the professor's remark: "By the way, if you can't get *Henry of Huntingdon* in the original, I am sure Mademoiselle Almedingen will translate the English version," and she turned to me: "Would you mind reading it first in English?" I had a library copy by me, and I read: —

". . . In the year 1096 began the great movement towards Jerusalem on the preaching of Pope Urban. . . . It was the Lord's doing, a wonder unknown to preceding ages, and reserved for our days, that such different nations, so many noble warriors should leave their splendid possessions, their wives and children, and that all with one accord should, in contempt of death, direct their steps to regions almost unknown. . . ." So I finished and translated it into Russian, but for several minutes my heart and my thought remained with Henry. In the next interval I turned to him again: —

"Britain is truly an island of the utmost fertility, abounding in corn and fruit trees, which are nourished by perennial streams. It is diversified by woods" — and, through the lattice of the somewhat stilted words, I saw the picture of a garden in Kent, with a prim, formal lawn, bordered by old-fashioned roses, a gray sundial in the middle, and a bit of box hedge dipping to where old apple trees were swaying in the wind. The air was full of lavender, freshly mown grass, and good, clear English speech. The blinds were down in the windows of a none too big Queen Anne house. An old sheep dog wagged his tail on the hot stones of the porch. Inside, in a room dim, cool, fragrant with dried rose leaves and beautiful with lovingly tended furniture, someone was bringing in tea, seedcake, scones, a jar of strawberry jam. . . . "Cousin Charlotte," my mother was saying, "it is much too hot for a walk."

But I was standing on the Nicholas Bridge, the Quay was empty, no steamers left for England any more, and someone's sardonic voice was asking just behind me whether I had actually joined the First Crusade. I turned round, my cheeks burning. The daydream splintered, a mood of almost wild nostalgia gripped me. To see a garden like that, to hear the sound of English speech, which was my own . . . and, inconsequentially, I remembered Professor Karsavin's sarcastic comment — "You had Serge Poltoratzky for your grandfather, I believe? Why, then, can't you write an essay in proper Russian?" and my halting reply that I supposed few people could be bilingual. "What a cosmopolitan muddle," he murmured.

But I was on the Nicholas Bridge, and the nostalgia was drifting into a stupidly sentimental channel: at that moment the height of all bliss was the very unlikely possibility of lying somewhere at peace, my cheek pressed against the English soil.

"And what is it all about?" asked Marie, deciding that she had waited long enough.

I can't really introduce her. It would take too long. Enough to say that she was a friend, belonged to my seminar, was a Jewess, recently converted to Christianity, and was supposed to be one of the most brilliant pupils at the Conservatoire — at least, M. Glazounoff said so. She played Bach, and, alone of all the people I had ever known, she never mocked me for my deafness of tone. She used to say that I "felt" music in much the same way as a blind person might be aware of color, and when she played, I never felt shut off from that world. Sound and harmony came near and allowed themselves to be interpreted in an undoubtedly heterodox fashion.

Rather brokenly I told her about Henry of Huntingdon and the imagined garden in Kent.

"I can't send you where your heart belongs," she said

slowly, "but I can offer something else. They have just opened a new variety theater at the New Port. There will be a concert tonight, and I have three free tickets. You and Esther are welcome to two of them. Here are the details: I have heard that two British merchant ships are in the New Port docks. Skippers and crews have been invited to the concert. You might hear English spoken once again — "

"Marie!" I clung to her hands, and she interrupted: —

"I have no conditions to make, but I suggest that it might be better if you didn't try to speak to them. As a matter of fact, I am not at all sure if it's wise for you to go at all. . . . Of course, Esther has sense —"

The evening came. Esther and I went to the New Port. Armed with our tickets, we passed the five sentry posts, and at last came to the front door of the hall. They let us go in, saying that the back seats only were free. All the front rows were reserved for "foreigners."

The hall was empty, and we had to wait a long time. Presently, the rows ahead of us began filling up. Taut in every muscle, I watched them coming in, but the lighting was rather primitive, and rapidly went from bad to worse. Burly shadows went on slipping into the seats ahead. My ears heard nothing except disjointed fragments of German, Swedish, and Spanish. Then suddenly I seized Esther's hand. A voice had said: —

"Rum kind of a place, eh?"

"Where? Where?" I whispered, and she muttered back: "About three rows ahead of us, I think. For goodness' sake, be careful."

The gaudily painted curtain went up. I believe someone in black and crimson tried to sing, and someone else, splendid in a brief pink tulle skirt, sketched a ballet dance. . . . There were a few crude acrobatic tricks. The audience grew noisy. Good-naturedly they did not expect much from a concert hall in the New Port. They clapped, shouted, and clapped again even when the brief pink tulle skirt missed her footing and fell in a most unballet-like posture. Then Marie came on and played two short pieces. For once I never listened to her; I lived for the intermission to come.

It came. Lights went up. A door just behind us swung open with a deafening rattle. Most of the "foreigners" trooped out towards the improvised bar at the end of the passage outside. I felt Esther's hand tugging at my sleeve, I heard her urgent whisper: "Here, they're coming. Be careful, they'll pass us in a moment." In her very anxiety she had raised her voice, and one of them heard it. He stopped, he swung round and called to the others. In less than half a minute they were standing in front of our chairs, five middle-sized, wiry, tanned, blue-eyed, slightly be-wildered Englishmen, one of them saying awkwardly: "One of the chaps told the mate here . . ." They had un-derstood there were no British left in Petrograd. "I am not British," I jerked out hurriedly. "I wish I were. . . . I can't get out, can't even send letters to England. . . . When you go back, give my love to England, please — "

We were more or less alone in the hall. It was all a matter of seconds rather than minutes. They did not stop long. They rummaged in their pockets, bent forward, and thrust a heap of things into my lap. One of them muttered that they'd stop by me again "later on." They'd take any letters I wished to send to England, and off they went. In my lap lay two crumpled envelopes, a sheet of paper, a pencil, two boxes of matches, and a packet of Gold Flakes.

In less than ten minutes the two notes were written, slipped into the envelopes, and hidden under my hand. I blessed the dim lights with all the fervor in my heart. The interval lasted for something like twenty minutes. At last a bell clanged somewhere, and the "foreigners" started trooping back to their seats. But the five Englishmen were not there. My heart danced a wild measure. Had someone seen? Had my crass selfishness got them into trouble?

Bless them whose names I never knew! They had waited outside for all the lights to go out. Then only, with the hall plunged into deep shadows, did they come in very slowly, and one of them brushed against my chair. I felt a rough hand close over mine, the letters slid out of my clasp, there was a quick murmur: "You bet they'll get there all right," and I was in the seventh heaven for bliss which lasted until the second intermission when someone sidled up to us, a sleek little fellow, his black hair carefully brushed and his khaki tunic trim to the rare point of elegance. "You are going to leave the building at once," he said, and involuntarily both of us got up and went out, and he led us down towards a door at the end.

"You spoke to the English sailors. You must leave at once. If I were not a married man with a family, I would have had you arrested. But you look very young, and I have a daughter about your own age," and he added, "You must never come here again. There will be other concerts, but you must never come to any of them."

"But — " I started, but Esther pulled me away, and in a few minutes we were out of the New Port. Then only did she say: —

"Didn't you realize that the little monkey in khaki behaved most chivalrously? We might not have got home at all. After all, you got your chance — so there is absolutely nothing to grumble about — "

Years later I discovered that those penciled notes had got to their destination. Bless them whose names I never knew!

3

ↄ∼ↄↄↄ∼ↄↄↄ∼ↄↄↄ∼ↄↄↄ∼ↄↄↄ∼ↄↄↄ∼ↄ

THE opened window was never really closed again, and once it was opened by someone who tried to persuade me that it was my duty to end my days behind the thick glass panes.

"You do know English," said one of the University officials, and I nodded.

"Well, we are saddled with someone whom you might try and cope with. He comes from America, but he was born in Poland. He has completely forgotten what Polish he ever knew. We can't make out what he wants here. You had better shepherd him about a bit — "

In a voluminous brown check overcoat and a gray Trilby hat, so big that it kept falling down on the bridge of his thin, hooked nose, he found me in the cloisters one morning, and swooped down on me with an embarrassingly straightforward question: "Are you the saved sister in this pit of iniquity?"

I knew him at once and disliked him just as promptly. "This happens to be a seat of learning. I suppose you would like to be shown round. Where shall we start?"

Instead of answering me, he delivered himself of an extremely tangled homily. In the clear sunshine of a March morning I could see that his eyes were of an unpleasant green-brown, that his mottled chin was weak and badly shaven, and that his long nose was suspiciously empurpled.

The pit of iniquity was inhabited by all those who were still completely in the dark so far as pure Communism was concerned, but his particular brand of Communism could never have come out of the Kremlin stockpot. Outwardly he did belong to "the party." If he had not, the Kremlin tin gods would never have allowed him to "gad about" in search of information. I had no idea as to what he could have said to them in Moscow, it must have been something muddling, but there were a few people who did understand English in Moscow, and I was puzzled. He styled himself "an advanced Christian Communist," and was most obviously and tiresomely proud of it.

"Yes?" I said with a weary politeness. "Well, shall we start now? The house in the corner is our library, and I could — "

"I am here to spread the theories of advanced Christian Communism," he said again, stubbornly refusing to notice the library porch.

"Most of our people are in the schools." I hurried him past the cloisters. "You might be able to get a chance later on. But I don't quite understand what your creed is. I happen to be a Christian, but I am no Communist — "

"You have to be both to be perfect," he insisted. "Sell all thou hast — "

"I've nothing to sell," I assured him. "I have had no possessions to speak of for something like four years." I glanced at his expensive overcoat. "It does cost money to travel about — I suppose — "

"I go about my Lord's business," he rebuked me, his voice oozing with solemnity, and I thought of a sleek tom-cat sitting on a sunny wall.

At last I discovered that there was nothing he really wished to see and nothing he wanted to hear. He kept on asking countless questions, but I doubt if he ever heard a single answer I gave him. He insisted on being given "straight spiritual data" about the students. I suggested that there were certain things which could not possibly find place in a formal questionnaire. He argued the point in a feeble way, and at last decided to appeal to the University.

He wanted a meeting summoned. I went to the man at the Dean's Chancery for permission to use a hall, and the lecture was advertised all over the place. About forty-odd mildly curious first-year students gathered together. For something like an hour the advanced C.C. spouted dreary and untidily worded nonsense about a Utopia that his distorted vision must have seen in a particularly muddled hour. By the end of the lecture less than one half of his audience were left yawning in their seats. The rest had discreetly vanished. When he had done he said ruefully: —

"They are benighted. They have not gotten a true angle on Christ."

"They are rather tired," I suggested. "They work hard

— often under impossible conditions. Some of them sleep four and five together in one small room. They often go hungry. They have got to study — they have also a thousand other things to do! Even if they are lucky enough to have a few logs for their stoves, those logs have been carted, sawn and chopped by their own hands. They lead a pretty hard life — "

"Christ's life was not easy." His revolting unctuousness made me explode: —

"That is not for anyone to say. . . . It's worse than cant."

He smiled gently and remarked that I was speaking "out of the darkness of my mind."

"All the same, I have hopes for you. Some day you'll see the truth, and then you'll work among them. Sister, you may yet be turned into a powerful transmitter. I am going to leave some books with you." But rudely enough I shattered his hopes by saying that I had no time left for extraneous reading.

"What's more, I hope I may not have to spend all my days among them."

On that he jumped to his feet, pushed his absurd hat to the back of his head, and stared at me just as though I had suggested committing a murder in broad daylight.

"You mean to turn your back on it all? Sister, it would be a grievous sin. I see clearly by the truth dwelling in me that you have gotten your work right here. You should not talk about running away — "

I realized that he had come from the Kremlin.

"My work is here," I shrugged. "I am not making any ridiculous plans for escape, if that is what you think. But

those you would like me to work among may be gone anywhere before long."

Soon after, the advanced Christian Communist shook the
cloister dust off his shoes, his data on our "spiritual levels"
left direly incomplete. "The pit of iniquity" continued its
work.

4

∞∾◦∾∾◦∾∾◦∾∾◦∾∾◦∾∾◦∾∾◦∾∾◦∾

FOR some time now, the *Rabfak* (Workers'
Faculty) had been known as the Second University. *Rabfak*
was in reality a glorified technical college. I once heard
a story that first-year students had to be taught their alphabet when they came in, but this may have been fiction. In
official verbiage our college came to be known as the First
University: we studiously avoided the numeral. *Rabfak*
men and women hardly ever came near us, except for isolated science courses, but we knew that they were privileged
members of the community: they appeared wearing "real"
boots, and when we chewed potato peelings, they had good
bread to munch.

Sometime in 1921 a third university was opened — for
the sole purpose of language study. By that time the Government policy of isolation had already veered in a different
direction. Decrees were published by the Sovnarkom, but
the Komintern was coming into its own. I remember public

meetings here and there; we had one in the courtyard of our college. There was a great deal of fiery talk about winning the whole world over to the tenets of Communism. Primarily, the Third University was meant to be a nursery for young Communists. It was as if the Commissar for Education had examined the globe, rubbed his hands, and shouted, "We are out to conquer the world, to spread revolutionary ideas in all countries. We can't do it unless our pioneers learn foreign languages. Esperanto won't do at all," and the scheme was launched — with a great many speeches, red bunting, songs, and copious quotations from Lenin, Marx, and Engels. The Third University was to have five branches — English, French, German, Italian, and Slavonic. All the lectures were to be given in the language of the branch. The vernacular was there on sufferance only — as a subsidiary explanatory channel.

They took an enormous house somewhere at the end of Kamennoostrovsky Prospect, near the Islands, once the fashionable suburb of St. Petersburg. Masses of students were enrolled, and a few college professors were "invited" to take their share in the work. They were to receive a modest enough salary, but the greatest inducement was the green ration cards. The green ration cards were a hungry dog's juicy bone in those days. The *utcheny payok* (scholars' rations) was not doled out in communal stores but on the college premises. No time was wasted in any queue, and the *payok* meant sugar and butter. The *Rabfak* had enjoyed it for some time. "They are issuing green cards at the Third University," I heard, and immediately afterwards someone said that there remained a vacancy on the lecturing staff: they had nobody for English medieval history and literature. I went home, reflecting on those green cards. I had no more private lessons at that time, there seemed no further chances of finding any, Esther's few marketable possessions were rapidly dwindling away, and mine had long since gone. They were issuing green cards at the Third University, and there remained one vacancy. I made cautiously impersonal inquiries. The appointment would mean four hours' lecturing every week. They had already fixed the timetable, and I discovered that the hours would not overlap with my seminar work. I paid a visit to the terribly efficient clerk at the Chancery. Yes, a vacancy still existed, but I found out that lecturers had to be members of the faculty, and nobody could be a member unless he had a degree. Yet it was more or less obvious that they wished to see the vacancy filled and, as a preliminary, I sounded my own professors. They said they would not have anything against my applying for the post so long as its demands did not interfere with my proper college work. But I could well see that none of them imagined me fully qualified for the appointment, nor did I see it myself. But I heard that a professor whom I knew slightly had been called to an important post at the Third. I went to see him.

"You want that appointment. . . . I can't have you unless you become a member of the faculty. When were you born? Goodness, you are barely twenty-three." He tugged at his untidy mustache, and I saw the green cards vanish in the mist.

"Do you think you could do it?" he barked at me.

"Do — what?" I faltered.

"Lecture, of course," he snapped. "You may know your history, but can you teach? And do you know literature?

Look here, I have no time to waste on you now. Come again in a week, and I'll put you through your paces — "

"I am not a member of the faculty, sir," I stammered, and he said again, "Come back in a week."

I went home and brushed everything aside for more than a week. I practically lived at the old Imperial Library. I read some Stubbs and Maitland, an unnecessary number of chronicles, Langland and Chaucer. I returned, and the fussy little man gave me about half an hour.

"That will do. Now, I have talked to the Rector. We have decided that a herring might be better than no fish at all. You are not even a herring yet — you are a miserable little shrimp. All the same, we are going to take your degree for granted and make you a member of the faculty — "

"Oh!" At that moment I quite honestly forgot the green cards, but he said drily: —

"You will have to win your spurs, of course, by giving a public lecture to the University. Would a month be enough for you to get ready?"

"Yes — yes." I swallowed hard, and he measured me with a fierce look.

"You don't sound too certain. However, get on with it. If I were you, I should write out the lecture from beginning to end. You'll be expected to speak for about an hour. Don't make it too thin in substance and don't finish on a well-padded cushion — they'd make mincemeat of you if you do that. Don't make it too long — none of us want to be bored. And don't let me down — I've more or less sponsored you. Now what about your subject?"

"Fourteenth century," I said rather gropingly. "People like Rolle — "

"Well, you'll have to begin by a concise preface on medieval literature. Don't take details for granted. The faculty are learned enough, but few of the students will have a single idea about it. Be sure of the facts, remember that you are a novice, avoid flowery conclusions of your own. Keep any personal fervor under proper control — we don't want a sermon." He waved a podgy hand towards his bookshelves. "Help yourself to anything you like."

I carried away a few volumes. That afternoon the desolate, half-ruined city seemed a good place to live in — its libraries were still there.

By degrees the theme gripped me hard. Little by little, the once madly coveted green cards grew paler and less significant. It was good to lose oneself — even for a few hours a day — in passages such as this one: "For love my thought has fast, and I am fain to fare away. I stand still mourning for the loveliest of lore. . . . The brand of sweet burning for it holds me . . . from place and from playing; till I may get a sight of my sweet one, who wends never away. In wealth be our waking, without hurt or night. My love is everlasting, and longs unto that sight . . ." but, reading my Rolle, I tried conscientiously enough to remember the professor's injunction about the avoidance of fervor.

The month was over all too soon. I knew it would be a University lecture, but I had not quite expected the hall to be so vast or so crowded. My courage was shredded long before I climbed the few steps to the desk. My sheaf of notes seemed astonishingly thin, and, even as the Rector was reciting something in Latin, I realized that I had forgotten half of my notes. More than the beginning of my carefully drafted lecture lay on a table in the house on the Moyka Quay. . . . Suddenly I knew that the hall was waiting. I cleared my throat. I was not even Daniel in the den of lions, but a limpet among whales.

There were gaps. There were awkward pauses. The remaining notes seemed too sketchy, yet I must use them, I dared not trust to my memory. I finished, and I knew the depths of failure in their silence. At last the Rector rose and addressed the hall. From my chair behind the desk, I tried to study the stuccoed ceiling. I could not gauge their reaction. The students kept still, and the faculty were well-bred men. In my presence, very coldly, without any enthusiasm, they voted for me. The Rector shook hands with me. I must stand up and thank them. I did so — in a shaking, small voice. Presently the hall must have become empty — the platform was an uninhabited island except for my sponsor and myself.

"You could not have done it worse," he said.

"Why didn't they vote against me?"

"Well, there is nobody else to do the work. Your delivery was ghastly, but you seem to know your subject. I suppose we could not have expected more — "

So began my brief academic career. It started in the summer and ended the following November. Throughout those months I received the green cards, but not a penny of my salary. When I left, it was still unpaid.

The first morning was a bed of thorns. The Third University premises were an unknown land to me. I had no wish to meet any of my new colleagues. I feared ridicule more than hunger. A frightened rabbit, I hurried under the great porch. On the wall, framed in black, hung the enor-

mous timetable. The names of subjects were picked out in
startling red. I noticed "Slavonic Language and Literature.
Serbian and Bulgarian," and even at a distance my own
name made me halt. Surely there was a mistake! I came
nearer and understood. Why couldn't the professor have
said: "Well, it'll be nice for you to work at the Third —
we have your brother there"? He must have been present
in that hall but I had not seen him, I had not spoken to
him. The place had been crowded with strangers — including him, my only brother. . . . The professor must have
taken it for granted that I knew.

Beyond the porch stretched a long, wide passage. I
hesitated. I might meet him any moment. Would we recognize each other? I had not seen him for more years than
I could count. I had heard about him. He had married that
girl — in the end. He had gone to Moscow, lectured, published books, written some good poetry. Infrequently
enough I had rather longed for him. The old dreams about
my father's friendship had somehow merged with an imaginary picture woven round that brilliant, enigmatic, hot-
tempered brother. So he was here, and nobody had told me.

I turned back to the timetable. I saw my own name. I
must find No. 7 Auditorium, give my first lecture. But I
could not move, I heard distant steps down the passage.
Doors opened right and left down its whole length. I saw
two very tall men at the very end. They were talking.
I could not see their faces clearly. They stopped by a door,
the taller of the two opened it and vanished. The other
came on towards me. I asked in a voice which did not
quite belong to me, "Please, where is Number 7?" He
stopped, his clean-shaven face kindly enough.

"Up the stairs, first door on your right." He added: "You are the new member of the faculty?"

"Yes —"

"Well, nice to have two of you here. Your brother has just gone into the Chancery —"

"Oh, yes, indeed —"

He bowed and passed on. I moved down the passage. Level with the Chancery door, I stopped again. "Open it, go in, say to him, 'George, don't you know me? Where were you the other day?'" something whispered to me, but I stood still.

The door opened. For a second I imagined myself back at Xénia: my father stood before me, the same leonine head, the same untidy hair and small beard, the same fierce black eyes. I had forgotten George was sixteen years my senior, I had always imagined him very young. The man I was looking at had streaks of silver in his hair.

"George —"

He knew me, of course, and I knew that he did not wish to know me. He stood there, looking at me from his great height.

"Well?"

I said very stupidly: —

"How many years —"

He said nothing at all. He was still looking at me. I ought to have said: "It is more than nice meeting again. What do old family quarrels matter now? You and I are alone, we both work in the same field. George, please, let us be brother and sister. You know there is nobody else." I ought to have said: "In this strange world one's own flesh and

[254]

blood should become precious. Do you think you could ever feel a little bit proud of me?"

Instead I said stupidly, my hot hands clutching the shabby attaché case: —

"So I am here — and you too — "

"Yes," he said at last, "it looks as though they were turning this place into a nursery." He added, "I was in the hall the other day. I did *not* vote for you."

"Why?"

Almost passionately I wished he would start a quarrel. Once he had slammed a door. I did not want him to slam a door now, but I wished he would get angry, do and say something, yet allow me to recognize a brother in him. But he was not angry. His olive-colored face looked closed-in and indifferent. He might have been speaking to an usher about a draft down the passage.

"Because I did not wish you here."

"Why?" I insisted.

He moved away.

"This is a farce," he said quite levelly. "Your life and mine have always been apart. Unfortunately, this place is not big enough. We might have to meet — as members of the faculty." He bowed. "This must be enough — for us both. Otherwise there is nothing we need say to each other," and he went.

Somehow I found the stairs, climbed them, came to a door, saw a program crudely typed in red ink. I read slowly and carefully: "Monday, 11–12. Almedingen, Marta Alexandrovna, M.F. English Medieval History and Literature." Further below I read "Tuesday, 3–4. Almedingen,

Professor Georguy Alexandrovitch. Serbian and Bulgarian Language and Literature." "They need not have given us the same auditorium," I thought.

I opened the door. The students were already waiting for me. My head bent low, my fingers fumbling with the clasps of the attaché case, I thought wildly: "Well, it is on a par with all other things. . . . Esther will understand . . ." But the students were waiting, and I must begin.

5

I NEVER went near the common room. Often enough, on the stairs, in a passage, I met George, and he bowed politely and never stopped. Nor did I wish to stop and talk any more. Sometimes we met in others' company, and discussed impersonal college matters. My other colleagues were nice enough to the youngest member of the faculty. Well-bred, almost paternal, they would stop and make brief, encouraging remarks. But I could never feel at home amongst them. Some of the things they said, however unwittingly, were so many thorns. The old man who lectured on German always brought George into his conversation. "What a brilliant brother you have, Marta Alexandrovna! . . . We are glad to have him here. Have you read his translations from Longfellow?" I had not, and said so awkwardly enough.

There were the faculty meetings, when the youngest member, her cheeks red, sat in some remote corner, clenching her hands and hoping that nobody would notice her. Voting had to be done on certain occasions and, the members being addressed in alphabetical order, my name came second on the list. The very first time I had forgotten that I was sitting among my peers and leapt to my feet when the Rector called on me. Someone behind remarked in an acid, sibilant whisper — "Sit down. You are not a student — here, at least," and opposite me I saw George's face, remote, closed-in. It would have been a relief to read irony in it. Those green cards and the happiness of browsing among the fragrant pastures of medieval England were paid for in bitter coin indeed.

Things were easier in the auditorium. I could afford to breathe there. Lecturing to my students proved a slow enough business: few among them knew English at all adequately, and I must stop, translate often enough, and speak slowly and distinctly for the others to understand me. Still, two or three among them were deeply interested in the subject. They asked for private coaching and later passed the first examination with full honors.

They were all nice, but somehow or other most of them remained so many blurs to me. I made no friends among them. I came and went to my lectures. I lingered in passages and auditoriums. I made no social contacts with either staff or students. I tried to meet George as seldom as possible.

Two or three among the students were fervent Communists. I did not understand how any knowledge of medieval England could possibly help them to develop any theories about the spread of Communism in modern England, and they admitted themselves that they did not know much about it.

"It is the State's business," one of them said. "We pay no college fees, we are lodged and boarded by the Government. If they have decided on a certain curriculum, we don't see why we should argue about it."

Years later, one of them came to England for a few weeks, and I ran into her in the North Room of the British Museum. She was traveling, so she told me, on no business connected with the Communist Party. She was no longer a member, and her admission carried conviction. She was now a teacher of English and German at some girls' school in Odessa. Her earlier Communistic ardor had burnt itself out.

"You couldn't have liked lecturing to us," she remarked over a cup of tea somewhere in Coptic Street. "Yet we liked you a lot. Goodness me, what a child you looked in those days! I remember your telling us something about Richard Rolle one morning. You sounded almost inspired. You talked about the divine love and so on. Some of us laughed afterwards," she added quietly, looking away from me. "I did not, though. I remember it was a Saturday, and that evening I went to Vespers, the first time in many years. You know, you didn't know a thing about lecturing — you were often tongue-tied, you blushed and stammered, sometimes we felt sorry for you. But all the same, you made us see things, somehow . . ." The chance encounter made me feel very humble.

6

~~~~~~~~~~~~~~~~~~~~~~~~~~~

I WAS then busy enough, but in the middle of it another unexpected demand was made on my time. There would have been no question of refusing the job thrust on me: it must be accepted by virtue of my being a citizen of the Republic.

In those days all private houses were strictly State property. No house, flat, or room, not a single square inch of space, could be let by private individuals. Each house had its own committee of tenants, all of them approved by the local commissariat. Remnants of *bourgeoisie*, intelligentsia, let alone old aristocracy, hardly ever served on those committees. The *domkom* was composed of sailors, soldiers, factory people, and their wives. They looked after the property and allocated what accommodation was available. Housing shortage considered, nobody had the right to unlimited floor space. Esther and I were lucky, so were the other tenants in our flat: each of us had a whole room to ourselves. I knew cases when a family of five and six people would be given one none too spacious room, and often enough single tenants had to stay content with just strips of floor space. Kitchens were communal, and all the tenants had to bear their share in strict rotation as regarded the cleaning of kitchen ranges, stairs, courtyards, and so forth.

But at least there was no nightmare of rent: the State charged nothing at all.

Over and above the house committee, who met at more or less irregular intervals, there was the house commandant. He or she must be at the beck and call of all the tenants. The *domkom* met, talked, spat all over the place, paid frequent and useless visits to the local commissariat, met and talked again. The house commandant had to work. He must keep his eye on everything, specially on such "repairs" as could be carried out, the shortage of all materials considered. He had to consider applications from prospective tenants, to issue ration cards once a month, and to see to it that none of the people under his roof enjoyed more floor space than they were entitled to. The business of the ration cards was the worst. It lasted about three or four days.

Properly speaking, the house commandant was not "available" except at certain defined hours, mostly in the evening, since it was taken for granted that everybody was at work by day. The house committee allowed him an apology of an office and an occasional supply of paper and ink. His work was voluntary in so far as he received no pay for it, but the appointment could not be refused. You were never asked if you would like to be a house commandant. You were merely told about it, and you were expected to begin work straight away.

I believe the *domkom* in the house on the Moyka Quay came to the conclusion that I alone among all the tenants had too much leisure on my hands. I did not discuss my Third lectures with anyone, they knew me only as a university student, and "study," as everyone knew, was child's play compared with hard manual work. One fine September morning I got up to find a dirty slip of coarse gray paper under the door of my room. This was the order to start the commandant's duties the following evening. I carried it down the passage to Esther's room.

"I suppose they wouldn't have me instead of you?" she wondered. "And if you refused — "

"They'd tell us to go," I said bitterly. "I've known it happen before."

Esther scanned the dirty piece of paper. The hardly legible writing said something about the office hours being from six to eight.

"If it were two hours only," she sighed.

"Well," I said, "I'll probably do the job so badly that the *domkom* will be glad to dismiss me by the end of the month."

The house was enormous. I think it had about one hundred and fifty odd flats, once inhabited by well-to-do families, whose place was now taken by a host of working people, with a very thin sprinkling of social "exceptions." One hundred and fifty flats had enough "floor space" to provide for a whole community. The block was a huge warren.

The commandant's office had once been a porter's cubbyhole, a narrow strip of a room with a badly fitting door, something of a window, an upturned crate for a chair, and a two-legged table. The dusty floor was littered with ledgers. My senile predecessor must have had a passion for slinging ink all over paper: the two ledgers I picked up bore ample witness to this, but I could not get much else from their blotted and bethumbed pages. All I knew was that several thousands of human beings had their habitat in the house and that, in some occult way, I was now responsible for the roofs, floors, windows, stairs, and doors in the building, also for the monthly ration cards.

Office hours? Well, there were not any. On rare occasions I found myself with an unexpected free afternoon on my hands, Esther away at the Academy, and the sailor's wife indulging in one of her parties. No serious reading could be done in my room. I tried Esther's den only to find that the party had decided to overflow into the bathroom, next to Esther's door. I seized a couple of books and made for my "office." It was fairly quiet there, but the door would not shut, and presently, some half a dozen tenants besieged the cubbyhole. *Historia Francorum* and my notebooks had to be pushed aside. Some of the callers were brief and definite: they wanted a windowpane mended or a leak seen to. But the majority crept in, themselves not knowing what they were after, and they usually blamed me for not telling them what it was that they wanted of me.

So I remember a fat, middle-aged woman in a dirty green shawl, who came one sodden October evening, a whining story on her lips. I listened for several minutes. Gradually, odds and ends of that plaint began dangling in my understanding. It was all something about a vixen, a real tartar she was and no mistake, and brand-new rep curtains, red they were, and a glorious deep fringe they had. The red curtains were in nobody's way, she could stake her life on that, and if the vixen said they were, it was the vixen's business, and, of course, the vixen knew where the red curtains were, she herself did not, not she, and she always spoke the truth and she never boasted about it either, and truth was truth, and her curtains had a lovely deep fringe to them,

[262]

and they had not been stolen but bought quite honestly with the commissar's knowledge, and that was the truth, and nobody had any right to object to her having them, and the whole world knew that any curtains had to be aired sometimes, and there was so much dust in the place, it was wicked, and the vixen's room smelt like a pigsty, but the curtains were hung out for an airing, not for the vixen's pleasure, and —

Here I broke in: —

"Who is the vixen? What has she to do with the fringe of the curtains? Where are they or where were they?"

She raised her fat red face at me and shouted in righteous indignation: —

"What is the good of you sitting here if you can't tell me where the curtains are? She stole them, and it is for you to find them. Now wait a second. I was telling you — "

I can't remember the outcome. I dare say the rep curtains, fringe and all, were found in the long run. Things usually were, though theft on a smaller scale was appallingly frequent, and there was hardly any way to check it.

On another occasion someone asked me to go and look at "that cursed roof. All the floodgates of heaven are pouring into the kitchen, and nobody cares."

I knew that roof well enough. I had sent in some four or five applications to the local commissariat. I had begged for the repairing order to be given, but they said the roof must wait. It was only a kitchen roof, and nobody lived in a kitchen. Now, it appeared that the room next to the kitchen shared in the deluge. The tenant wrung her hands and spoke of her daughter's cough. I went there at once. She ran beside me, muttering: "You don't mind me dragging you all this way." She lived at the opposite end of the block. "Come to think of it, you look tired enough. Never mind, a bit of tarpaulin might stop the hole. And I will find you a slice of cabbage pasty now that you have come all this way — "

I gratefully munched the cabbage pasty, offered on a piece of dirty newspaper for a plate; I sat on some sodden piece of furniture which might or might not have once been a chair; I examined the very obvious damage, heard the child's rasping cough, and I promised to get the tarpaulin. To my surprise, the authorities decided to have the roof repaired, kitchen and all, and the greatly exaggerated story about it went all over the block. The huge human warren proved itself human indeed.

From day to day I never knew what might happen. A house commandant before our time in the ground-floor flat had had to tackle a peculiarly foul murder, and I prayed that none might come my way. Sometimes for days on end it was merely the routine job of allocating accommodation, sending off applications for urgent repairs, and nothing much else. Yet to offset the monotony there were evenings when routine kept far away, and men, women, and inquisitive, frank, and friendly youngsters trooped in just for a chat. There were lengthy, complicated family histories, detailed narratives of ailments, accidents, births, and deaths. There was also common gossip, gathered in market places and bread queues.

"There you are," mumbled an old baker, stroking a bushy gray beard. "I have heard my woman tell she'd heard them say in the Sennaya there was an earthquake somewhere. And we never heard a word of it. . . ."

"Where?"

He gestured vaguely.

"Far away, over the sea somewhere — else we would have heard something. The English King has perished and the American President, and all the rest of them. Now they say there will be freedom over the whole world. But I don't believe it, I said to my old woman that nobody could get anything out of an earthquake — "

"Stands to reason you can't," they all agreed chorally, and a hunchback of a cobbler chimed in: —

"An earthquake is nothing. Why, the other day I heard a fellow say that over there they had stopped walking and riding altogether. Always up in the air they are. You get up into one of them machines, and away you fly to dine thousands of miles away. That is life, I reckon — "

"Well, the air has no frontiers," someone suggested. "You are free to go anywhere — unless they have sort of traced frontiers in the air — "

"What are you talking about?" The cobbler looked as offended as though the air belonged to him. "The air is not, in a manner of speaking — like a couple of fields with a hedge between them. How could there be frontiers, I ask you — blockhead?"

"Well, then, anyone might come and fly here for their dinner — "

"Tosh," said the man of the earthquake story. "What should anyone come in for? Fly a thousand miles for your dinner and get a plateful of *wobla* soup for your trouble?" And he spat on the floor.

Sometimes visitors came in, carrying small bundles in their hands. There followed mutterings, nods, nudges, and reminders about keeping my own counsel, since all gifts to officials were vetoed. The bundles were pushed under the table, and the donors hurried away. Alone, I unwrapped them. Usually they contained chunks of good country bread, hard-boiled eggs, a. few potatoes, boiled in their jackets, or else a nice pickled herring or two. Once I came into the office to find a large pie under the table. A scrawled note lay on the top: "On our honor, this is beef, not cat." Esther and I did not laugh that night, as we sat and feasted; genuine beef was the rarest delicacy in those thin days, even horseflesh was becoming something of a luxury, and the note, with its astonishing candor, shone rather like a candle would in a darkened room.

One evening a working woman, still young in spite of an aged face and silver in her brown hair, caught me just as I was leaving "the office." She said the accommodation given her was rather cramped. She reminded me that the *domkom* had often enough promised to reconsider the allotment. Would they do something about it? It seemed an urgent enough case: there were five of them, husband, herself, and three children; all the space they had was a narrow slip, used as a box room by former tenants. Sometimes they left the door open, and the eldest boy slept on the staircase landing, but this would be impossible now that the winter days were drawing in.

I remembered that case. I had sent in three or four applications already. I said I would try and make them hurry.

"No, there is no hurry now," she said listlessly. "I just came to remind you, that is all. Nothing much can happen now — there is Manka pregnant by Mishka, the fourth month gone she is. She will be all right. I will have her sent to a home, and my old man took the strap to Mishka, but looks to me you can't blame them. They are my twins." And she added almost conversationally — "Still, you might ask them to hurry up. The room does not look friendly — somehow — "

I could not tell her I was sorry — so much of an insult there would have been in the least expression of sympathy.

A great deal of that work must have been appalling, maddening, and bewildering. But I have forgotten all the tragedies, always excepting that granite-faced mother and her unfortunate twins. There must have been a host of exasperating days, when all the imaginable floors, roofs, stairs, landings, and doors in the world seemed welded together in a common and mysterious conspiracy, and were determined to tumble down together, as some gigantically-scaled gesture of an inanimate but nonetheless fiendish poltergeist. There must have been a great many days when, after a few hours of the office, I returned to Esther and to my den, loudly wishing that I had never been born, so tiresome, muddling, and maddening were the demands of the tenants, so weak and equally maddening were my inexperience and inability to answer those demands.

Yet most of those things have faded with time; loud, raucous voices of dissatisfied men and women have become mere plaintive murmurs, and I can't say I remember anything violent happening in the office except the night when a drunken foreman from the Putilovsky metalworks stumbled into the room, shouting that he had lost his ration cards. I told him I could not give him another set. He caught hold of the door, all but tore it off its uncertain hinges, and swore that he had never lost the cards, I had not given them to him. I showed him his own signature in the ledger. He retorted it was a forgery and launched a volley of unprintable abuse, shaking his fist in my face, and I felt frightened, when his wife appeared in the doorway, and the roaring lion shriveled into an almost pitiful lamb.

The foreman, however, was unlike the rest of them. In that great warren men and women slogged on with a well-nigh incomprehensible courage. Like that widow of thirty-odd, mother of seven children, who had long been trying to get an extra inch or so of floor space for her brood. The commissariat people kept refusing her plea, saying that overcrowding could not be helped. The night she came to hear about the result of something like the seventh application, I shook my head.

"I am afraid no luck at all! Of course, I will go on trying, and perhaps something may happen — "

I quite thought she would burst into tears. She said briefly: "Ah, well, things might always be worse than they are. Thank you for trying."

She may have come again, but I was gone. The *domkom* dismissed me as peremptorily as they had appointed me, and a burly peasant from the Orel Government stepped into my shoes. I met him once, and I disliked him greatly. He fancied he had a tin pedestal under his huge feet. He always used the first person plural about himself, signed his name with a ridiculous flourish, and roared like a goaded bull whenever the tenants' importunity exhausted his short-lived patience. He did not endure, however. Evidently his lordly habit of using the first person plural led him to a perfectly logical assumption that "we" were entitled to a double set of ration cards, and the *domkom* disapproved of such logical applications. The story came out and, in spite of his peasant antecedents, the man from Orel got six months' penal servitude. He should have got much more for having browbeaten and bullied men and women who asked for so little and gave back so much.

7

ONE early Sunday afternoon I was tramping home along the wide pavements of the Alexeevskaya Street. It was in the late autumn and, though no snow had yet fallen, still it was possible to smell its coming in the crisp tang of the air. The day was sunny, the few trees in a garden on the way stood, etched like so many knightly sentinels, against a very pale blue sky, torn here and there by drifts of fleecy clouds. These changed their form so swiftly that I lost all hope of learning them. At last, a drift of ivory gray floated away from its brothers and, for something like a few seconds, remained almost motionless, a piece of carved ivory against pale blue velvet. I thought it looked like a bridge. I could almost imagine the delicate edging of a parapet, the curves of slender arches and . . . But here the bridge grew into an indeterminate lump of cold rice pudding, its ivory and faint primrose were gone in wet gray, and, disappointed, I turned round the corner.

"I have lost my way, I think — if you please — "

I stopped at once. Since the evening at the concert hall in the New Port, I had heard many tantalizing rumors about "foreigners" coming to the city, and I had tried not to think of them at all. They were like that cloud — a lovely, fairy bridge one moment, a dull, colorless lump the next.

But now, having halted, I must turn round and look at a very tall man with a deeply bronzed face. He wore a heavy overcoat of obviously foreign make. He looked a sailor. He proved to be one. But I trod warily.

"Why did you speak English to me?"

He took off his hat and bowed. There was a faint touch of irony in his smile.

"But, obviously, this is the language the lady understands — "

Pinned to the sadly frayed lapel of my coat was a tiny Union Jack, made of various odds and ends of ribbon that Esther had once found in a workbox of hers.

"Yes," I replied. "It was stupid of me to ask. You've lost your way. Where do you want to get to? I am afraid there are no trams running in this part of the world — "

"I have walked from the Baltic Docks. I am a captain of a Dutch boat. Permit me." He handed me a card. "I am seeking a restaurant — "

I would have liked to laugh, but I did not. He seemed so very much in earnest.

"There is no such place — not here anyway. You might find a few cafés on the Nevsky, but you would not get a meal there. I believe there is something like a buffet for foreigners, but I don't know where it is."

"In that case I must go back to the boat — "

"I am afraid so, but it is rather a shame — having had to walk all this way for nothing — "

"A walk always does much good to a sailor," he smiled. "I never get enough — what do you say — constitutionals. Thank you very much. You are so kind," and he was turning away with a bow when a daring idea leapt into my mind. I knew Esther would be at home. I did not know if our larder were empty or not, but I said: —

"Well, my friend and I live quite near. We should be glad to have you, though I can't promise you much of a meal."

"Oh, no." His hesitation was so obvious that I broke in: —

"Things aren't as bad as all that. Both of us get rations of a kind. You aren't likely to eat us out of house and home — "

"Pardon?" He raised his hat again, and I must render the idiom into something he could understand.

Esther looked slightly bewildered, but he spoke exquisite German to her, and she laughed at my daring. "Inviting a guest to a meal! *Liebchen* — is there anything fit to put on the table?" I left them together and rummaged in a cupboard. That poor famished Dutchman certainly did not sit down to a feast: a few *rissoles*, made of frozen potatoes, fried sparingly in some forgotten variety of vegetable oil; *wobla*, the famous Soviet ham; some black bread, and acorn coffee was all we could offer him. But his manners were those of a prince. The coffee drunk, he produced some cigarettes and said quietly: —

"I shall not forget to tell the newspapers in my country about the most interesting meal I have ever had."

We sat round the oil stove and pelted him with questions. From him we heard facts about Versailles and President Wilson's idea about a League of Nations and the beginning of disarmament conferences. Yet it was obvious that he wanted to ask us about our own conditions, and once or twice Esther checked my flow of curiosity, but I heard him say he had been to England recently, and the last shreds of good manners left me: he must tell me about England.

He was a man of few words, with no narrative power in him, and I gathered little more than a string of names from his talk, but even such a paltry crop seemed rich harvest to me. Regent Street, Piccadilly, Hyde Park; there were gorgeous flower beds in Kensington Gardens, and you could take a bus and ride to Richmond Park, once the property of kings. The Dutchman in him remembered Kew almost glowingly.

"Tell me more, please," I begged, and Esther frowned, but he reassured her.

"The young lady would be happy to see the little flags in whole streets, is it not so?"

"Go to England? Shall I ever?"

He rose and asked Esther's permission to call again. I drew a crude plan of the neighborhood for him. He left, and that night neither of us could go to sleep. The oil stove had gone dead and cold, but we sat there and talked about "the West."

"In a way," Esther was saying, "I wish all these people would forget Petrograd is on the map. They do leave so much *Sehnsucht* behind. I wonder if it might not be better to forget the outer world altogether. Shall we ever see it?"

"This is not like you," I retorted. "How could we ever

forget that world, a place where plugs and drains are in order, where nobody pesters you just because your nose isn't shaped in the proper proletarian way? I am sick of the very word. . . . Peasants are not proletarians — they are gently bred. . . . Forget a world where no time gets wasted on bread queues and — "

"Well, he said they were rationed in England," Esther reminded me, "and London had those ghastly air raids — "

"But it is all over," I argued. "They have had peace for three years. And with this business starting in Geneva and disarmament talks, it looks as though peace had come to stay. Here, say what you like, we are bang in the middle of a military camp. . . . The whole creation must have been started for the benefit of the Red Army. . . . The civil war is over, but no, they must go on hugging every soldier as though he were the most important member of the community. They feed him, clothe him, pamper him. . . . Yes, clothe him," I ended almost viciously, "and look at the rags we've got to wear. . . . Forget a world where you need not walk about in tatters?"

My clothes were certainly comic. The boots were made of carpet strips, my chemise had once been a sheet, my flannel blouse a pyjama coat. About seven materials had been used by Esther for the skirt I had on: black and brown serge, some plaid stuff, strips of rather shabby green velvet, and a hem of navy-blue cashmere.

"And you are not a bit like yourself either! You are whining," said Esther, and we decided to go to bed.

Within two days our Dutchman came again. His pockets were bulging. He told us he was not allowed to bring any "real parcels" from the ship. So he had emptied all his pockets before going ashore — "and then I packed them with some things you might like to see. . . ." Silent, fascinated, we stood and watched him delve into his pockets. There were matches, cigarettes, soap, two packets of biscuits, a small tin of cocoa, some sugar and salt. Under his great-coat he had slung a small canvas bag with two half-bottles of whiskey and a small tube of aspirin tablets.

I ran into the kitchen and rummaged for a kettle. Grannie and the sailor's wife watched me in silence. I came back from the yard, a filled kettle in my hands, and I heard the sailor's wife say: "Aren't we getting grand, Grannie? Visitors, and foreigners at that! I had better drop a hint to my man. . . . High time this flat were properly searched! I'd say they had bags of foreign money under their beds. . . ."

I ran back to our room.

"She says the place ought to be searched. . . . She must have eavesdropped again."

"Don't worry." Esther was calm. "By the time they have issued a warrant or whatever it is, the food'll have gone. All the same," she turned to the Dutchman, "I don't think you'd better come here again — "

"This is good-bye." He spoke ruefully. "We are leaving soon — tomorrow."

He could not stay long, he said, there was urgent business waiting for him on board, and, somehow, we felt we could not build enough conversation with the few straws of trivial remarks. I thought of Esther's words about *Sehnsucht*, and understood them. We could offer him nothing but thanks, and when he rose to go, we went with him halfway down to the docks.

We had forgotten to padlock the door of my room, and

we found the table cleared on our return. Not a single package was to be seen. In the kitchen we saw Grannie sniveling over a bowl of gruel and mumbling something about the sailor's wife, who, on hearing our voices, promptly bounced out of the room and accused Grannie of having stolen our treasures. They took to quarreling, and we left them to it. For something like an hour they went on wrangling in the kitchen, and then were friends again, doubtless busily sharing the loot from our room.

It was, after all, a trivial detail. The gifts brought by the Dutchman were unexpected and unearned luxuries, and, strictly speaking, we were no worse off than before. Nonetheless, their disappearance depressed me. The very coming of that Dutchman had suggested a generously opened window. Now he was gone, his gifts too had vanished, and the window was shut with a bang.

I flung myself into my work. I came to a stage when dangerous retrospection crept round the corner, and it had the vague shape of a white and frightened face. Sometimes, when my eyes refused to wrestle any longer with the barbed script of some medieval manuscript, and when the brain rebelled, clamoring for a brief respite, I would put my head down on my folded arms and think of the things gone before.

Such moods came and went, but on no single occasion did they carry me right to the very edge of absolute despair. Something always stood in the way, a barrier between that edge and my foolish, tired self; something always pulled me back, convincing me, beyond all doubt and questioning, that, deep below the surface of our chaotic life, some worth-whileness, not to be captured into words even in the clearest moments, had its abiding home. And if this were nothing more than an illusion, woven on the loom of a tired mind, why, then all the great fundamentals in life might seem equally illusory.

8

"YOU have a coat for the winter," said Esther, "and very little else. I cannot put another patch on this skirt. You'll have to stay indoors all tomorrow. This blouse can't be worn another day, and flannel will not dry quickly."

"Ah, yes, I have got a coat." I brought it out, the last remnant of the pre-1917 days — a cheap enough astrakhan jacket, an aunt's gift. "But it will have to go if they cut our rations again."

"Nonsense. We must keep it. And I mean to turn those curtains into skirts. You know — the ones in my room. I wish I had some dye. . . . That purple may be a bit startling. . . . But at least they'll be warm — "

"They'll look beautiful," I assured her, but she stamped her poorly shod foot.

"It's the boots. . . . I have nowhere to go to except the Academy — just over the bridge, and you have miles and miles every day. These boots won't last more than a month. Let me have a look at your feet."

Carefully I took off the rug and linen boots she had

made for me to wear through the summer and autumn.

"Why didn't you tell me before? We should have got a pair of *valenky* weeks ago —"

"We can't afford them."

"That's neither here nor there. That's why you've been limping. Goodness, your left heel is quite raw!"

"You are limping too," I said almost crossly. "Anyway, those *valenky* rub one's heels just as much."

"Yes, but I can bandage your feet first. The boots could not be worn with bandages inside."

She got rid of her gold watch, and two pairs of thick fawn felt *valenky* were bought from a private speculator after a few hours of sharp bargaining. They were good, strong *valenky*. They reached up to the knee, and the first time the sailor's wife saw me wearing them, she clapped her hands and shrieked: —

"Wasn't I right? Foreign money! Bags of it! Those *valenky* must have cost millions and millions! Why, they've got leather soles to them! If only my man could keep sober enough for me to tell him."

Grannie also joined issue against us.

"Felt *valenky* and a fur coat, and some people have not a rag to their backs! Selfish, I call it! They would not give an honest woman a chance to earn a few bits of pink paper. . . . They would not let me clean their rooms. . . . Misers, I call them. . . . Taking bread out of other people's mouths," grumbled Grannie, herself wearing a tweed coat with a suspiciously smart fur collar.

"These *valenky*," said Esther, "ought to last well after Christmas, and it would be idiotic to look further ahead," and, the wardrobe question settled more or less satisfactorily, we "settled down" to face the fifth winter of isolation.

Chapter Eight

"GIVE US
THIS DAY..."

1

~~~~~~~~~~~~~~~~~~~~~~~~~~~~~~

YET both of us had forgotten that set-
tling down was more or less impossible in a chaos. Famine
was in full swing in the country, and the city could not
escape it. Early enough in the autumn I lost all my private
pupils. All of them paid in kind, and none had enough to
satisfy their own hunger. The ordinary University rations
were getting smaller and smaller.

"It is beginning to look as though we had a thin winter
ahead of us," I thought the day when they refused to let
me have the usual student's cards.

"You do get scholar's rations elsewhere, don't you?"

I replied that I had never made a secret of it. Those were
extra rations for extra work, but it did not concern them.
I was not entitled to a double set, and it would have been
futile to start an argument. The scholar's allowance was
good, but hardly adequate on its own, and it did not in-
clude bread. So I ran from pillar to post, lodging one protest after another. My case was a good one, but protests
seemed vain. The larder stood empty; without the least
warning the green card *payok* was suspended for a fort-

night — owing to transport difficulties. The little Esther had from her Academy would not have kept a dog alive for a week. She had a few things she might have bartered against food, but that autumn of 1921 a particularly frenzied war was being waged against all private trading.

One Sunday afternoon Esther ran into my room.

"The Americans are here. . . . Darling, wouldn't there be a chance for you? They've taken a big house on the Morskaya. I've seen some of their cars. . . . It is the American Relief Administration, they've already begun calling it ARA for short — "

"What do you mean — a chance for me?"

"They'll want interpreters. I heard someone say they haven't brought their own staff — "

"What spare time have I got?" I said moodily.

But the Americans were there, and the air rang with endless stories about the *Amerikanzi*, the salaries they paid and the food they gave. The house on the Morskaya was supposed to have a canteen where they fed their half-starved personnel twice a day. There were legends about freely given woolen stockings, shoes, and blankets. Every queue discussed the American theme, and even at the Third I heard about tins of condensed milk and flitches of bacon.

A few days later Esther and I sat down to a supper of a rye rusk apiece. Our breakfast had been the same, and the midday meal had consisted of a halved *wobla*. The next morning I went to see my professor. She suggested that I might look on what job I could get with the ARA as something like a cure. "It need not necessarily take the whole of your time — and after all, a brain must have food." That afternoon I went to the Morskaya.

I found the place seething with men and women, all busy, hurrying, unconcerned. I edged my way to a counter, and a tall man asked me what I wanted. I very nearly blurted out, "Why, food, of course," but I managed to control myself and said I wondered whether they had any vacancies for interpreters. "Upstairs, first door on the right, ask for Mr. Saunders," and he was gone like lightning.

I found Mr. Saunders. The room was so warm that it made me feel dizzy. "I've come to — " I said, and he pressed the bell. A girl came. He spoke to her. I could not hear much. A minute later I found myself in the canteen. A white-coated man led me to a table. Almost unaware, I drank hot soup and ate white bread. Condensed cream, lavishly poured over the pudding, made me cry. But the canteen was empty: the white-coated man had vanished behind the screen, and I hurriedly finished the pudding.

In the room upstairs they told me they wanted no interpreters in Petrograd. Their Moscow office, however, was badly understaffed. The question was shot at me like a bullet — when could I start?

"Tonight, if I were free — "

"Aren't you?"

I explained about the Third. Mr. Saunders telephoned, and a reedy, sandy-haired *tovaritch* came into the room from the other wing of the building. Speaking in execrable English, he said that the Third people could be "squared up in a jiff and no mistake." All those professors and people had to do what they were told. I was mobilized by the ARA, and that clinched the matter for everybody.

I felt uncomfortable, and Mr. Saunders said quietly: —

"We don't mobilize anyone. We want volunteers."

The *tovaritch* ignored the remark and hurried away, repeatedly assuring Mr. Saunders that everything would be "O.K., first class, for sure, yes, sir," and I felt more than uncomfortable. The faculty, as a body, had been fairly decent to me; the reedy *tovaritch* would send them something of a military order, typed, stamped, and sealed in the best Tcheka fashion. Mr. Saunders was a stranger and a foreigner; such things could not be explained to him. A paper was given me, and I signed it. They talked about salary, expenses, and an immediate food draft. In less than an hour I got home, a little boy behind me pushing a well-laden sleigh. I paid for the hire of the sleigh with a small tin of condensed milk. Esther was in, and together we hauled the food draft upstairs. Sugar, flour, condensed milk, salt, cocoa, bacon, and corned beef! I looked at the floor strewn with packages and reflected that all of it could be left behind in Petrograd. The thought brought comfort: whatever happened at the Third, however officious and difficult the *tovaritch* was, Esther would not be hungry for some weeks.

They had also given me two blue blankets, and Esther promised to turn them into a coat and skirt. But I must travel to Moscow in my purple velours garments! My scant possessions went into a small wicker basket, tied round with a rough hempen rope. The train, leaving Petrograd late at night, was supposed to come to Moscow early in the morning, but the chaotic transport conditions meant that food must be taken for the journey. My protests notwithstanding, Esther dipped into the bag of flour and started making some buns.

"We are all getting cynical." I talked whilst she was mixing the buns. "The country is in the grip of the worst

famine ever known. They have some data at the ARA, and
photographs, too. There is supposed to be cannibalism east
of Kazan. Does this worry any of us? I am going to work
with the ARA for no other reason than the monthly food
draft. I suppose I ought to pretend that I am terribly upset
about the interrupted work at the Third. But I am not.
It is all bunkum. I just don't want to be hungry any more.
I howled over my pudding at the ARA."

She argued that this was natural.

"If I were you, I should stop thinking about motives,
reasons, and all the rest of it. Get on with the work. You'll
come back to your books all the better for a change — "

Next morning I had an awkward interview with the
Rector of the Third. He had received a letter from the
tovaritch, a badly worded, official "order," directing the
Third to release me from my duties under some vague
threat or other. The Rector thundered that the college was
no soap factory, nor was he a subservient manager.

"I don't mind if the whole world hears of it. . . . It is
preposterous — "

I told him I had applied for the job. I had explained about
the *tovaritch* and the attitude of the Americans.

"I should have come here in the first place. I am sorry.
. . . Things have been rather difficult — "

His face suddenly cleared, and he made it all the worse
for me by talking about a great and humane effort. The
tovaritch and his outrageous letter were forgotten. The
Rector, easily imagining himself in an auditorium, discoursed
on the noble task ahead of me, begged me to be careful in
areas where typhus and plague were raging, and assured
me that they would all welcome me on my return. Crimson with shame and an unquiet conscience, I left his study.

That evening I started for Moscow, traveling in a train largely made up of cattle trucks. Mine was a proper coach, packed more closely than any sardine tin. My small bundle of food proved useful: the train stopped often enough, but not a crumb could be bought at any station. More by luck than anything else, we reached Moscow in the late morning. It was Sunday. No bells were ringing. The station suggested a heap of badly painted bricks dumped somewhere in the heart of a desert. The streets were more or less deserted, their pavements gaping with holes, and the roads were ankle-deep in gray, slushy snow.

I could see no droshky, and, the basket dumped at my feet, I finished my provender standing in the porch: the waiting rooms were all locked. The basket slung over my back, I tramped towards the ARA Headquarters. In a tidy enough office, the officer in charge greeted me genially, but he looked perplexed. He was not sure if I would be needed, but even if they wanted me they could not house me anywhere in Moscow: conditions were far worse than in Petrograd, and that was saying a lot.

"They might want you at Kazan, but there is no train running tonight, and we haven't got any room at the center —"

I sat, the wicker basket at my feet. I could see myself in the train back to Petrograd. . . . No vacancy there. . . . So the maddening round would start all over again, and perhaps the green cards would be worth something later on. Suddenly I longed for the flat, Esther, the Third, even Grannie and the sailor's wife. That life, whatever its hardships and worse, had been so familiar. Moscow's hands seemed like clenched fists.

And in a chair at the big desk sat the American, obviously puzzled, not knowing what to do with a young female about whom they had heard nothing at all. At last he remembered that the committee room was unoccupied. It was very big, he said, but he might be able to get hold of some wood for the stove. He quite thought that there was a sofa of sorts in a corner.

The room was indeed enormous. The logs of wood, obtained after hours of frantic search, were pitifully few. But the sofa was there, and I spent my first night in Moscow under layers of thick blankets, brought by an ARA orderly. Nonetheless I got up frozen to the marrow of my bones. A jug half filled with water had been left on the table. The water was ice.

I got up, wondering about Kazan. But apparently they needed someone in Moscow, and I stayed on. The committee room gave me shelter for a few more nights, and then I got a room in a flat not far from the Headquarters. My landlady was a young nun, recently exiled from her convent. She worked as a nurse in a typhus hospital. She was very pious, but not at all sorry at having been sent away from the nunnery. "Candles, incense, and psalms from morning till night — I would rather worship my God in some other way," she declared, and added: "I see you have got some cigarettes. Could you spare me a few?"

She smoked, quite unconcerned. She was still wearing her black habit, a voluminous veil, and heavy square-toed boots, such as were worn by all Russian nuns.

"Where are all the other sisters?" I could not help asking. She shrugged.

"The young ones got jobs of one kind or another. We

must all live. The others — well, I could have wept for them. . . . Two or three managed to get shifted to another nunnery; they could not start a life in the world, you see — much too old and set in their ways — " She smoked on.

"What a tragedy — " I murmured.

She looked at me curiously.

"Yes — but there were other tragedies — in the old days. . . . An aunt of mine was a nun at a small convent in the West, somewhere, and a pogrom happened there. Well, she thought Christian charity was her duty and befriended some Jewish children, but do you think the police thought that was Christian? Not they! They came to the nunnery all right, and the mother superior went all to pieces, and the Bishop was against the nuns. You have no idea. . . . Holy Russia! Holy Police — I should say — " and she made a vague unhappy gesture.

"But look at it now — " I ventured.

"Yes, look at it now — martyrs in their hundreds. . . . All the same, the old days weren't always happy."

2

❧❧❧❧❧❧❧❧❧❧❧❧❧❧❧

I FOUND no interpreting work in Moscow. My task was mainly distribution of food, medicine, and clothes. Food was doled out in poorer districts, and its distribution carried a certain amount of red tape. This was necessary: supplies were limited. Yet all the formalities notwithstanding, there were cases of flagrant dishonesty, and some people managed to get much more than their share. By some mysterious means, *Amerikanskye* sugar, bacon, and corned beef crept into the Moscow markets. Formalities were almost doubled, but no measures could prevent a certain trading in condensed milk and cocoa.

The city was a revelation. The first impression of that desolate station and forlorn streets was soon to be dispelled. If Petrograd was more or less a derelict churchyard, with her closed shops, her absence of traffic and markets, her charred ruins and nightly blackness, then Moscow was very much like a fair in full swing. I trudged along the Tverskaya Street and the Kuznetzky Bridge, silent and astonished, remarking the innumerable shops, stocked with food, tobacco, footwear, clothes, and even furniture. True that prices were prohibitive, except for foreigners and speculators, but things could be bought, and even my own slender exchequer occasionally permitted the purchase of a bun or a packet of German cigarettes. At night the streets were flooded with light, and wherever you went you heard scraps of foreign speech. Moscow was swarming with foreigners. *Burobin, Buro Inostranzeff* (Foreigners' Bureau), had just been opened to look after their interests. *Burobin* was a bank, a store, an estate agency, a post office — all in one. Some people whispered that it was also a disguised offshoot of the Tcheka and that every foreigner had his shadowy familiar from the Loubianka. This may have been so — but I never traced any evidence of it.

Yet in spite of the glitter, the traffic, the laden shops, and the spectacular sights, Moscow was far grimmer than Petrograd had ever been — even in the very depths of her silent dereliction. Moscow was the center of the Government. Moscow had the arrogantly white walls of the Kremlin, once used by the Tsars, now the home of Lenin and the seat of the Sovnarkom. Armored cars slid up and down the streets. Heavily armed sentries paced to and fro in their appointed places. Moscow had Butyrki and the Loubianka, before which the most terrible stories of Gorochovoya and Shpalernaya in Petrograd paled into contemptible insignificance. Moscow was indeed alive, but her life was fever, dread, and also fatigue. Moscow was like a blinded old woman placed in front of a picture and ordered to admire it volubly and endlessly.

I received a regular salary at the ARA. My board was free, and the nun-landlady accepted no other rent than an occasional parcel of food and some cigarettes. So for the first time in many years I had money to spend. Near the Arbat, on the pavement market, I saw a pair of gorgeous brown silk curtains. A shriveled little Tartar sold them cheaply enough. My landlady told me of a dressmaker near the Tverskaya. I went to her. She fingered the stuff in a slow, unhappy way, shaking her gray head over the darkly shimmering folds.

"Looten from some palace or other, I dare say! Well, well, so you come from Petrograd. I'd much rather be there than here, for all I am a Muscovite by birth. But I can't get a permit to leave Moscow. They don't like anyone leaving here. They must have the city full of people, they say, to make a good impression on foreigners. Good impression — heaven forgive them! Moscow is a churchyard for all the shops and theaters and restaurants, and they are dancing in the churchyard, and there are thousands of waifs dying all over the place. . . ."

"I saw one of them yesterday."

"One?" She almost smiled. "You couldn't count them — if you went away from the boulevards. They're hustled away from the boulevards, you see; foreigners must not meet too many of them."

The one I had seen was a thing rather than a human child. Its head and body were wrapped in some dark tatters. It crouched behind me as I came out of a shop, a small bag of buns in my hand. Then it pounced forward, agile as a monkey, wrenched the bag out of my fingers, and vanished into the dark mouth of an alley off the street. The only impression I had was of terribly protruding cheekbones, two live coals for eyes, and a great running sore across the chin.

In Moscow the vanished aristocracy of Russia went on living out their squalid existence. In Petrograd you never heard much about them, at least not in the world I lived in. But in Moscow they seemed everywhere, crushed, piteous, and almost forsaken. It looked as though the same city which had once surrounded them with Oriental splendor were now determined to hug them closer and closer to her own thin and hungry breast, sucking their mind and blood. Some among them may have been harsh, blind, and even cruel; but the penalty they were now paying seemed out of all proportion to whatever they may have been or done. It was a death sentence, spread over an undefined period. Most of their men were gone by now — either perished or escaped. The women remained, hiding in squalid attics and cellars of the Moscow slums. At least, they hid whenever the tired flesh could endure no more. Otherwise they came out, and sometimes you passed them in the streets, unalive, haughty, cloistered in a world all their own. A few of the younger ones became piteously "acclimatized," flaunted a certain amount of bravado, took whatever jobs came their way. One or two of them were at the ARA. But they remained a minority.

There was something else in Moscow. Fantastic, macabre stories were often whispered round the canteen table. Voices must fall to a whisper once that topic was broached. In Petrograd, even in bread queues, it was never mentioned at all. But Moscow was different, she was tossing about on a feverish bed, and things were spoken which might have remained unsaid in healthier surroundings. Here, in the old city, that subject sooner or later crept into every whispered conversation.

"They" were all alive. They had all escaped early in 1918 — through the Black Sea. They were now living in England. After all, the King of England was his first cousin, it seemed natural that they should have sought and found a refuge in England. The Dowager Empress was the sister of the Queen Mother. Yes, so ran one variant of that universal story, they were all safely in England.

There were other versions. They were not in England. They had been all killed long ago, here, in the very heart of Moscow, in a cellar of the Boutirky Prison. Their bodies were burned immediately afterwards, but one of the executioners went mad and broadcast it all over the city.

I brought some of those stories to my landlady. Whatever her opinion of the old nunnery, she seemed a safe enough listener. One evening she offered me a widely different version. She had heard it from an exiled abbot, who lived outside Moscow and whose brother had been in close touch with someone who knew. "They" were living in the country, safely hidden away, leading ordinary peasant lives. They had sunk the last shred of their identity among peasant folk. The young nun added: —

"After all, it happened once before. What about that hermit in Siberia, he who had once been Alexander the First?"

Fantasy throve and grew apace. Of the incontrovertible facts about the tragedy enacted one day in July 1918, in a cellar in Siberia, none of us had even an inkling. In my turn, I brought the nun's story to my fellow workers in the ARA. At once the theme of the sunk identity gripped them. Yes, it must be true, and they repeated the story to others, my brief variant enriched by a profusion of gratuitous detail. "They" were all safe, somewhere in a village, worlds away from the fevered, dangerous turmoil of any city. They lived in a common *izba*, had a patch of arable land, and the children worked in the fields. More fertile imaginations were not slow in supplying still further details: the village was somewhere in the south, near Simbirsk, or perhaps further still, round about Tsaritsyn.

Sudden, fantastic, whispered stories somehow fitted into the background of Moscow, that unreal and hurried life, glittering and tangled, terribly tense, in very truth a cemetery turned into a fair ground.

So we distributed cottonwool and corned beef, saw tragedies every day, lived our own small-scaled lives in what then seemed undreamt-of luxury, but the famine and its host of familiars, plague, typhus, and worse, danced its own measure at no great distance from Moscow. In fact, often enough the grim steps echoed down the closed-in alleys off the boulevards, and forgotten people died a slow and lonely death in their forgotten homes before the kindly hands of rescuers could be stretched out to save them.

3

I HAD not been with the ARA for more than a month when I found myself switched off in a different direction. The ARA was not alone in the relief field; several other bodies had come both from the United States and from England, and the British Relief Mission was among them. Dr. Farrar came with it, and he found that he could not do much without an interpreter. The ARA lent me to him. With Dr. Farrar work became interesting. Typhus and plague were then raging in the famine areas. Dr. Farrar started studying conditions in outlying hospitals, and I followed him on those excursions. I knew nothing of his work in detail, but I saw him often and often with timid mothers, shrinking, frightened children, young people and old, all trace of health and hope wiped off their gray, thin faces. He could not speak a word of the language, nor did he say much to me. Somehow this did not matter. A gesture, a touch, a look, above all, that smile of his — all those worked their way into their hearts. In their frozen inarticulacy they often went away without a word of thanks being spoken, but their gratitude obviously touched depths no mere spoken word could have reached.

Was it a fortnight or three weeks? One morning Dr. Farrar had a headache. We stayed indoors, and he began dictating a long bacteriological report. I knew no shorthand, and it progressed slowly enough. Once I apologized for my inefficiency. He smiled and said he liked working slowly.

"I couldn't rush today. My head's getting worse again."

Late that evening he wanted to write a letter to his wife. I gave him some paper and his fountain pen, but he could not write more than a few words. I left him at that place on the Sofiyskaya Quay, and the next morning I found a German Red Cross sister at the door. She said I had better not go into the room.

"We think he has the typhus." She spoke in clipped, broken English. "You will not wish to catch it also."

I halted in the doorway. Dr. Farrar's bed had been pushed into the middle of the room. He was unconscious. I turned and saw that the sister's large blue eyes were clouded with tears.

"He's been doing more good here than anyone else I know," I faltered, and she wrung her hands.

"*Ach,* it is always so — "

It was a few days before Christmas. The ARA center had planned a real Christmas for all its workers. I believe it was Christmas Eve or the day after that I called again at the Sofiyskaya. The sister looked graver than ever.

The next morning I came to the ARA center for a hurried breakfast. An officer said, passing by the table: "Guess you've heard? The Doc died early in the morning — "

A breakfast of coffee and rolls was a very rare luxury, but that morning I ate nothing. I went to the Sofiyskaya. In the hall, an enormous wreath of evergreens was propped against a table. Pale winter sun caressed the words, stamped in silver on scarlet silk, *Dem Helde für Russlands Leid*, and a sister tiptoed in the hall.

"This is so true," she pointed at the lettering, "but you must take great care. The typhus is so everywhere. The lice, they bite everyone — "

I could not consider the lice and their fatal bites. I thought of the man from England who had come to help, who had brought and given so much. They gave him an important funeral with music and horses and guards of honor. We tramped all the long way to the Lefortovskoe Cemetery. A member of the British Trade Mission read the committal service. It was so cold that when we got back to the Mission house in the Povarskaya for lunch, I could not hold knife and fork for several minutes.

The ARA suggested that I had better return to Petrograd. But the dressmaker's assertion was proved true: they did not like people leaving Moscow, and I could not get my permit for several weeks. I filled in the gap by doing odd secretarial jobs at the British Trade Mission. Very odd they were indeed, because my typing could not be worse! Once I wasted a whole morning over a single sheet of foolscap. The document, whatever it was, would be sent to the Foreign Office. When it was done and I handed it over, there came a deep sigh from the head clerk in the Chancery.

"You are soon going back to Petrograd?" he inquired politely.

I told him I was only waiting for the permit to leave Moscow.

"I am at the University — " I added.

"Yes, I know. . . . Do go back — for goodness' sake! I think you'll be much happier there — "

He might have added that the Chancery people would be much happier without me, but he did not. Somehow this heartened me, and I attacked the next sheet with a greater zeal than ever before, but I suppose the result was the same appalling smudge. I remembered Stepan and his wrath over an ancient typewriter. At the Mission the typewriter was a magnificent shining thing, but I was at a loss about the changing of a ribbon.

At last the permit came and I went back to Petrograd. After Moscow it seemed a paradise. Nonetheless, the twin monsters, famine and typhus, were very much there. I got back in January 1922, returned to my own college for the seminar studies, and also worked for the ARA, on the Morskaya Street. One morning I got up with a headache. I went to the ARA and they sent me home. Our flat was not too far away. Somehow I managed to get home, hoist myself up the stairs, open the door, and tumble into bed.

A louse must have bitten me somewhere. They suggested to Esther that she should send me off to one of the typhus hospitals and, had she agreed, I might not have come out. People died like flies in those hospitals. There were not enough doctors. The supply of medicines was negligible.

For three weeks I was unconscious. When this was

over, I wondered whether my body was made of frangible spun glass. At the least movement, the glass seemed to break with an exquisite pain. During those weeks of convalescence, temperature fell to normal in the morning. In the afternoon I was plunged back into a furnace, and talked "most varied nonsense," as Esther told me much later.

That illness wrought an incredible change among the tenants. The workman's wife had always been more or less decent, even though she had kept aloof. Now she began sharing milk and eggs with Esther, and made her husband walk on slippered feet. She was truly a heroine: during the first spell, as I learned much later, I used to scream often enough, and my shrieks terrified her so that her baby arrived almost a month too early.

The sailor's lady did not share her lavish rations with anyone, but she curbed her tongue, refrained from slamming doors, and put a stop to her man's drunken orgies. Grannie emerged from her den, washed her face and hands in cold water, and told Esther that she had nursed her own mother about fifty years before. If it had not been for Grannie, a few friends from college, and the woman whose memory proved long enough to remember a piece of tarpaulin, Esther would not have had much sleep all those weeks.

I lay convalescing, and Grannie, her face almost clean and a shawl pinned under her chin, sat by my bedside and talked. She stayed on even when I slept, but she must have fought down her predatory instincts: not a crumb was missed in the room after her visits. From her I heard the story Esther had hoped I would never know.

[298]

"The sister" (they always called her that in the flat) "was out of the room for a few minutes. It was long ago, you were so ill then that all your wits were scattered. She came back and found you standing on the window sill. The window had been wrenched open. Well, had she screamed, you would have tumbled down. She came up so quietly and tried to get you down. You fought her. You need not look at me like that, I am telling you that you did not know what you were doing. A woman I know had her lad down with typhus at the Obuchovsky. His ward was on the third floor, and he went slick through the window, all his bones smashed to pieces when they found him. Well, typhus folk are like that. It is the madness in the blood all boiling over, so to speak. Well, you fought the sister like mad, but she got you down somehow, and once on the floor you collapsed as though you were a balloon and a pin had pricked you. I came in, and between us we carried you to bed. Yes, she is a good woman, for all she is a foreigner — "

I could not comment on the story, nor could I ever tell Esther I had heard it.

I once asked Grannie if there were a mirror in the room, and she looked uncomfortable.

"She said I was not to give you one — "

I threatened to get out of bed and find one myself; she grumbled and protested, but at last she found a hand mirror, put it face downwards on the bed, and slipped out of the room.

I picked it up and I was glad to be alone. I saw a stranger's face, white skin drawn tight over the bones and the eyes grown to the size of two Bavarian plums. I stared, wondering where I had last seen something like the face before me. I remembered soon enough. A blurred picture of a mortuary near Moscow came into my mind, the mirror fell on the bare boards, and I wondered about the splinter of glass.

4

～～～～～～～～～～～～～～～～～～～～～～～～

My relief work was over. They had kept my place at the ARA, but purely office work seemed almost childish after the Moscow experience. Besides, I knew no shorthand, my typing was fourth-rate, of bookkeeping I knew nothing, and interpreting was not wanted. I hoped I might be sent back to the famine area, away from the safe and polite world of ledgers and typewriters, but my illness put an end to such hopes. I had spent about five months away from the University, and I knew that the widely different experience of relief work would, in a way I could not yet gauge, help me with my academic work. It had been getting almost fossilized, self-centered and limited. But I had met people in those five months, I had seen human nature at its best — for all the appalling environment.

For to the Russians the relief brought far more than material benefits. It was a generously opened window, which made it possible for countless people to remember once again that all was neither cruelty nor fear nor yet injustice in the world, that there were still some folk living in it who held kindness above other things, who were willing to help and expected nothing in return. All selfless giving to a Russian, whether he be externally pious or not, embodies the spirit of Christ. That much the relief achieved for many and many, and for this alone it deserved unconditioned gratitude.

As concerned myself, I went into it cynically enough. Because of one clerk's obduracy and another's spitefulness, half the food I was entitled to no longer reached me. Hunger becomes more than unpleasant after a few years' acquaintance. With no high motives I went to have that first interview with the ARA people in Petrograd. Even the college work, once so passionately beloved, could be swept aside without a moment's consideration and almost without regret. I wanted food, and that summed up all my needs. I traveled to Moscow, my mind indifferent to the sufferings of those same people whom the ARA had to come to rescue from the grim clutches of starvation. I belonged to that organization, but its ideals were still remote. I started my work in the same spirit, thinking far more of the twelve-o'clock meal in the warm canteen than of the tragedy writ large upon a young woman's face, whose hair gleamed silver under a patched rag of a shawl, and whose cheeks were wet with tears when I handed her a parcel of food. "I shall eat it," she whispered more to herself than to me, "but my dead son cannot see it," and I turned to the next applicant almost impatiently.

Yet such an attitude could not endure. There was something in the very idea of the Relief that brought it down. Months later, I realized that a strangely moving evangel was graven in the heart of that strange and difficult country. I was no convert to it, but I learned to be ashamed of that earlier, coarse-veined cynicism in grabbing hold of a job for the victuals it offered. Somehow, it was good to feel ashamed.

These thoughts came in the spring when I received my first letter from my aunt in Italy — the first after five years' silence. The letter had been sent to the British Embassy in Petrograd, and traveled to Moscow and back to Petrograd again, and its journey took about four months. It was a necessarily cautious letter, but it had a postscript: *"Veux-tu venir ici — chez moi?"* I read again this seemingly casual invitation to come and visit her, and fingered the flimsy sheet, and dreams came knocking at my door once again. "Impossible! Italy — and a decent life!"

People were not allowed to leave for abroad in those days. I remembered I was due back at college very soon. I began thinking about the next year's work. I put the letter and its postscript out of my mind.

5

AT the Third they told me I had better resume my work in the autumn. At the First I was reminded about the finals in the summer and my own seminar work. Somehow, one term jumbled into another. The green cards were now definitely a thing of the past. There was nothing but the very meager student's *payok* to depend on. Esther's own allowance had by that time dwindled to little more than a neat little set of pale pink cards — issued with a maddening regularity once a month. On paper she could get a lot. In grim practice, however, her allowance meant a very occasional pound of black bread and something like a handful of the "Soviet ham."

"Well, it looks like living on dry bread through the summer," I remarked, but Esther was busily rummaging in the drawers of her chest.

"The other day I heard that they have started to run trains to Kolpino again," she said, and I stared at her.

"Well?"

"We are going there."

"To speak German?"

"To get some food."

At that time there were practically no more markets left in the city. But, as Esther said, an occasional train went from Petrograd to Kolpino, some fifteen miles or so to the southwest, where the German colonists still lived on the land given to their forebears by Catherine the Great.

Those expeditions were vaguely dangerous. Railway tickets must be bought with a certain amount of cunning. Then we had to run the gauntlet of several sentry posts at the railway station. It was no use going empty-handed to Kolpino, but bulky parcels might not be taken out of Petrograd. The German colonists were no philanthropists; they had flour, potatoes, and butter to spare, but they would not part with their victuals for nothing. The first time we journeyed down, we had a small silver saltcellar and a pair of onyx links, once the property of Esther's father, and we got to Kolpino without any mishap. We drew a blank at the first farm we came to; they merely asked us to go away, they never had any dealings with speculators. We trudged on across a muddy field to the next farm, and there the door was slammed in our faces, not a word spoken by the fat and glossy-faced *Hausfrau*. I began wondering whether all the stories about the German colonists and their readiness to help were so many fables, my feet hurt me, and the sun was very hot. But Esther would not give in. She made me march for another mile and there a squat, whitewashed farmhouse had its doors opened in a friendly enough fashion. A middle-aged woman came out, asked us in, and suggested a rest. As soon as we were in, she began laying the table. We protested, and she silenced us by a shrug. In less than half an hour we sat down to a meal of hot boiled potatoes, drenched in milk, a dish of fried eggs, and real coffee.

"Eat more, please," she went on insisting in her very broad German. "We had a good harvest last year, and the crops are promising to be fine again. You look honest enough to me — not like some of those people from Petrograd who come here and look as though they would rob us of everything — if they knew the way to set about it."

We finished, produced our saltcellar and the links, and from a genial hostess she became a shrewd business woman. Yes, she supposed she liked the links well enough. Come to think of it, a son of hers was getting married in the autumn, and the links might make a nice wedding present. But she was afraid she could not really afford to buy them. Esther said: —

"You are so kind." She smiled and bowed, and the woman smiled and bowed back. "We have wasted so much of your time. Well, would you like to have those things for a small bag of flour and about ten pounds of potatoes?"

The woman got so angry that I thought she meant to hit Esther. Certainly, she banged her fist on the table.

"Do you take me for a decent Christian woman or a thief? I can guess the value of your things, but I don't know if I can afford them. . . . A bag of flour, a few potatoes! Mad — are you?" She thought hard for a moment. "Listen, I can give you a bag of flour, a sack of potatoes, some butter, and a round cheese. I wish I could offer more — but I dare not. Of course, you can't take it all back tonight. You will have to come again, once or twice, perhaps. You will be welcome," she bowed to Esther, "and perhaps you will stay the night next time."

We returned to Petrograd, knowing that we had a friend at Kolpino. She kept her word, and she fed us each time we journeyed down to collect the installments. When these were finished, she said she had no more to spare, but if we had any other trinkets, she could put us in touch with other women in the neighborhood and she herself would see to it that we were treated decently. So in the early summer months of 1922 we made friends with four or five families at Kolpino.

Those excursions into the leafy lanes and fields, dotted with clover and poppies, to the white and gray farmhouses would have been wholly pleasant were it not for the nightmare of the return journey. To the very end I could not get used to it. To the very end I began shivering as soon as the train drew near the big, gloomy station in Petrograd.

No foodstuffs could then be imported into the city, such was the law, and the armed guards, dotted all over the platforms and sometimes beyond the barrier, were there to catch all trangressors of the law.

Once we traveled back, some flour, butter, and cheese for our illicit luggage. It was early in May, I believe, but a bitter northeasterly wind was blowing hard, yet we must take off our coats and wrap the treasured packages in them. The small train went on, jolting all along the line. At last it came to a dead halt about half a mile from the Petrograd station. Our carriage was crowded. An old woman in a corner crossed herself. She was certain the train would very soon be raided by Red militiamen. Trains were often stopped outside stations for no other purpose. It was wicked, she mumbled on and on, people were starving in the city, and not an egg, not a single pound of potatoes, could be brought in from the country.

All of us were common transgressors. All kept still as though the woman's plaint did not concern us in the least. Our own seat happened to be in the corner by the window. Suddenly Esther whispered to me in English: "Try the door handle, will you?" I did, and found that the door was unlocked. Usually, they had them locked from the outside — so as to prevent people from getting away along the line. The train kept still. Daylight was getting dim. I threw a doubtful glance at the fairly high embankment, grown over with stumpy and prickly undergrowth, but Esther went on whispering: "I believe there is a path just underneath. We're in the last carriage. It's about half a mile from the city, and I know the country. These people are all right. They'll probably come along too, and be glad of the lead.

Come on, you jump first, find your feet, and roll right down — we mustn't be noticed — it isn't as steep as it looks — " and we jumped, and got back to the city by devious ways, the cheese having lost its earlier shape after rolling on its own down the embankment.

Never were we actually stopped by the sentries. However hot the weather, Esther wore her heavy coat and, probably, her brief white veil earned her a certain amount of respect from the soldiers. Certainly she always carried much more than I did, potatoes and eggs and butter, all in tidy little packages, stowed away so cleverly that, looking at her, I wondered whether she had not dropped them on the way to the station at Kolpino. Her manner was superbly reassuring. She walked, head erect, tendered her ticket with a smile and a brief remark about the weather, and sometimes received a cheerful grin in return. I tried to imitate her, but my knees would not stop shaking, and I knew that my face got whiter and whiter each time we came near a barrier. Esther was once chaffed by a sentry: "Eh, you, sister, a fine nurse you are! Look at that girl — face like chalk," and she parried it by blaming the sultry weather for my pallor.

"Come on," she urged me as soon as the train halted. "Oh, darling, why must you be so frightened? We are not doing any wrong. That law is too wicked to be kept — "

"But — but — " I said, feeling the packages round my waist, "suppose a bit of string gave way."

"Suppose the skies came down," she mocked. "Come on. It would have been over by now if you'd hurried —"

So she gave me of her own spirit, and sometimes a thin wisp of courage crept into me. But usually this happened only with the last barrier left behind. We stalked down the Nevsky, two lawbreakers, still at large and unashamed of our transgression.

6

That summer, I remember, came with a strange suddenness. Before we knew where we were, the tall, heavily girthed limes in the Summer Gardens were all powdered with the delicate green of young leafage. The passing of five years had doled out some mercy to the charred ruins of houses, burned down in 1917, and here and there a wounded wall stood, its nakedness covered with bold shoots of creepers. Grass sprang in between the fissures of pavements once tortured by machine-gun bullets, and grass grew here and there on the Nevsky Prospect, now hardly disturbed by traffic, except for very occasional cars — "foreigner — or else a commissar" — there were no other owners of cars in the beggared city.

St. Isaac's Cathedral had not yet been turned into a museum, and on Saturday evenings the voices of men and boys, chanting "Magnificat," broke through the great bronze doors and stole away down the reawakened river. Under the great pillared dome of the Cathedral of Our Lady of Kazan, the frayed, faded colors of vanished regiments still hung over General Koutouzoff's humble tombstone. My old school, Xénia, now housed the Labor Commissariat and was still called "Palace," *Dvoretz Truda*. On one occasion I passed through the great doors, but the alien spirit within soon drove me away, my now forgotten errand unaccomplished.

In the pearl-white evenings the Neva slipped back into her sapphire sovereignty, and pale gold lay spilt all over the dome and the slender spires of SS. Peter and Paul Cathedral across the water. Clumps of crocuses had come and gone in the college gardens, and a professor's intrepid wife watched a bed of white tulips break into life. Neglected, partly ruined, her drainage an ever-crying disgrace, her streets mostly deserted and her palaces silent and lonely, Petrograd never lost some of her loveliness; she still gave joy with the curves of her Quays, the arrowy reaches of her wide avenues, the leafy wealth of her several pleasances. Remembering the hot, feverish, walled-in temper of Moscow, I knew myself loving more and more this paler, far more enigmatic city, once known as the Venice of the North.

Yes, that summer came suddenly, bringing with it the city's six weeks of white bridal, when sunset was married to sunrise within one brief half hour of delicate pearl-white light.

The summer came and brought in her hands a mood of homesickness, sharper than any known before, a longing for some staple anchorage in life. The sum total of the year just gone seemed so much of a paradox: so much done and undone at the same time. The twelve months were strewn with oddly assorted litter: attempts to get food; crude ways to settle the clothes problem by means of curtains, sheets, and blankets; hosts of acquaintances — made in a queue, in an overcrowded tram, just anywhere. Work

at the Third and my brother, alien and remote; seminar
studies; the ARA in Petrograd and Moscow; trains, over-
heated rooms, the smell of Lucky Strikes, food drafts, sewn
into unpleasantly rough canvas, lice and bugs, carbolic,
hospital wards, typewriters, trains again. . . . Back in
Petrograd, and typhus, mainly remembered as short red and
violet waves of intense heat. . . . Excursions to Kolpino
and college work again. . . . Gregory of Tours and Wandalbert. "There is nothing new in Wandalbert's definition
of Time, but, being a poet, he clothes old ideas into a new
dress." But how did he clothe them? Finally, Henry of
Huntingdon — "Britain is an island of unbounded fertility,"
but he also wrote to his friend Walter: "Reflect . . . how
worthless is this present life, and since we see that even the
most powerful, who were in possession of the fullest measure of its wealth, accomplished nothing, and that we ourselves accomplished nothing, let us seek another way of
life in which we may expect happiness and shall not
fail. . . ." Ah no, even Henry offered but cold comfort —
sometimes.

What a littered year! The finals began in June, and I
passed them, but I can't remember much about them. Then
I settled down to Kolpino and to my thesis, when the
cough, which had never left me since an earlier illness, began
keeping everybody awake at night. Esther remembered that
a good German doctor saw people at a hospital where she
had worked. I went there early one morning. After about
twenty minutes he put down his stethoscope and said
kindly: —

"Would you like me to send you to the Health Commission?"

"Is anything the matter?"

"Well, they might find you eligible for something like a year in some sanatorium in the Crimea — "

"Is anything the matter?" I felt I must know, but he was evasive.

"I don't think another winter here would do you much good. The South might put it right — "

"Put what right?"

"Your left lung is not all it should be. Well, would you like to send a report to the Commission?"

I said I could not go anywhere before November — at the earliest. I had my thesis to think of. Also the people at the Third expected me to begin my lectures in the autumn.

"Of course, they might decide against sending you anywhere," he said a little curtly.

I waited for about a fortnight. A brief chit from the Health Commission summoned me to go there the next morning. A young and serious doctor sounded me, and passed me on to someone else. Within a week I was called for the interview with the Commission. They were kind enough, but, unlike the German, they were outspoken. They received me in a large sunny room. There were about ten of them, and a vase of roses stood on the table. It was very pleasant, reassuring, and terrible at the same time. They offered me a chair and said that I had t.b. in the left lung. They thought they would have a year's vacancy in a sanatorium not far from Alupta in the Crimea. The chairman added: —

"In such a case you would be expected to go at the end of August."

"My degree," I faltered, and he smiled not unkindly.

"A degree would not be of much use to a corpse. An autumn here will most likely land you in a cemetery. But we are not forcing you to go. Take a week over it and let us know, will you?"

I thanked them. They were really very kind. I turned my back on the table with the pale yellow roses in the middle. I found Esther waiting for me outside.

"You are going to the Crimea," she said. "Now what about seeing that very nice man at your college? He will give you good advice about the thesis — "

I went to see him. He proved helpful indeed. He said I might take several books from the college library and finish my thesis at the sanatorium.

"After all, the faculty keep it for about six months before you are allowed to defend it. In your case, they won't refuse to wait for a year — "

"It is nearly finished," I said miserably.

"Then leave it here. It will be nothing but a year's delay — "

Still I could not decide. At the sanatorium, I knew well, I would not meet many people of my own world. Most of the candidates were recruited from the working classes. Even with my thesis finished, I should have to work hard to keep abreast with the seminar studies. There would be little privacy at the sanatorium. I had heard enough about conditions there. Oranges and sun and plenty of milk. . . . But I wanted books and a room to myself. At last, Esther put an end to all my hesitation.

"Either you leave for the Crimea or I apply for a nursing job in the country. I simply refuse to stand by and watch you go under — just because you will be a donkey.

Imagine what next winter may be like! And you coughed blood the other day. Grannie saw you wash a handkerchief in the kitchen."

"Grannie had better mind her own business. If I go and you are here alone, what will you do?"

"I have not got a bad lung. Well, are you going?"

"All right — but I'll hate it just the same — "

"Hating it won't do much harm to your lungs."

I duly applied for the vacancy at the sanatorium. That same day I returned to find a visitor, a girl from the Third, who rushed towards me with the day's great news: —

"They have started issuing foreign passports. I hope to get to Berlin in the autumn. Isn't it a miracle?"

"Is it?" I asked almost indifferently.

But that night I took out my aunt's letter and read the postscript: *"Veux-tu venir ici — chez moi?"*

I realized that I had never answered her. Stamps were prohibitive and, moreover, there had not been anything to say.

Chapter Nine

...AND SO
TO FREEDOM

1

~~~~~~~~~~~~~~~~~~~~~~~~~~~~~~~~~~~~~

ESTHER came into the twilit room, stood behind me, and looked at the letter lying in my hands. Then she said in a strangely detached voice: "Well, Italy might be better than the Crimea, don't you think so?"

"If they ever let me go," I said, "I would never come back, and I could not do it. I have you, and you are all I have in the world —"

"Put that letter away," she suggested. "You might try and buy some stamps and write her a nice little letter. After all, she must be feeling anxious about you —"

"I suppose so —"

We ate our supper. Neither of us mentioned foreign passports, and both thought about them hard enough. Washing up our few chipped crocks, I said to Esther that Italy might certainly be better than the Crimea if she only decided that she preferred Germany to Soviet Russia.

"Well, of course I do." She turned away to fetch a towel.

Days passed, and neither of us mentioned those foreign

passports. Often enough I dreamt of them. I knew that Italy indeed would not be like the Crimea; once over the Russian frontier, I would turn my back irrevocably on the country which bore me. But, of course, all those were so many daydreams. I had not the slightest idea whether I should be found eligible for a foreign passport, nor did I make any inquiries. By virtue of my college appointment I was a state worker, and state workers were unlikely to get abroad. The Soviet Government, for all the blunders they were making, were most emphatically not fools, and they must have been aware that few of those who applied for foreign passports had the least intention of ever returning to Russia.

But one day my professor said unexpectedly: —

"I know you are leaving for the Crimea in August, but even a sanatorium sometimes suffers from food shortage. Why don't you apply for a foreign passport? You might go to France or Italy?"

"They'd never let me go."

"You might try."

That evening I told Esther about it.

"Well, I've heard that three or four students at my 'Academy were refused permission to go to Venice. But they said they wanted to study mosaics — you would go for your health, and that might make a difference. Now the first thing is a letter to Rome. Perhaps your aunt might be able to pull a few wires."

"Esther, you know what it means if they do let me go —"

"Of course I do. You'd be the greatest fool in the world if you ever returned —"

[318]

"And what about you?"

"Must you talk like that? Let's take one thing at a time. I'll try it myself later on. But do tell me something about your aunt — "

I could not tell her much. Aunt Hermione had been an exotic meteor in my childhood, but my mother's eldest sister was a stranger. She went to live in Rome about 1870, married an Italian soon after, and had never left Italy since his death in the early nineties. I had corresponded with her from childhood, but my letters had always been dictated by duty.

"I heard people say that she was very beautiful in her youth. My uncle was a pure-bred Roman, he served in the Papal Guards, and they lived in their own palace. My mother always said that a Roman *palazzo* could not be anything as grandiose as the palaces in St. Petersburg, but, all the same, her life and ours could never be compared. Her world would be quite unknown to me — even though she is very poor now. There was a lot of trouble with her in-laws after my uncle's death. . . ."

"Have you got a photograph?"

"Several." I went to fetch them, and Esther looked at the faded portraits of a small, slight woman in a court dress with a long train and a tiny coronet on her head.

"I am glad you won't have to enclose those in your application. That is counterrevolution with a vengeance — "

"They'll want to know where I am going to — "

"I suppose they will — "

I had not much of a hope, but nonetheless the very next day I sold a pound of rye bread to a woman in the flat above and got enough "pink paper" to buy the stamps for a foreign letter. It was not easy to write. I knew the censors would read it. I must be at once clear and noncommittal, I must give my aunt an idea that I wanted to come to her, but I must not show my eagerness in any way. I suppose I achieved it in the end, since the letter reached her.

2

FROM several unofficial sources I gathered the information I needed. Such a lot had to be done before the foreign passport was issued that my heart quailed at the idea of sending in the preliminary application.

The first stage meant going to the Smolny, the Petrograd off-shoot of the Central Executive Council in Moscow. There I must ask for the preliminary application form — not for the passport itself but for the permission to apply for the passport. This application would go to the Tcheka. The Tcheka alone would decide whether I was eligible for the passport.

The form was a questionnaire, printed on four foolscap sheets, and it demanded an "unequivocal and detailed" answer to every question. For some days I toiled over them. At the very first glance it seemed that "unequivocal and detailed" answers to some of the questions would be more or less beyond me. "Was your paternal grandfather a worker for the revolutionary cause?" I knew little enough

about him. He had served in the army and died comparatively young. He may have been a Liberal, but even this
seemed improbable: the mildest form of Liberalism had
never marched together with the tradition sponsored by
his regiment. I put down a brief negative and left it at
that.

A girl from the seminar helped me to complete the form.
We had heated arguments. I said I was not going to put
my signature under any lies. "Everybody knows it is no
use lying to the Tcheka people. What they don't know
about you is not worth knowing." She agreed with the
principle, but argued that a first cousin could not be considered as one's family. A question asked whether any
members of the family "had suffered the supreme penalty
under the present regime," and a first cousin of mine had
been shot in 1919 "for counterrevolutionary activities."

"I should say no," she suggested. "Anything else would
damn the application at once. If they question you later
on, you might always get out of it by saying that you
had no idea the question included cousins and uncles —"

But I filled the two dotted lines with the full name, re-
lationship, and the date. She looked at what I had written
and said: —

"Well, they might give you a passport on the strength
of this answer alone. They don't want mad people to stay
here. . . . You are as mad as a hatter."

The application was sent early in June. We waited. We
went on waiting till the middle of August. I was supposed
to be leaving for the Crimea on the nineteenth, and I
burned my bridges by telling the Health Commission that
I had changed my mind. We waited and waited.

The Smolny people sat there in their awful and distant glory. They had received the application, but if I wanted to know the answer, I must visit the Smolny. It lay roughly about four miles' distance from my house. Occasional trams were running at the time, but their fare was prohibitive. Twice a week I trudged to the Smolny, always starting in the early morning, a book under my arm. As one week followed another, Esther said that the fare to Rome would not be as much as those tram fares, had I allowed myself to indulge in such a luxury.

Those biweekly excursions had something epochal in them. I set forth briskly enough and tramped along the Nevsky, my heart full of wildest hopes. Three or four hours later I returned the same way, all the hopes burned to cold gray ashes, a mere handful of ashes on the once proud hearth of my dreams. There were days when I must tramp home, having seen some "refusal" scenes at the Smolny. Those were the worst days. It was so easy to imagine the same treatment meted out to me at the end of the long waiting spell.

Nobody could ask questions at the Smolny. We were all ushered into a room where an unpainted wooden partition separated us from the typists at their work. A narrow door led to that room. The walls were colored dirty pea-green, the floor was bare and the windows grimy. It was a waiting room, but there was neither chair nor bench to be seen.

That flimsy wooden partition was our Mecca. Badly typed lists of "successful" names were posted against the rough deal boards. As soon as the door opened, we rushed to them. We scanned those lists, our eyes filled with an almost elemental hunger. On some occasions no lists were pinned at all, and then we merely huddled together and waited as patiently as we had all learned to wait. It struck noon. We had been there since nine o'clock. Nothing had happened and nothing would happen; the office closed at twelve, and we went away, trying to hope against hope.

Few people talked loudly in that room. Some faces bore a strained, broken look. It was a room of splintered hopes and of hopes fulfilled almost miraculously, of hearts beating high and hearts almost shattered in some abyss of black despair. All those who had never had any chance of escaping "across the Gulf," and who were now longing for some legitimate opportunity, came into that room. You could not scrutinize them closely: there was something wounded in their eyes.

On rare occasions some bolder applicant would dare to knock at the partition. Then a crimson-lipped girl in a white peasant blouse and cropped hair came out. "Who knocked? We are busy. What do you want? You have no right to make all this fuss. We know nothing about your application. Sent it four months ago? Well, you might have to wait four years longer, for all I know — "

Once I witnessed an unexpected diversion from the ordinary theme. A quiet, middle-aged woman knocked at the partition. The crimson lips came out, glanced impatiently and shrugged. All of us waited for an outburst, but she spoke quietly enough: —

"Isn't your name so-and-so? Well, this is none of my business, but I'd better give you a bit of advice. Your name is not here and, what is more, it never will be. You'd much better stop coming here."

[323]

The applicant's lips moved, though we could hear no reply. The door banged to. The woman tottered into the passage outside, and I followed her.

"Forty years ago," she said softly, "I was a pupil in these same walls. . . . Well, I never expected anything else. It is not as bad as it might have been. My daughter is in Brazil, but I am certain I would never have got there." She smiled bravely: "I trust you will have better luck."

I was not so sure, and at last I felt it would be better to keep away from the Smolny. But it was August, the college was closed, my thesis nearly finished, and desultory reading seemed barren of all profit. Besides, those lists, pinned to the partition wall, haunted me day and night. I let a week go by. Then I decided to go again, but I had started late, and the lists were already out when I got into the dismal room. A group of men and women stood scanning the names, and from the doorway I heard someone's peevish voice: —

"I can't read this one, Pavel. Something foreign, isn't it? Al — Alme — Never mind, it is not ours. And now I have dropped my spectacles. . . . Let's find them and go home. Oh, goodness, will our names ever be out?"

Someone, but surely not myself, crossed the room and read the name typed in pale violet ink on the gray paper. Someone's trembling hand knocked at the partition and raised the latch. Someone's eyes saw a room crowded with typists. The windows were clean — and the hot August sunlight drenched the vast room. Nearest the door the girl with the bitter, crimson mouth jerked up her head.

"What is it?"

"My name is out —"

"Is it? Well, why don't you say so? What is your name? Yes, your application has been approved. Here is the permit to apply for the passport, but you need not go mad over it — you have not got it yet and you might not get it at all — "

"What do I do next?" someone's very thin voice stammered out.

"Room 89, second floor." She turned her back and added over her shoulder, "And don't come bothering us here again whatever happens."

Upstairs a man clerk, quiet, timid, but friendly, seemed more than human by comparison with the crimson-lipped virago. He offered me a chair by the desk. Patiently and at great length he explained the further procedure. But formalities were like sawdust to my mind. "Freedom! Freedom! Freedom!" something rang within me, and I stared at a slim bunch of lilac-colored asters on the ink-stained desk. "Asters in an old jam jar. . . . Never mind the jar. . . . They are flowers nonetheless." But formalities must be listened to, and I grasped that an application for a foreign passport had to be accompanied by all my personal documents, four photographs, and a set of fingerprints. I must also get two "responsible citizens" of some recognized public position to be my guarantors. Those would have to sign various documents to vouch for my political impeccability. More signatures, more photographs, more everything else. . . .

The gathering of that documentary harvest took about a week. At last, armed with a bulky dossier, I returned to the Smolny. In Room 89 a second application form was handed to me. I took a rusty pen and wrote along the dotted line that I wished to leave for Italy on six months' sick leave. The friendly clerk blotted the paper and dispatched me to another room on the third floor. There a man with a lemon-colored face and a great deal of acerbity in his manner took all my papers and flung the narrow slip of a receipt across the counter. He scared me, but nonetheless I ventured to ask him: —

"How long do I have to wait now?" and for the scowl he gave me, I might have inquired about an earthquake or a murder.

"Am I an almighty commissar to answer such questions? I would not tell you if I knew, but I don't know. The papers are now going to Moscow, and we have nothing more to do with them. Besides, you seem convinced that you will get your passport in the end. I wouldn't be so sure if I were you. The Kremlin refuses as often as the Tcheka does. Next —"

I went home, my enthusiasm somewhat cooler, but Esther said that waiting was tedious only for those who had nothing else to do. "And you are going to be busy."

I made myself read history harder than ever before. An Englishman who had come to Petrograd to work at a shipping office offered his services as postman, and my letters to Italy now went through Finland and Denmark. I wrote asking my aunt whether she could arrange an Italian visa. Wisely enough, she left the question unanswered in her own letter, but my friends at the British Mission in Moscow soon wrote to say that a visa was awaiting me at the Italian Legation.

Yet a visa was useless without a passport, and the Kremlin remained silent. Again I started dreary journeys to the

Smolny, but the wheels of the Foreign Commissariat ground very slowly. The tired, impatient clerks kept telling me they had nothing to report. Sometimes they added that they might not hear anything for months — if at all. At last the lemon-faced clerk sneered and suggested that I had better stay away from the Smolny till about Christmas. In despair, I went down the stairs and knocked at the door of No. 89. The friendly clerk suggested that if I really wished to speed things up in Moscow I might go there myself and see if something might not be done on the spot. "Have you got any influential friends there? If so, they might be able to hurry things through for you. Of course, you would not mention that the idea was first given you at the Smolny — "

I thanked him rather listlessly, and went. The idea was excellent, but I did not see how I could do it. I had no money for railway fares. Money had indeed been promised me on loan from one of the Relief Missions — for the purpose of getting to Rome, but I could not begin spending it on a trip to Moscow. But Esther reminded me that, a few days before, we had received food drafts through the ARA, sent by some friends from England and Germany. "A bag of white flour will easily buy the return ticket."

I reminded her that it was no longer safe to go to a market. "They've forbidden all sale of foodstuffs. . . ."

"Pouf!" she said. "If it comes to that, it isn't safe living here at all, but we have done it for more than five years. You leave it to me. I suppose there is a place in Moscow where you could stay. I am afraid the flour won't run to much more than the ticket — "

I remembered the young nun I had stayed with during

my work at the ARA, and I wrote to her. As it happened, I never stayed a night in Moscow.

Esther sold the flour, and the money for the ticket was there, but it took me another week to get the permit to leave Petrograd. I had to go here, there, and everywhere trying to get it. In those days it was impossible to leave one town for another without a permit. My efforts were necessarily hampered by the fact that I could not disclose the real reason for wishing to get to Moscow. At last they gave me the permit after I had stated my desire to study certain manuscripts in a Moscow museum. The day before the permit came, I heard from a friend at a relief mission. A check for the journey to Italy was enclosed with the letter. But the passport was not there. . . .

The permit to leave Petrograd arrived on the eighteenth of September. The very next day I was fortunate to get a ticket for the night express to Moscow, and on the twentieth I laid siege to the office of the Assistant Foreign Commissar, armed with an introduction from the Head of the British Trade Mission. That letter, I thought, would be used as a trump ace. Earlier in the morning I had been to the Passport Department of the Commissariat, only to hear that my application would be considered in the usual way. "It may take months, perhaps a year; we can't tell anything definite," they had told me politely enough.

Now I reached the inner sanctuary. Several clerks in turn informed me that the Assistant Commissar was too busy, that he was abroad at a conference, that he was away on sick leave, and, finally and simply, that he would not see me. But somehow or other I got past the clerks and found myself facing one of the private secretaries, a fairly well-groomed young man with a supercilious manner and a shocking near-gentlemanly accent. I told him I had come to see the Assistant Commissar, and he minced that many people said that. The Assistant Commissar had important work to do and he could not grant interviews to people who did not matter.

"Anyway, what is your business?"

"I have a letter from the Head of the British Trade Mission — "

He hesitated. His abruptness changed to something oily and far less pleasant. Could he see the letter? I showed him the envelope and turned it round to make him see the British Lion engraved on the flap. He spoke almost silkenly: —

"Of course, I shall take it to the Assistant Commissar at once —"

I clung to my letter with both hands. It was not to be given by anyone except myself, and I said so.

He looked me up, he looked me down, he sneered, and he shrugged. We were in an immense room, crowded with typists and clerks, and I suddenly knew that the click of numerous typewriters had ceased. Then the secretary turned on his heel and left me without a word. I heard a typist giggle. . . . Someone said "Sh," and the clicking noise started again. I stood in the middle of the room, the precious letter clutched in my hands. In a mirror I saw myself — purple coat and skirt, a shabby broad-brimmed hat and curious, homemade footwear, largely strips of old carpets and what not. Under the black brim, the face looked white. I wished I might slap my own cheeks, to give them color, and I thought about the young nun off the Arbat.

[329]

"I think I have got some cigarettes for her . . ." And then the secretary was back, saying curtly: —

"Come this way —"

I went with him to a small, modestly furnished room. Behind the desk a little bearded man got up with a surprising bow. A chair was pushed forward. The secretary scowled behind his chief's back and vanished. I handed the letter to the Assistant Commissar. He read it slowly once, twice. Then the thick sheet of cream paper fluttered down on the desk. He leaned forward and gave me a peculiar searching look.

"You are not a British subject?" he asked in passably good English.

"No —"

"Then why this?" He tapped the letter with a well-shaped, well-manicured forefinger.

"Well, I am known there. My mother was British before her marriage. We've always had links with the British. Also I worked at the Trade Mission last winter —"

"I see." He studied the letter again. "You worked there! What exactly was your work?"

"I — just typed — odds and ends of things. I can't really remember —"

"Wouldn't you like to go back there later on?"

"Go back! Well, no, I don't think so. I've got my University work. It's history —"

"History? Don't you know languages?"

"Yes, about six —"

"Six? Languages — " he spoke reflectively, "are a very great asset — at least, they should be."

"I suppose they are — but I've chosen something else."

[330]

"You look young enough." He almost discomfited me by his smile. "Young people often change their minds. And don't you think it might be rather nice to get work at some foreign legation or other? I suppose you had interesting work at the British Mission?"

"Well, I loved working there. But then, of course, I have always been happy among the British — "

"Quite, quite. . . . Tell me — did you ever have to type anything about the Ukraine — or the economic conditions here — or the Far East — for example?"

I blinked. I swallowed hard. I laughed.

"I am sorry, Comrade Assistant Commissar, but I am afraid you are under the impression that I was someone's confidential secretary there. I was nothing of the sort — only a very ordinary and incompetent typist — and that for no longer than a few weeks," and, whilst I spoke, there flashed in my memory visions of several ruined sheets of thick foolscap paper, all marked "strictly confidential." Their contents I had entirely forgotten; they might or might not have been important. They were confidential, and were meant to be forgotten as soon as they were typed.

"Quite." He smiled again as though my reply had been a reassuring one, and studied the letter for a third time. "I see that you want to go to Italy for six months' sick leave. Well, there is no reason why you should not go. We are always ready to do anything for our British friends." He folded away the letter and added, speaking with an emphasis it would have been impossible to misunderstand, "If on your return you find that your college work is not — er — remunerative enough — you will remember to come back and see me here, you understand? Foreign languages are a far more important asset than you seem to realize — "

"It is most kind of you, Comrade Assistant Commissar," I replied, my face wooden.

He pressed the button, and the secretary came in.

"Citizen Almedingen's papers," he said curtly. "Ah, you have brought them. Nothing has been done so far? Have a foreign passport made out at once."

He rose and shook hands with me. In less than half an hour I left the great building, the foreign passport in my hands. I spent the rest of the day in Moscow, saying good-bye to a host of acquaintances at various relief centers. I also went to the British Mission in the Povarskaya, and there it was suggested to me that I had better go by sea to Stettin and then overland through Austria. "It is much safer than trying to go through Poland. The frontier is so far away, and nobody knows what might happen before you get to it — "

3

THE same night I traveled back to Petrograd. According to the instructions received in Moscow, I handed my passport to the local Tcheka headquarters for "a final inquiry," and then I went to book my berth for Stettin. I was not quite certain about the date of my departure. I had a vague idea that it would be ten days or a

fortnight. I almost hoped for something longer than a fortnight. Things grew so desperately final. . . . But at the
shipping office, the Norwegian clerk handed me the ticket
and smiled: —

"Leaving on the twenty-fourth! Don't you wish it were
tomorrow instead?" and the shabby purse in my hands clattered to the stone floor.

Three days only! They were crowded. I went to the
University. I heard from the clerk at the Chancery that
my thesis would be safe. "They have given you a degree
at the Third. . . . Probably the faculty felt that they could
not go on having an undegreed member in their ranks."

I heard it and, unseeing, unhearing, I rushed into the
cloisters. I had a wild impulse to burn my boats once again,
to tear up my passport, and to face a succession of hard
winters. After all, I had a niche there, and I loved the
exquisite enigmatic city of my birth, un-Russian, alien, like
myself. I loved the college, halls, cloisters, library. . . .
At that moment I even loved the Third — in spite of my
brother's presence. . . . I had the whole of my lifework
all but mapped out there. . . . But the impulse was brief.
Common sense came back with a strange warning: "Don't
be a fool . . . Medieval history . . . the University won't
have room for such work in a few years' time. . . .
You are going to Italy, and you shall go to England later
on — " This was at the end of 1922. By 1924 my premonition was to come true: humanities had no longer any
room in the Soviet scheme. . . .

Those three days sped like arrows. I knew that, in spite
of the six months' sick leave, I would never see the country again. A host of friends at college and elsewhere had

to be seen. A crowd of apparently trivial things demanded to be done. My packing was necessarily a sketchy affair, since too much luggage would have aroused suspicion. All my possessions went into one small, battered fiber suitcase. My leather-bound copybooks, full of sentimental verses, my diaries, all the family letters and photographs, I left in charge of an English friend who promised to send them later on through Denmark. My books, rescued by Esther from Madame X's flat, had to be left behind. They seemed more precious than ever before, but at that time not a single printed line could be taken out of the country. Nearly all my funny ersatz wardrobe would also be left behind. Arrangements had been made for my check to be cashed in Berlin, and, "What an orgy of shopping you'll have!" said Esther. "Think of it — to be able to buy anything you like — without cards or permits — "

"Yes, shopping," I said stupidly. I could hardly grasp the mere idea at first. We had not known real shopping for more than five years. . . . I began thinking about it, however, imagining a real coat and skirt I would buy in Berlin, stockings, gloves, a real blouse instead of a converted pyjama jacket.

Admittedly, all those were trivial considerations. But I had to take refuge in them during the last three days spent on Russian soil. The nights seemed endless: excitement made sleep nearly impossible. I had to take refuge in trivial things — for there was Esther.

We had been close friends for a little more than two years, yet we were bound together by links which could not be sundered. I owed my very sanity to her, and I could leave her nothing except a little money, the old fur coat, and a few odds and ends. . . . I was leaving her — to what? She promised again and again to get out as soon as she had got me off her hands. She talked about her sister in Sweden.

But even in 1925 her letters still reached me from Russia. They were very brief. She had never talked much about herself, and in her correspondence I found the same dearth of personal details. I knew she could not be candid because of very rigid censorship, but I wrote time and again, begging her for a crumb of news. Towards the end of 1925, when she had not written for some months, I had a letter from a college friend. She mentioned Esther, and added that her position was "desperate." Apparently, owing to her muddled national status (she was born in old Kurland, now Latvia), she had not been able to go anywhere. I knew enough about her reluctance to become Lettish: she was a Baltic German, and the idea of becoming a Lettish national always repelled her. I wrote again and again, but there came no reply. Owing to my virtual escape, the official channels of possible information were closed to me. Unofficially, I continued trying to trace her for several years, and every fresh inquiry ended in a cul-de-sac. She had left the house on the Moyka: nobody knew more than that. . . .

"I'll be all right," she kept saying to me during those three days. "There is no question about it — it is your duty to go. You nearly died last winter — if you but knew it. I feel sure that, if you stayed on, you'd go under before very long. You are not a weakling, but your strength is very near the breaking point. You must not worry about me — "

But I did.

"Esther, if it had not been for you there would have been no college — there would have been nothing. . . . And it all seems so futile — so final. . . . I shall never be able to pay you back — "

"You have paid me back, *Liebchen*." She gestured me away. . . . "Do you imagine I did not feel richly rewarded the day they made you a member of the faculty? All your successes were mine. . . . And don't talk about me. . . . I did little else except bully you into the University. . . . My bullying would have been little use if you had been a lazy dunce. . . ."

All the same, I worried, and, had it not been for her own iron reserve, I suppose I should have gone to pieces during those three days. She, however, kept me on the go the whole time; she continued reminding me that so-and-so had not been seen yet, that I had apparently forgotten this and that and the other. She had not had much of me during those three days.

The third of them broke at last, and Petrograd decided to make me remember her loveliness for a long time to come. It was a pale blue morning, cold but not frosty. Streets, houses, bridges, and, above all, the river, were bathed in the pale sunlight of a Northern autumn day which had primrose, gold, and gray in its texture.

I had still many places to go to, and, wherever I went, landmarks known and loved since childhood smiled at me through the gossamer sunlight. Here was the darkling green-russet splash of the Roumiantzeff Square, its onee formal beds and paths now patches of rank weeds. Here stood the house where Cyril had got his midshipman's shoulder straps. I wondered if the old model of a frigate still hung in the refectory, but the gates were closed as I went by. Here, at last, was the Smolensky Lutheran Cemetery; I read my mother's name for the last time, and I turned back to hurry through the last good-byes. A few college friends promised to come and see me off in the evening. In my room the slender fiber suitcase was already strapped, a red, home-woven blanket folded on its top. Esther was getting something of a tea meal ready. The boat, bound for Stettin, was to leave at dawn the next morning, but we were told to be at the pier not later than six in the evening. Those last few hours had wings. I walked about the room, my very last perch on Russian soil, fingering now a book, now some trifle possessed for years and years. I could not say much, but Esther made some fresh tea, cut me a bacon sandwich, and made me eat it.

"The food you are leaving behind," she said briskly, "will keep me for nearly a year."

"You promised you would try and get out at once — "

"Of course. . . . Then I will leave it to someone else in my turn — "

I ate and drank in silence. I watched Esther cut some more sandwiches and fill a small bottle with cold tea.

"That's for our supper," she explained; "I expect we shall be kept hours at the pier. We can carry the suitcase by turns — it is light enough. I think we'd better start at five. It does not matter when we get there — and I am sure you will want to have a long look at every house on the way — "

All too soon the clock struck five.

"Come on, *Liebchen*. Where is your coat and hat? Are you sure you have not forgotten anything?"

[337]

"Esther — " I began lamely, and she shook her head.

"You are not going to be either maudlin or sentimental. English people seldom are, and you ought to think of that. You have had more than five years of sheer hell, you have got through it all, and now it is over, and you are going away, and you are lucky — "

"I know I am. I want to get away most terribly, but it's you."

"It's nearly ten past five," she said, and I walked by her side down the English Quay and across the Nicholas Bridge. I could not look at any of the houses. I even forgot to say good-bye to the river.

We came to the pier. The wind had dropped. The September evening was warm enough. . . . There were about two hundred of us going away. We all huddled on the Quay, sitting on our luggage and trying not to worry too much about our passports. Twilight fell all too rapidly, and in its shadows the last glimpse of the Quays I was ever to have, vanished.

The boat was there, but nobody could get on board except by passing through a roughly timbered shed which had another door opening out on to the gangway. This was the Tcheka shed. There, in dim candlelight, sat the men in whose hands lay the final decision of our several fates. One by one people went in, as a man in khaki appeared in the narrow doorway, facing the Quay, and called out each separate name. As they went in, we watched the gangway, trying to gauge the length of time each person was kept in the shed. Now and again we could see someone waving to us from the lower deck. But soon it grew darker and darker, we could no longer distinguish any figures passing up the gangway, and the boat was so dimly lit that we had to give up trying to peer through the shadows.

The few friends who had come to see me off left, and I was not sorry to see them go. Every minute, as I knew well, might be the last one. There were millions of things I wanted to say to Esther, and none could be said. We just sat and shivered, because the night was getting colder, and she talked about everything under the sun — except herself.

My own turn came somewhere between three and four in the morning. I was one of the very last to be called in. When my crudely mispronounced name rang from the doorway, we both jumped to our feet. Esther handed me the suitcase. She would have no further chance of seeing me. We had only a few seconds left. We could not kiss. We shook hands, and she said: —

"*Gott sei mit dir, Liebchen. . . .*"

I stood still, my hand clutching her cold fingers, but once again my name was called, and I hurried forward. Suitcase in hand, I entered the shed and faced the long low table, where five men and three women sat and watched me in silence. The table was littered with papers. They were all smoking, and the air was thick with the acrid smell of very strong tobacco. There were a few thick candles stuck into empty beer bottles. . . . I came nearer the table, and the last act of the five years began with a simple enough question: —

"Where are you going?"

"To Italy."

"By what route?"

"By sea to Stettin — then overland through Austria to Rome."

"What address are you going to in Rome?" and I gave it to them.

They glanced at the papers before them, there followed a brief pause, and then the chairman shot another question: —

"When are you going to resume your lectures at the University?"

"On my return." Here I noticed that at one end of the table a woman was busily scribbling down my replies.

"Do you know Italian?"

"Yes."

"Have you been there before?"

"No."

"Are you going to engage in any political work in Italy?"

"I am a scholar. My subject is history. I don't meddle with politics."

"The British helped you get this passport in Moscow, didn't they?"

"They gave me a letter of introduction to the Assistant Foreign Commissar. He helped me to get this passport without delay."

"What made you go to the British for help?"

"I had worked for them before. At the commissariat they told me that I might have to wait a year for a passport. My health is none too good. I could not stand another winter here — "

"Because of the economic conditions in this country?" The question was asked quietly, but in spite of fatigue I saw the trap and tried to avoid it by replying: —

"Certainly not. Because of the state of my health."

"We see that the Health Commission had accepted you as a candidate for a year's stay at a sanatorium in the Crimea. You were due to leave in August. What made you change your mind?"

This was a question I had not expected. I dug my hands deep into the pockets of my coat and said that I thought the Italian climate would be more certain than the Crimean. It seemed an idiotic enough answer, but they accepted it. Probably they in their turn were getting tired of a long night's work.

"Have you any friends in England?"

"Oh, yes — "

"Why aren't you going to England?"

"Partly because of the climate. Also because my only relative lives in Rome."

"She is a woman of title."

"She married a man of title."

"Do you share her political and social views?"

"I have not yet met her. I don't know what her views are."

"You understand that you have promised loyalty to your own Government?"

"I am bound to — holding this passport," I said, remembering my secret decision to tear up the passport immediately on crossing the Italian frontier.

There was another pause.

"Have you any movable or immovable property in Italy?"

"None."

They stopped looking at me and began whispering among

themselves. I imagined it was over. But the chairman picked up a scribbled sheet of paper. I heard him say: —

"Where are you going?"

"To Italy."

"By what route?"

We had got to the middle of that infernal questionnaire when I knew my head was beginning to swim. I could see a blur for the table, and the few candles became so many spots of swaying light. I wondered if they ever meant me to have my foreign passport. "But I shall get out just the same — I'll tramp all the way to Finland," I thought vehemently, and an automaton's mouth moved steadily enough: —

"Partly because of the climate."

"She married a man of title."

"I have not yet met her. I don't know what her views are."

But the automaton's voice seemed on the point of vanishing. Once or twice the chairman said icily: —

"We can't hear you. Can't you speak louder?"

At that moment something I could not account for whipped my more than shredded energy to a new life. My voice rang loudly enough when I replied for the third time: —

"I am a scholar. My subject is history. I don't meddle with politics."

They exchanged glances and whispered comments. A woman shrugged. The chairman said gruffly: —

"That will do. Sign here for your passport."

In about ten minutes they had examined the contents of my suitcase, had me searched for documents and foreign money, and then, swaying a little, I found myself groping up the gangway. An officer piloted me to the dining salon. I must have had a meal, but I remember nothing of it, and even the shining cutlery and spotless napery made no impression on me. A stewardess came and shepherded me to the cabin. I had not the energy to undress, and was asleep as soon as my head touched the pillow.

I woke about lunch time, had a bath, and came on deck. The boat was cutting through the dark gray waters of the Gulf of Finland. The captain saw me and waved from the bridge. Presently he came down and grinned.

"Yes, it is all safe. All is behind you now. Good, is it not?"

I could only smile. Adequate words would not come for several years and when they came they rang an unexpected note. They could express little else than very broken thanks for all those yesterdays, full of horror and of splendor also, now laid aside and yet still living, for an experience which came and left a truth graven on the consciousness. That truth, however, could not be told in my own words. Saint Paul's must be borrowed for it: "For I am persuaded, that neither death, nor life, nor angels, nor principalities, nor powers, nor things present, nor things to come, nor height, nor depth, nor any other creature, shall be able to separate us from the love of God."

DATE DUE

12/7			
GAYLORD			PRINTED IN U.S.A.